The Artemisia Files

THE ARTEMISIA FILES

Artemisia Gentileschi for Feminists and Other Thinking People

Edited by Mieke Bal

The University of Chicago Press
Chicago & London

The University of Chicago Press, Chicago 60637
The University of Chicago Press, Ltd., London
© 2005 by The University of Chicago
All rights reserved. Published 2005
Paperback edition 2006
Printed in the United States of America

14 13 12 11 10 09 08 07   3 4 5

ISBN-13: 987-0-226-03582-6 (paper)
ISBN-10: 0-226-03582-4 (paper)

Chapter 1 was adapted from a paper given at the international symposium
entitled Artemisia Gentileschi: Taking Stock, held at the St. Louis Art
Museum, St. Louis, Missouri, September 13, 2002. It was first published in
Norma Broude and Mary D. Garrard, *Reclaiming Female Agency: Feminist Art
History after Postmodernism* (Berkeley and Los Angeles: University of California Press, 2005), copyright © 2005 Norma Broude and Mary D. Garrard, and is
reprinted here with the permission of the University of California Press.

Library of Congress Cataloging-in-Publication Data

The Artemisia files : Artemisia Gentileschi for feminists and other thinking
    people / edited by Mieke Bal.
        p.   cm.
    Includes bibliographical references and index.
    ISBN 0-226-03581-6 (cloth : alk. paper)
        1. Gentileschi, Artemisia, 1593–1652 or 3—Criticism and interpreta-
        tion. 2. Feminism and art. 3. Art criticism—History—20th century.
        I. Gentileschi, Artemisia, 1593–1652 or 3. II. Bal, Mieke, 1946– .

    ND623 .G364A94 2005
    759.5—dc22   2005000617

♾ The paper used in this publication meets the minimum requirements of
the American National Standard for Information Sciences—Permanence of
Paper for Printed Library Materials, ANSI z39.48–1992.

CONTENTS

ILLUSTRATIONS

INTRODUCTION

Although Artemisia Gentileschi worked as an artist during the seventeenth century, "Artemisia Gentileschi" is a fabrication of the last
decades of the twentieth. During the era of feminist revisionism of
the art-history canon, she was (re)discovered as one of the great
artists of baroque Italy only after having been invented as one of
the first women making great art. Thick files on this painter grew
and flourished. The structure and use of those files are deeply problematic, for they anchor all consideration of her work in the life
story, revised and revived through myths of women and sexuality.
This book is an attempt to go through those files once more, to
work through them, so to speak, and file them away so that we can
finally look at the paintings without scandal and sensationalist
prefigurations in our minds. It also aims to provide an understanding of the files themselves, to engage the current discourses on
Artemisia Gentileschi, and to consider these seriously as documents of our time. They are documents, by extension, of how our
culture thinks about art. It is a proposition of this book that the
ideas at issue here are widely applicable as thoughts about art in
contemporary culture.

While many writings in traditional art history developed a discourse that tended to undermine Gentileschi's art, feminist histori-

ans sometimes came close to heroizing Gentileschi the artist. The former discourse diminished her artistic merit; the latter foregrounded its excellence. The tendency to minimize Artemisia Gentileschi the artist is still current. This is done either by attributing some of her best work to her father, Orazio, or by ascribing to her artistically dubious works more likely to have been made by other artists. One of the pioneers of feminist art history, Mary Garrard, has gone a long way to redress these wrongs. A new contribution by Garrard's hand opens the current volume.

Diminishing the importance of Artemisia's work is also done either by neglecting, ignoring, or denigrating works. Babette Bohn's article here takes up one such case. This denigrating discourse has also sexualized the artist to the point of explaining her art if not through, at least systematically with reference to, the artist's rape by her tutor Agostino Tassi. Nanette Salomon and Griselda Pollock discuss this almost inevitable, yet fatal, sexualization.

If the traditional art-history discourse, which diminishes Artemisia's merit, continues to need addressing and redressing, the feminist revisionist discourse that tends to heroize her also invites critical reflection. Feminist art historians were the ones who wrote Artemisia into the canon as a great artist. But since they, too, work within art history, the attempts to save her work from sometimes prurient biographical fallacies needed to take issue with that dominant discourse, and, as a result, partly collude with it. It is a significant aspect of this volume that it is opened and closed by two pioneers in feminist art history, who represent very different, at times even antagonistic, approaches. If this volume has an innovative contribution to make, it is primarily because these two writers come uniquely together in a still different project for a common goal: to take stock of, revise, and where necessary overcome the Artemisia files.

One such file contains documents of popular culture. Indeed, popular culture has produced semibiographical novels, plays, and, more recently, a film of the "biopic" genre. This film in particular occasioned a new flurry of writings about what Griselda Pollock here calls "the art/life problem." These artifacts of feminist revisionism heroize Gentileschi through a discourse of victimization. The transcripts of her rape trial became required reading for everyone wishing to write about her work. Given the presence of these documents on the cultural scene, what can art history do? To ignore them would be to disavow both the cultural figure of "Artemisia" and art history's past collusion in building up this figure. Taking that figure for granted, however, would unquestioningly reinforce stereotypes of the worst kind. This tangled issue is taken up by Griselda Pollock in the final essay of this volume.

For many, the exhibition during 2001–2, in Rome, New York, and St. Louis, of the combined oeuvres of Orazio and Artemisia was a unique opportunity to see and assess her works for themselves. The success of the exhibition demonstrates that a large public is interested in moving on from the files to the work itself, in shifting its cultural agency from gossip to eye-witnessing. The authors of this volume have taken the opportunity offered by this exhibition to rethink "the Artemisia files." They critically engage rather than simply reject the ways this exceptional artist has been treated thus far.

As this brief account intimates, each of the six essays brought together here engages with one of the commonly practiced approaches to Artemisia Gentileschi's oeuvre, which are also approaches of art history in general. Through the Artemisia files, we also reflect on the ways in which art history as an academic discipline is imbricated in larger cultural ways of dealing with art. Such approaches range from attribution, judgment, and personal confrontation to historical contextualization, exhibition, and popular rewriting. Each of these approaches is taken on, and a serious engagement with each yields a critical revisionism of the approach itself, without altogether disavowing its *raison d'être*. Together, these approaches revisit what academic art history, museum culture, and popular culture have created and called "Artemisia."

One problem encountered by feminist studies in the visual arts is, indeed, the recurrent temptation to call a woman artist by her

given name rather than by her surname or full author name. The
title of the film discussed in the final chapter of this book repeats
the infantilizing familiarity, by calling itself *Artemisia*. Yet within
the space of only a few years, while the major exhibition of the two
Gentileschis traveled from Rome to New York to St. Louis, the
shared surname became the subject of a shallow battle over the relative merits of father Orazio and daughter Artemisia. From that
point on, the name acquired a different connotation, akin perhaps
to Michelangelo (Buonarroti), Rembrandt (van Rijn) or Vincent
(van Gogh). From what Griselda Pollock, together with Rozsika
Parker, with great effectiveness, mockingly called "old mistresses"
(Parker and Pollock 1981) to Mary Garrard's elegant title *maestra,*
naming women among the venerated old masters is necessary yet
not entirely comfortable. Since we were aware of the tension inherent in the use of the first name, both the presence of Orazio on the
stage and the potentially positive, canonizing connotations have
made us feel a bit more relaxed about avoiding the clumsy reitera-
tion of the long full name.

The recent exhibitions, the appearance of the film, and the continued production of novels, as well as the production of contemporary art responding to Artemisia's work, have all given us reasons
enough to consider the Artemisia files as precious documents
straddling the edge between academic thought on art and the attitudes toward art in Western culture at large. The 2001–2 exhibition
has occasioned critical work of high standards, which—together
with and in the wake of a recent catalogue raisonné (Bissell 1999),
two in-depth studies by Mary Garrard (1989 and 2001), and many
articles—represents a provisional overview of what is thought of
Artemisia's production as an artist. It is in acknowledgment of this
state of the files, as well as with a sense of urgency derived from the
current reputation of the artist as these events have established it,
that we offer these *afterthoughts*—in the double sense of the word.

So allow me now to explain why, after all these writings and
events, we still feel that this book is called for. What makes the catalogue of the exhibition mentioned above, *Orazio and Artemisia*

Gentileschi, both remarkable and particularly precious is the overt disagreement among the curators on some controversial cases. The Metropolitan Museum of Art is holding up somewhat of a tradition: already in the exhibition entitled Rembrandt/Not Rembrandt, such controversies were played out overtly, for the eyes of the public. By virtue of this openness, which takes the public seriously to a hitherto unparalleled degree, the two entries, by Keith Christiansen and Judith Mann (2001), on the painting of *Cleopatra* in the Morandotti collection in Milan (either 1611–12, or ca. 1620; see fig. 10) together constitute one of the most impressive files in our possession, demonstrating not only how uncertain attributions can be, but also what kind of arguments can prevail in each case.

Christiansen attributes this painting to Orazio, Mann to Artemisia, and both are totally convinced they are right, as were those who, before them, attributed the work to either artist. Together, these entries suggest how different the ways are in which art can be analyzed, and how, accordingly, we have conceived the present volume as a response, not only to Artemisia's artistic accomplishments but also to the discourses that frame them. Therefore, I briefly analyze here the modes of argumentation at stake, hoping to offer through this small case study a concrete rationale for the present volume.

Christiansen's entry is first, and hence, I start with his. He begins his argumentation in favor of Orazio's authorship with a comparison that barely obscures his underlying judgment: "The first [objection to the case for Artemisia] is that the *Lucretia* and the *Cleopatra* are painted in completely different and, to my mind, incompatible styles—the one hard and schematic, the other luminous and richly descriptive" (97). The argument rests on two assumptions: that the attribution of the *Cleopatra* depends on that of the *Lucretia* (unquestioned as Artemisia's; see fig. 3) and that stylistic difference is best cast in evaluative terms separated by opposition. Both assumptions seem questionable to me. If the question of authorship were really open, other stylistic features as well as other comparisons could have been brought in. The choice to make a comparison with the *Lucretia*, another figure of a suicide by a woman, is more thematic and, as such, gender-based rather than stylistic. It is taken from the same passage in Garrard (1989), in which she attributes both of these paintings to Artemisia, an attribution against which the author argues in the passage quoted. Garrard did ground her attributions in considerations of gender, and extensively argued these before making the statement of attribution against which Christiansen's entry advances this oppositional argument. But if one rejects these considerations of Garrard's, then the comparison between the *Lucretia* and the *Cleopatra* itself needs to be argued anew.

The second assumption is equally dubious, because circular in logic. Only for someone who already believes that Orazio is the superior painter would the alleged higher quality ("luminous and richly descriptive" over "hard and schematic") lead to a change in attribution. Christiansen further sustains his reattribution on the same page with other evaluative qualifications, such as "unadorned approach to naturalistic painting," concerning which he alleges Orazio's *Madonna and Child* (fig. 38). Here he contradicts Mina Gregori, whom he quotes as mentioning, in favor of Artemisia's authorship, an "expressive concentration" unusual for Orazio. But expressive concentration is not a fact of naturalism at all. Rather, it is an issue of the dramatic power of the representation, not of its painterly mode. Nor does Orazio's skill in naturalism invalidate Artemisia's, or her capability of depicting expressive concentration.

Christiansen's attribution is based primarily on *judgment*, and this judgment depends rather heavily on a circularity that declares Orazio the better painter and the best paintings, therefore, Orazio's. This circularity becomes evident a bit later when he sees in the *Cleopatra* a "subtlety and rich variation for which I can find no ready comparison in Artemisia's work at any phase." He is writing here about the handling of the white linen sheet and red drapery. Thus style, in the tradition of connoisseurship, is located in the less important areas of the painting—less important for the representation, which is Artemisia's primary strength. His comment is also blatantly dismissive of Artemisia as a subtle colorist. The first three articles in this volume each address the issues that leap off Christiansen's page. Elena Ciletti shows that Artemisia was, indeed, precisely the brilliant, rich, and subtle colorist that Christiansen will not see in her because he already "knows" that such brilliance is evidence of Orazio's authorship. Nanette Salomon critiques, and offers alternatives to, the compulsion to judge comparatively—the compulsion, as she says, to put "versus" between two artist's names. Mary Garrard reiterates her strong case for this *Cleopatra* as the work of Artemisia, here on the basis of the overdetermined motif of the *hand.*

This hand is, indeed, a site where many possible considerations meet. Its depiction as expressive concentration, to reiterate Gregori's phrase, is both dramatically and stylistically remarkable. But it is also a *narrative* element of great originality. And this is the domain of Judith Mann's argument for Artemisia's authorship. She calls her ground of attribution the painting's "interpretive tone." This apt phrase integrates style and narration. It also takes the painting out of the obsession with the nude, without denying that it is also just that. In her entry, she first analyzes how the painting is unusually forceful in its choice of narrative moment. While most depictions of Cleopatra's suicide show her either committing the act or writhing in agony immediately afterwards, here, the figure is both determined, as revealed in the firm grip of her hand—in a Garrard-type argument—and pausing, before putting the snake on her breast, as if contemplating her decision and its implications. This choice of moment is consistent with other Artemisia paintings, such as *Jael and Sisera* from 1620 (fig. 34), to which Babette Bohn's contribution is devoted, and *Lucretia* from ca. 1621 (fig. 3), another case discussed here by Garrard.

Bohn is interested in the former painting because it has been discussed so little, and has been denigrated when discussed. Neglect, denigration, and disattribution are, indeed, three out of four ways mentioned above in which Artemisia's achievements have been minimized. In the framework of the controversial attribution of the

Cleopatra, the reattribution to Orazio by Christiansen and also, apparently, by Bissell (during his remarks at the symposium in St. Louis), and the neglect or denigration of the *Jael and Sisera* become subject to suspicion on similar grounds. In both cases, the writers appear blind to an aspect on which Garrard and Pollock, each in very different ways, have insisted: Artemisia's innovative interpretation of the narrative. In particular, I am struck by the profoundly meditative, at times philosophically urgent suspensions of narrative flow.

Indeed, Garrard, in a recent monograph (2001), devotes generous attention to this in her analyses of two versions of the penitent Magdalene, in an exercise of the gender-aware, feminist attribution she invented and has promoted during her career. Rather than preaching to the converted, Garrard's recent book will doubtlessly convince those who had remained skeptical about her earlier book (1989) of her argument that neither the theory nor the practice of attribution are gender-neutral. Griselda Pollock, who closes the present volume, is equally fascinated by the remarkable choice of moment, arrested and arresting, in the *Cleopatra.* In *Differencing the Canon* she brings in the gripping tale of the dead mother and muses on the problem of feminist desire and the relation between art and biography, which in this volume she renames the "art/life problem" (1999, 138–58). Like Mann, she is sensitive to another narrative subtlety, the gap in the drapery. Christiansen may find the handling of the drapery too subtle for Artemisia, but if I may borrow his discursive mode, the handling, *through* the drapery, of narrative temporality is more subtle than anywhere in Orazio's oeuvre.

The gap is a narrative prolepsis, or narrative forecasting. It announces the arrival of the women who are to discover Cleopatra dead, and who will kill themselves in turn, a scene following the suicide proper on its heels, and one that Artemisia depicted some ten years later. Together with the contemplative moment, the proximity of the snake, whose slit red tongue is already directed to the queen's white breast, and the hand's still-firm grip that holds the snake at bay, this gap functions as a temporal gearshift, from near-standstill to acceleration. Announcing, through the figure of prolepsis, the fatal moment, it gives incredible depth to the figure's ultimate moment of power and self-determination. The intensity and overdetermined meaning of this moment of suspense can be said to "foreshorten" time.

Mann's short entry hints at a form of attribution that parts ways with the judgmental connoisseurship of the Masters of Taste with whom Salomon's contribution to the present volume engages a dialogue. In spite of vast differences that separate their practices, both Garrard and Pollock have clearly been influential in developing this mode of thinking about art. Attentive not to why a work must go to the master already declared superior but to what is most distinctive about it as a complex, intellectually subtle work, Mann makes her case in my opinion much more persuasively than Christiansen. Not because it is a feminist argument, for no feminism is needed for good thinking. The entry is simply more solidly grounded in the painting. This leads to another issue that underlies this volume.

Many of the contributors write, at one moment or another, that "just looking" at the paintings was a wonderful experience, and that the exhibition facilitated it. The idea that a "fresh look" at the "paintings themselves" would offer fuel against old myths and obscuring judgments is not at all obvious. Indeed, such an idea can easily be misconstrued as a return to formalism. Nothing is farther from the truth, however. I cannot claim, for example, that Christiansen has looked less hard than Mann, that Mann's argument is more convincing because it is more directly based on looking. Both, I suppose, looked equally hard, but saw different things. For, as his discourse demonstrates, Christiansen looked at the painting through colored glasses: what he saw was Orazio's superiority. That the painting passes muster as a great painting, therefore, almost automatically makes it an Orazio.

Mann's look, although no less colored, is colored by something else, something that is not inherently evaluative. Her glasses are steeped in a feature of the painting that is inescapably essential to it: its narrativity. Why didn't Christiansen pay much heed to that aspect, in spite of its obvious relevance? I cannot speculate on his motivations, other than to say that the absence, in Orazio's entire oeuvre, of original narrative interpretation might have something to do with it. Hence, Mann's focus is derived from the painting, Christiansen's from the painter—to whom, therefore, he already must have ascribed the painting before he started that particular looking.

If, then, the case of *Cleopatra* is a file where Artemisia, art history (more generally), and (even more broadly) good thinking come together, it shows the path this volume seeks to follow. First, we discuss attribution, art history's foundational discipline. Closely following is the issue of judgment, partly imbricated with attribution, but also a more largely cultural attitude. In the third contribution that tricky phrase, "just looking," is brought into interaction with an overtly personal account, a staple of feminist scholarship that may at first appear to be the opposite of that unhampered look. The issue of exhibition is central to the fifth contribution, partly analyzing the 2001–2 exhibition, as exemplified in some of its juxtapositions and wall labels.

A less celebrated—indeed, often ignored—painting is central to the fourth chapter, which is devoted to a classically contextual interpretation. Here, for those who claim the rights of history, a demonstration of the compatibility of history and "just looking," will strengthen the underlying claim of this book that the Artemisia files are food for thought; occasions for and triggers of "good thinking." Thinking is not the privilege of academics. In the last chapter, art is set in the context of, and perhaps seen as, popular culture. In the face of popular acclaim, *Artemesia*, the Merlet film, is even more urgently in need of such good thinking.

Thus summarized, these six chapters each touch only obliquely on an aspect of the culture within which, before all else, Artemisia's work belongs: what is usually indicated by that notoriously unclear term *baroque*. This term appeared in the subtitle of the exhibition, while it had been studiously avoided in the title of an earlier exhibition, The Genius of Rome, at the Royal Academy in London in which Artemisia's work appeared. In both cases, the period or style

denomination enjoyed a self-evidence that seemed to make definition redundant. Yet in much of Artemisia's work the "baroqueness"
of, in particular, the compositions is so characteristic that ignoring
that aspect is already glossing over what could instead be a hallmark
of her work.

Without embarking on an extensive exercise in defining the baroque, it seems useful to indicate briefly how that term can help—
rather than hinder, through its vagueness—our understanding, especially of Artemisia's conception of narrative representation. This
is a key aspect that several contributions to this volume discuss, especially with regard to her two paintings of Judith killing Holofernes, which Elena Ciletti analyzes in great detail. Without pre-
empting later arguments, it seems clear that the striking directness,
the frontality that is almost brutal, especially in the earlier version,
have something to do with the conception of storytelling that underlies the compositions.

This conception is what makes Artemisia's work baroque. To be
sure, who says "baroque" thinks, primarily, of drapery and its folds.
Irving Lavin once stated that drapery, that icon of baroque art, was
a device to create "the almost hallucinatory relationship between
past and present that is a hallmark of the period" (1995, 5). The hallucinatory quality of that relationship—a quality that, like a drapery, deprives perception of its object—is the compelling philosophical feature with which to approach Artemisia's most gripping
paintings. I say "philosophical" because this conception of perception entails an entire vision of humanity, relationships, and the
world. As I have discussed extensively elsewhere, such essentially
baroque features as the fold, the oscillation between the macro-
scopic and the microscopic, the porous delimitation of the do-
mains of vision and discourse, the spatial thickness between two-
and three-dimensionality, the incongruous detail that spills over
into the entire image, sensuality, and mirroring constitute not only
thematically nameable baroque motifs, but also more pervasive,
less clearly noticed, yet crucial visual "discourses" (Bal 1999).

Bracketing the ornamental aspect of exuberant baroque form,

the philosophical heart of baroque culture lies in a vision that integrates an epistemological view, a concept of representation, and an aesthetic, all three of which are anchored in the inseparability of mind and body, form and matter, line and color, image and discourse (Bal 1999). The problems of knowing the baroque characterize contemporary understandings in the cultural disciplines as well as in baroque philosophy: the problems, respectively, of being "enfolded" in what one is studying, of embodying it as a way of fully grasping, of deciding the relative importance of unpresuming elements through a process of wavering in scale, of articulating engagement as a way of knowing, and, finally, of understanding the self/other dialectic of the mirror that threatens to conflate the subject and the object of knowing. Hence, to recognize that the criteria we bring to bear on our understanding of Artemisia's work cannot be severed from who we are, today, is fundamentally a baroque way of thinking.

Perhaps we can call this an intellectual style. "Style," then, cannot be a purely aesthetic concept. It refers to cultural attitudes and states of consciousness that encompass intellectual and aesthetic, political and scientific assumptions and thoughts. Artemisia's "interpretive tone," as Mann calls it—her particularly poignant interpretations of narratives, now turned acutely dramatic, as in the *Judith*s, then meditative and philosophical, as in the *Cleopatra* and *Jael and Sisera*—is therefore a more comprehensive, intellectual as well as aesthetic mode of specifically baroque art.

Keeping these remarks in mind should make it easier to see the unity in diversity of the present volume. In each of the six chapters, one aspect of our culture's intercourse with art is foregrounded, critically engaged, and embedded in other considerations. Each chapter focuses primarily on single motifs, themes, or paintings. Chapter 1 is written by the leading Artemisia scholar of our time. In "Artemisia's Hand," Mary Garrard, author of two books on her work, revisits the discourse of *attribution* that can make or break any artist. She looks at Artemisia's depiction of hands as a sign both of her expressive predilections and of her own artistic "hand." The strong and forceful hands of Artemisia's women, she contends, serve both as a hallmark of her abiding interest in expressing female agency, and also as a tool of connoisseurship that can help clarify her oeuvre.

Comparing the depiction of female hands by Artemisia and by her father Orazio makes it possible to resolve certain vexed attributions, such as the Genoa *Cleopatra* discussed above, in her favor. Garrard rejects other paintings recently attributed to Artemisia— in part because they present women with unusually weak hands or with no hands at all—and suggests that these attributions are not only influenced by gender-biased preconceptions, but that they also stem from a desire, found even among Artemisia's contemporaries, to repressively "feminize" the artist's image. Thus, Garrard tackles two of the four strategies for mitigating the artistic achievement of this artist. This microcosmic study exemplifies a dynamic that Garrard has described elsewhere in a macrocosmic framework: that the transgressive power of Gentileschi's art has brought forth cultural repression. In partial compensation for that repression, Garrard offers three new examples in works by or about Artemisia in which the artist signals her presence to us through subtle and witty gestures of the hand.

Attribution is closely linked to judgment. But judgment is not limited to attribution. It is a much more pervasive, almost compulsive, response to art, which pronounces first and foremost on aesthetic quality. Nanette Salomon addresses the issue of *judgment* in her contribution, "Judging Artemisia." This chapter examines the conditions of judgment as an art-history trope, through the lens of the critical fortunes of Artemisia Gentileschi. The changing terms of judgment are analyzed from two critical moments: the late sixteenth century (its earliest formal articulation) and the late twentieth and early twenty-first centuries. Moreover, an analysis is proposed of some key works by the artist, an analysis that offers an alternative to the competitive practice of judgment so endemic in the field of art history and particularly pervasive in the scholarship on Artemisia. Whereas Garrard discusses a range of paintings,

Salomon focuses on two series: one consisting of three different depictions of the oft-exploited theme of Susanna and the Elders, the
other on depictions of Judith killing Holofernes. These two series
will return in other contributions, and thus constitute a kind of
test case for the various approaches discussed and practiced.

In "'Gran Macchina è Bellezza': Looking at the Gentileschi *Judith*s," Elena Ciletti offers a close reading of the visual strategies of
four paintings by Artemisia Gentileschi: the two *Judith Slaying
Holofernes* works, in Naples and Florence (Uffizi), and the two *Judith and her Maidservant* canvases, in Florence (Pitti) and Detroit.
These are Artemisia's most celebrated and popular works, and they
seem to have become besieged by their notoriety and the vast interpretive possibilities they have inspired. Endlessly scrutinized for
what they might say about the artist's psychobiography and about
her multifaceted connections to her (and our) social, artistic, and
cultural contexts, the *Judith*s have often come to be more looked
through than *at.* The Gentileschi exhibition at the Metropolitan
brought all four paintings together, along with related works by
Artemisia's teacher and father, thus offering an opportunity to redress this imbalance via extended immersion in their materiality
and visuality.

While Ciletti is not suggesting that these complex works can or
should be "contained" in their physical qualities alone, it seems
productive to focus on their formal tactics in their interaction with
the author, who offers a personal account of her recent renewed encounter with the works. She has been helped in this task by Federico
Della Valle, a seventeenth-century Italian dramatist whose characterization of his heroine Judith's physical beauty as a "*gran
macchina*" (a great or impressive instrument of war) encouraged
her to think of Artemisia's Judith images in terms of their powerful
aesthetic machinations per se. On their own terms and in comparison to related works by her father, Orazio, and other contemporaries, these paintings may be seen as sophisticated and astute exer-
cises in the deployment of beauty. They therefore provide visual
support for the modern, feminist-inspired advocacy of Artemisia

Gentileschi as a major painter. This approach can be characterized as an account of visual narrative, where color as much as composition directs the viewer's gaze.

An even more monographic contribution, by Babette Bohn, represents the *historical* approach as it contextualizes a single painting from a variety of perspectives current in its time. In "Death, Dispassion, and the Female Hero: Artemisia Gentileschi's *Jael and Sisera*," Bohn takes on not a celebrated but a denigrated, little-discussed, single painting. Indeed, as mentioned above, Gentileschi's painting of *Jael and Sisera* has received curiously little attention or acclamation. Although it represents a woman's triumph over a man, a quintessentially Gentileschian subject, no one loves this picture or cites it as exemplifying Artemisia's heroic women. On the contrary, it is either discussed in neutral terms that avoid a full consideration of its subject, or denigrated as a disappointing picture that somehow never achieved the *frisson* of her contemporary *Judith Beheading Holofernes*. Bohn argues that the *Jael and Sisera* exemplifies the artist's capacity for original invention, fidelity to a biblical text, and virtuous depictions of women in a quieter mode.

Art is not only presented through scholarship, but also in *exhibitions*. These, too, determine to a large extent how culture at large comes to view an artist's work. In "Grounds of Comparison," Mieke Bal analyzes exhibitions in order to examine the pros and cons of comparison, that trope of judgment and hierarchization. She examines three cases of comparison, so as to exorcise its negative—antivisualist and judgmental—aspects, and to enhance its positive potential as a method of analysis, understanding, and, simply, looking at art. All three cases involve exhibitions where different forms of comparison steer the visitors' engagement with the art.

In the first, The Genius of Rome: 1592–1623, the ground of comparison is the master-student relationship: Caravaggio is the master, Artemisia the student. Judgment is based on chronology and cast as master-student influence. In the second, Orazio and Artemisia Gentileschi: Father and Daughter Painters in Baroque Italy, the theme, as the title overtly suggests, is the father-daughter relationship, and the ground of comparison is age and authority, again cast as influence, compounded with issues of attribution. The third is Kathleen Gilje's exhibition entitled Susanna and the Elders (Restored), staged around a single artwork. Here, the ground of comparison is the question of rape, and the comparison takes the form of quotation, commentary, and reframing in the present.

In the last chapter of this book, "Feminist Dilemmas with the Art/Life Problem," Griselda Pollock takes the 1997 biographical film (biopic) about the painter Artemisia Gentileschi by Agnès Merlet as the starting point for several interrelating arguments about the troubled *relations between life and work,* biography and art, fact and fiction, history and truth, and document and text. She addresses both fictions concerning the artist and the legal histories of her case to stress an ethics of reading rather than a politics of truth.

Pollock argues with and, at times, against Merlet's feminist critics. She responds to those who critique the film for its radical "distortion" of the "truth" of the key event, the rape of the painter by her teacher. This event has figured in the literature on the artist as the defining "fact" from which interpretations of her work stem. There have also been new-historicist readings of the legal evidence. These readings dismiss the idea of rape in our modern understanding of a sexual violation with traumatic personal effects. Reading for the historically and culturally specific social conventions and value systems in which premarital sexual assault was framed and the subjects involved in it discursively fashioned through testimony, Pollock states, new historicists practice a mode of reading texts rather than of using documents as evidence, while still claiming a truth status for their interpretations. Their work, with all its still-open questions about the register of subjectivity and embodiment, is being used by revisionist art historians of the Gentileschis to entirely discount as anachronistic the feminist interpretations of Artemisia Gentileschi's life and work as a site of feminine subjectivity and patriarchal violence.

Taking on the feminist desire for ethical narratives that function in our present of encounters with paintings and their inherited framings, and seeking also to maintain a theoretical self-awareness of the ethics of situated reading, this chapter replays, or plays back, across the historicist debate an analysis of the first fictional response to the Italian painter, a 1947 novel by the art historian Anna Banti. Pollock argues that this is an exemplary text in its self-critical engagement with its own desire, projections, identifications, and acceptance. Yet, she maintains, the novel makes the case that thinking about the lives of women in the past does matter—and is a necessary, if challenging, part of a contemporary, critical self-fashioning of feminine subjectivity and creativity.

Each chapter of this book, then, constitutes an engagement with an "Artemisia file," a discourse through which the twenty-first century has acquired its image of "Artemisia." Neither rejecting nor endorsing these discourses in any simple way, the essays look back in order to move on. Knowing that we cannot ignore the cultural traditions that have produced the Artemisia we think we know, the authors think through what it means to fall back on the common paradigms of dealing with art. They also attempt to contribute—from within those paradigms as much as from within an oblique perspective critical of them—to a further, deeper, and more engaged understanding and appreciation of the paintings, to a way of looking that is committed to what art is, can be, and does.

One last note: Artemisia's paintings derive a lot of their effect from their exuberant colors. Unfortunately, we could not reproduce color images in this book. For those interested in pursuing the colorism of these paintings, the catalogue of the recent exhibition will help (Christiansen and Mann 2001).

Mieke Bal

ARTEMISIA'S HAND

Mary D. Garrard

Art historians who are normally careful connoisseurs seem to crumble at the alleged sight of Artemisia's face. The *Portrait of a Female Martyr* (fig. 1) is one of several paintings that have recently been attributed to Artemisia Gentileschi and identified as images of the artist herself. Another is the *Portrait of a Woman Playing a Lute* found at the Villa Medici at Artimino (fig. 2), presented in the 2001–2 exhibition entitled Orazio and Artemisia Gentileschi: Father and Daughter Painters in Baroque Italy and its catalogue as a self-portrait of the artist (Christiansen and Mann 2001). These two works are very different in style, however, and the faces somewhat divergent in physiognomy. The very possibility of recognizing Artemisia's image in a painting, it appears, must trump serious considerations of style and other factors crucial in the practice of attribution.

We may reasonably ask whether there are quite so many self-portraits and self-images as have been claimed. The compulsion to identify Artemisia herself in every woman's face she painted, despite the lack of consistency among the faces in these images, may well be influenced by gendered preconceptions. One is the cultural habit of seeing woman as object-to-be-looked-at, the site of scopophilic pleasure. A preoccupation with the female body in

1

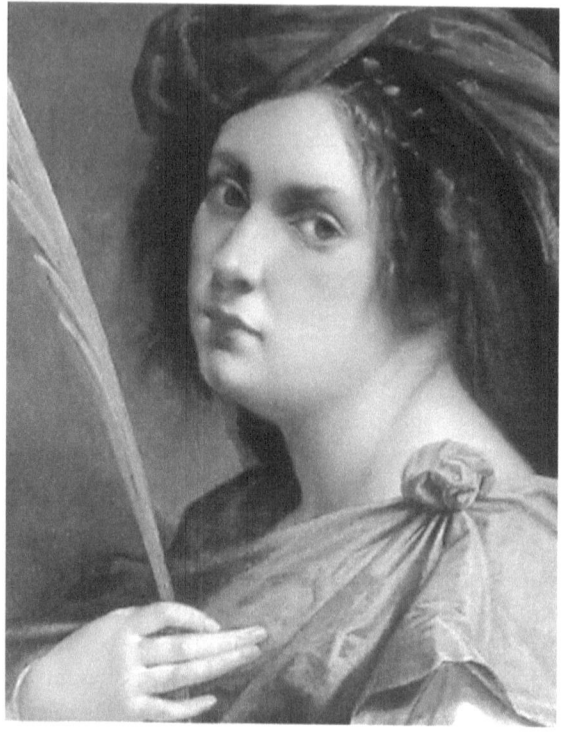

Figure 1. Attributed to Artemisia Gentileschi, *Portrait of a Female Martyr*, ca. 1615? Private collection.

these terms led many early modern writers to fixate upon women artists as objects of beauty rather than as active agents, a way of thinking that has by no means disappeared in today's world. A related gender stereotype, female narcissism, lurks behind the suggestion that the young Artemisia, locked in a claustrophobic Roman household, became obsessed with her own features and painted them repeatedly. This was recently proposed by one art historian (Cavazzini 2001, 291). Such gendered assumptions are all the more dangerous when unacknowledged, because they silently buttress attributions presented as value-neutral and thus affect the defining of Artemisia's oeuvre and artistic identity.

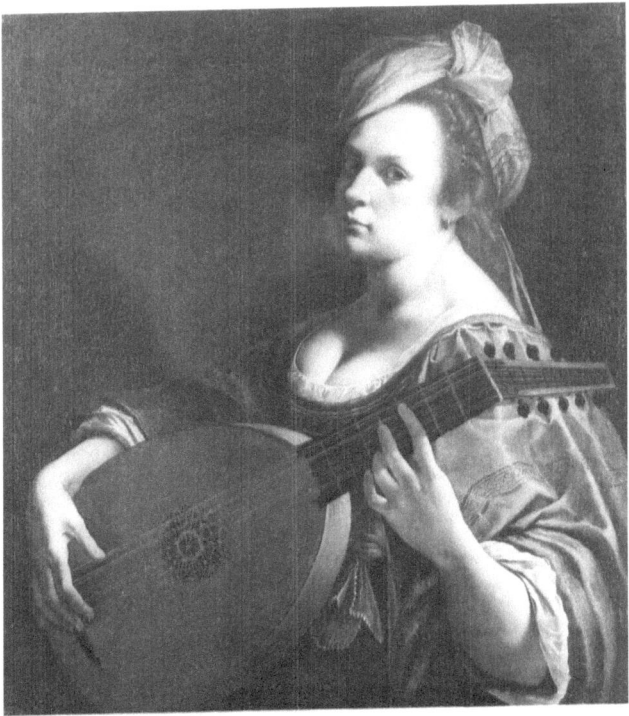

Figure 2. Attributed to Artemisia Gentileschi, *Portrait of a Woman Playing a Lute,*
ca. 1615–17.

As a way of challenging certain recent attributions on grounds
that might help establish broader criteria, I propose that we turn
away from faces, and look at *hands,* which have been an unexam-
ined aspect of Artemisia's distinctive style. It is a tenet of traditional
connoisseurship that the depiction of hands can be an identifying
trait of an artistic "hand." Giovanni Morelli and Bernard Berenson
argued that the hand ranked somewhere below the eyes and mouth
in revealing the descriptive habits of individual artists. These connoisseurs focused, however, on the static details of fingernails,
wrinkles, or the shape of a thumb. Max Friedländer, another eminent connoisseur, more astutely observed that "the hand speaks

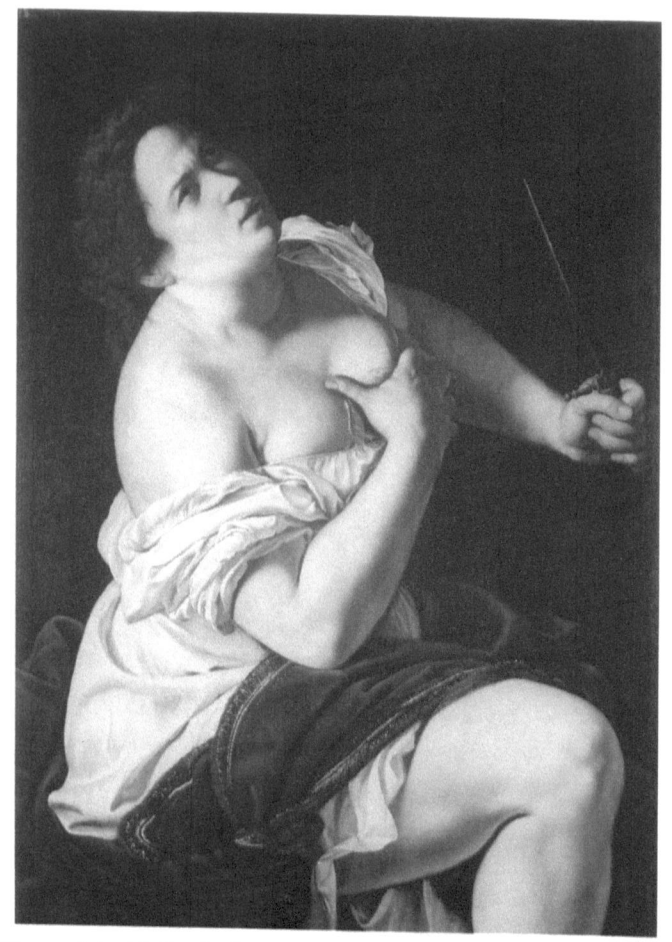

Figure 3. Artemisia Gentileschi, *Lucretia*, ca. 1621. Detail.

more through its movement than through its shape" (Berenson 1902, 134–36; Friedländer [1942] in Vaccaro 1996, 148).[1] Indeed, the hand speaks *both* through its movement and shape, but we in the twenty-first century are positioned to take this consideration further, for hands in art are shaped and move according to a variety of social preconceptions.

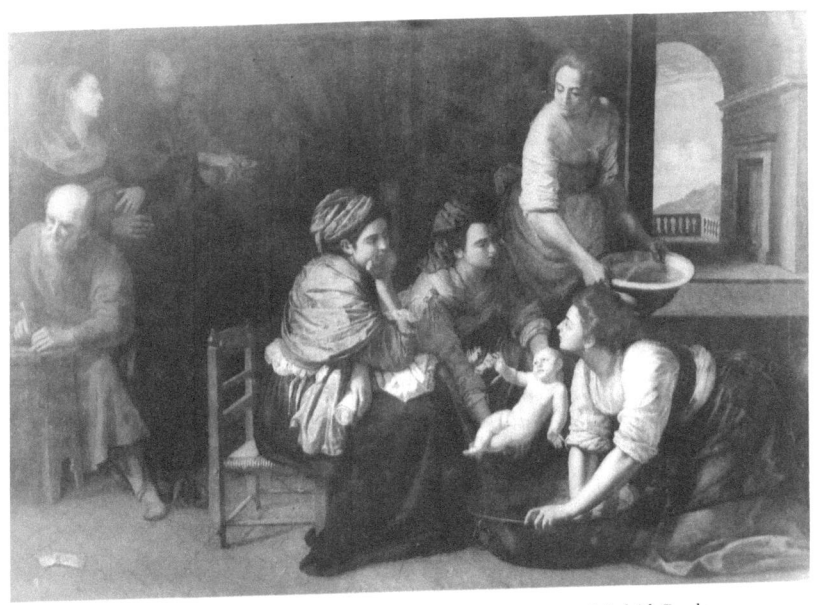

Figure 4. Artemisia Gentileschi, *Birth of St. John the Baptist,* ca. 1633–35. Madrid, Prado.

Like faces, hands have a gender dimension. They are the locus of agency, both literally and symbolically. In the early modern period, when the only female agency that signified was located in the womb, it is not surprising that some female artists, as if to compensate, depicted female characters with unusually strong forearms and firm hands, whose agility and grip express the women's power to act upon the world. Artemisia, above all, gives us such figures. It is through their hands that Artemisia's women take on the world and confront adversity. Looking at the Uffizi *Judith* (see fig. 24), we fixate upon the bloody decapitation, achieved with surgical skill by two coolly detached women, but we rarely comment on those supremely competent hands, wrists, and forearms that carry out the determined minds' command. In Artemisia's world, female figures hammer and paint, grab and hold, push and shove, with extraordinary ease. Their hands and arms are exceptionally strong, more than adequate for the job to be done. Lucretia, for instance (fig. 3), clutches both breast and sword with an anxious energy that doubles the tension shown in her face. The midwives in the *Birth of St. John the Baptist* (fig. 4) barely *have* faces, but they all have powerful forearms that move the basins around the space as capably as they got that baby born.

Perhaps the most capable hands in all of Artemisia's oeuvre are those of Abra in the Detroit *Judith* (fig. 5). These large, strong hands lead us into the picture at its base, the viewer's point of entry into this large painting, establishing the theme of female power to be amplified above. Gently but firmly, and with an ease that bespeaks self-confidence, Abra's hands close the sack around the ashen head, indifferent to the blood that stains their fingers. Our eyes are led from Abra's hands through her arms and gaze, upward, to the most dramatic display of gestural rhetoric in Artemisia's art. Judith's flamboyant gestures are dramatic, but also subtle. With her right hand, she claims authority, gripping Holofernes's sword with unusual determination. The angle of her wrist echoes that of the defeated general's empty gauntlet on the table, as if to mock his loss of power and flaunt her gain of it. Judith's left hand sweeps expansively across her body, impelled by the blade-like curve of her shadowed arm; her flat palm rises rhetorically into strong light to shout, "Stop, I hear something." This arresting gesture dramatizes, not the women's power, but their vulnerability. It's a visual cry of alarm at a moment of danger.

Hand movements that sustain divergent aspects of the narrative are to be seen in other works by Artemisia. Lucretia, for instance, weighs her decision and its consequences through contradictory gestures: the raised left hand that holds the dagger introduces the dismal prospect of suicide, while the right hand that clutches her breast and palpates the nipple recalls the ongoing biological cycle about to be interrupted by the drastic action that patriarchal morality requires. And look again at *Susanna and the Elders* (see fig. 17) as a narrative completely mimed in the movements of the six hands clustered at upper center. Through gesture, the elders express male bonding, conspiracy, and silencing, while Susanna's two-handed gesture conveys her intimidation and desire to escape. Yet these hands do more, for while the resisting right hand next to the twisted head conveys Su-

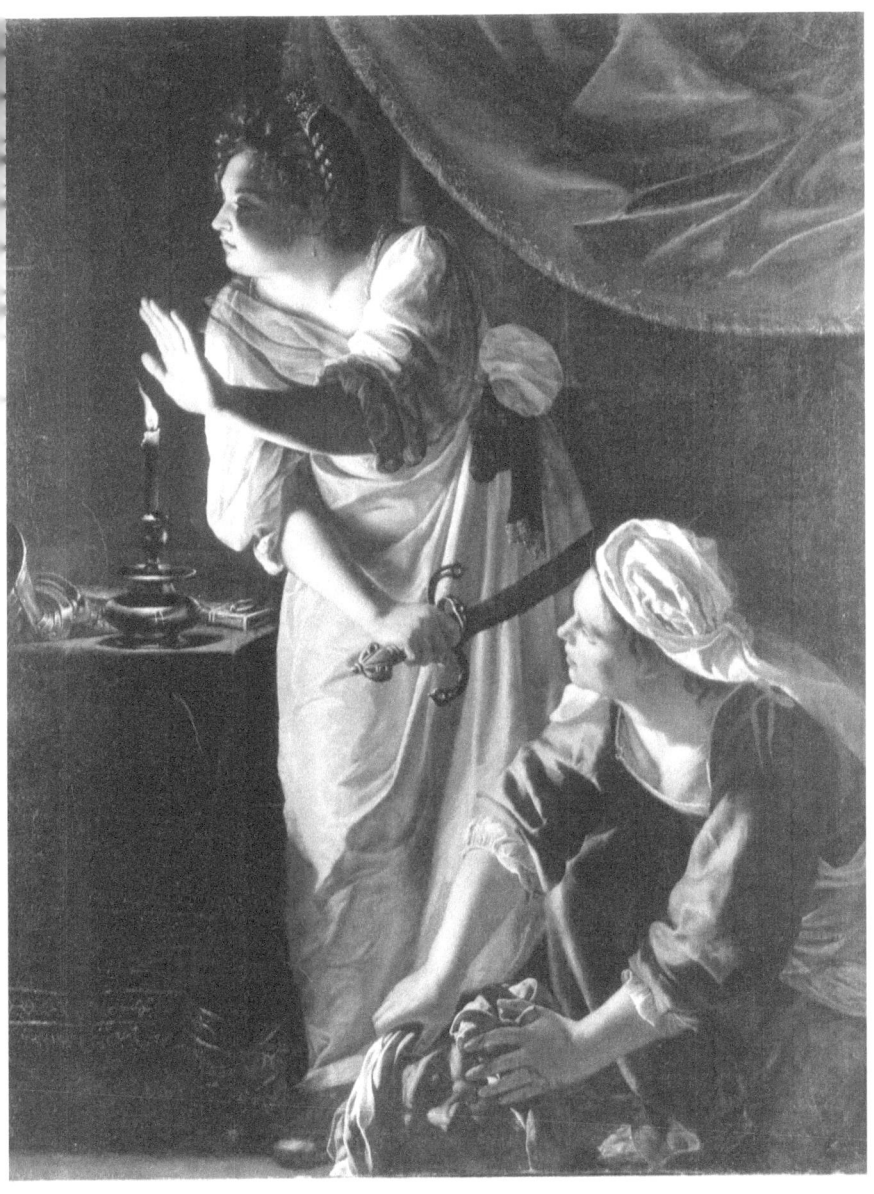

Figure 5. Artemisia Gentileschi, *Judith and Her Maidservant*, ca. 1625. Detroit, Institute of Arts.

sanna's fear and aversion, her left hand springs upright, relieving the torsion and compression of the head and right hand, and hinting at a resurgence of will and autonomy that the story in fact doesn't allow.

❦

Artemisia's women exert pressure with their hands. Their fingers grasp objects firmly and make a fist. They have full rotary motion in the wrist, and their wrists break backward to show the strain of exertion, just as men's wrists do. If, as seems likely, Artemisia modeled Judith's hand in the Naples and Uffizi pictures (see figs. 22 and 24) on the male figures in Orazio's *Crowning with Thorns*, this proved to be an effective strategy for empowering her women. For, more than anything, it's the breaking wrist that convincingly signifies both *agility* and *agency*, words linked by their common root, *agere*—to set in motion, to drive, construct or build. Orazio treats female hands differently. His women are typically given light work; they have a soft touch. With very few exceptions, Orazio shows women with hands that hang, relaxed and graceful, bend forward limply, or barely grasp a heavy object. His tendency to turn active figures into still lifes has been noted, but not the gendered differential that exaggerates this effect in his female figures. Artemisia's women have normal human hands that function as signs of female agency; Orazio's women have feminine hands, signs of female passivity.

   In presenting women's hands as objects of beauty or signs of passivity, Orazio follows the lead of many a Renaissance artist—Raphael and Bronzino, for instance—who give us female hands that are white, smooth, and soft, their fingers long and delicate, tapering toward the tips, just as the cinquecento theorist Agnolo Firenzuola prescribes in his treatise on the beauty of women (Firenzuola 1992, 67). The self-conscious display of a woman's beautiful hands, sustained in the seicento by artists such as Guido Reni and Domenichino (fig. 6), was fueled by a literary tradition derived from Petrarch, in which the perfect woman is described through poetic tributes to the beauty of her body parts, itemized

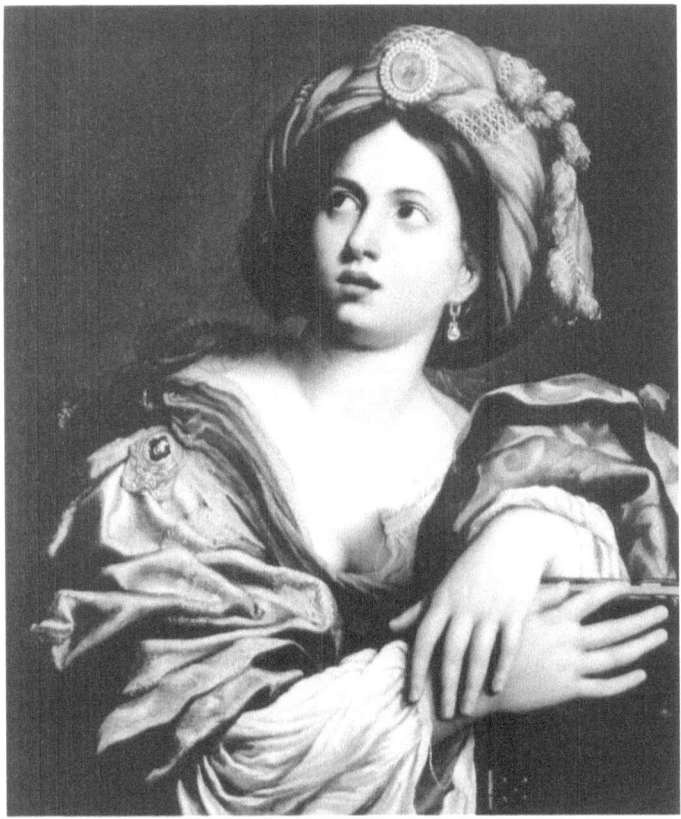

Figure 6. Domenichino, *The Persian Sibyl,* 1581–1641. London, Wallace Collection.

fetishistically. In art influenced by this tradition, when women do things with their hands, it must be ineffectively.

Orazio's *Lute Player* in the National Gallery (fig. 7) seems disposed for the display of one beautiful hand. What action we see is barely credible, for it's not easy to play a lute while supporting it lightly with a thumb on the back. Male lutists, whether seen frontally or, like Orazio's lute player, from the back (compare Paul Bril's *Self-Portrait* in the Rhode Island School of Design), typically grasp the instrument more vigorously and have actively moving, jointed fingers. The

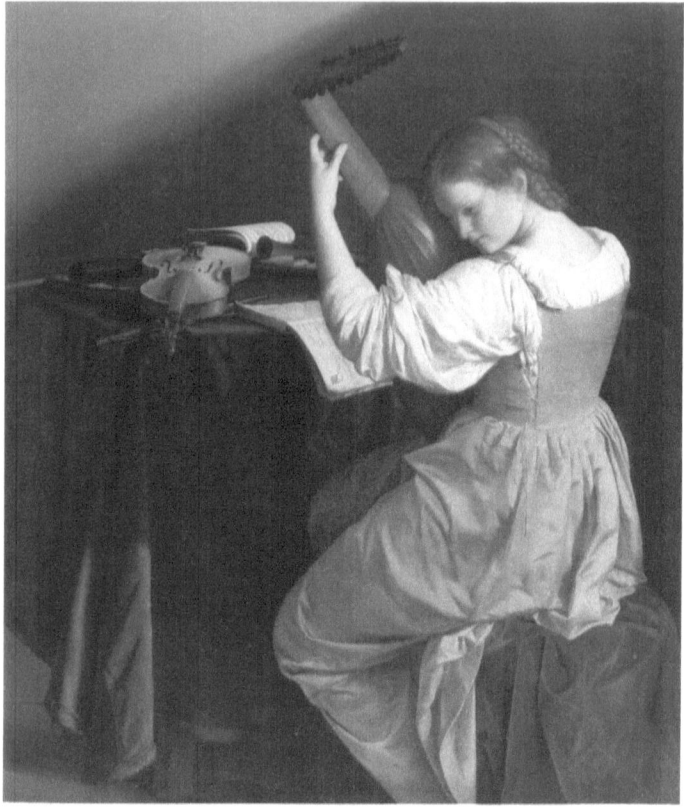

Figure 7. Orazio Gentileschi, *Lute Player,* ca. 1612–15. Washington, DC, National Gallery.

hands of female lute players, by contrast (e.g., see Carlo Saraceni's *St. Cecilia and Angel* in the Palazzo Barberini), are arranged to show off their beauty; they barely move, and they pose self-consciously. (One qualification: in the pictorial world of Roman Caravaggesque realism, "low-life" women often have strong hands, and they sometimes play lusty songs on lutes just like the men, but largely they do nefarious or shady things, like picking pockets or telling fortunes—female agency here is shaded by moralizing stereotype.)

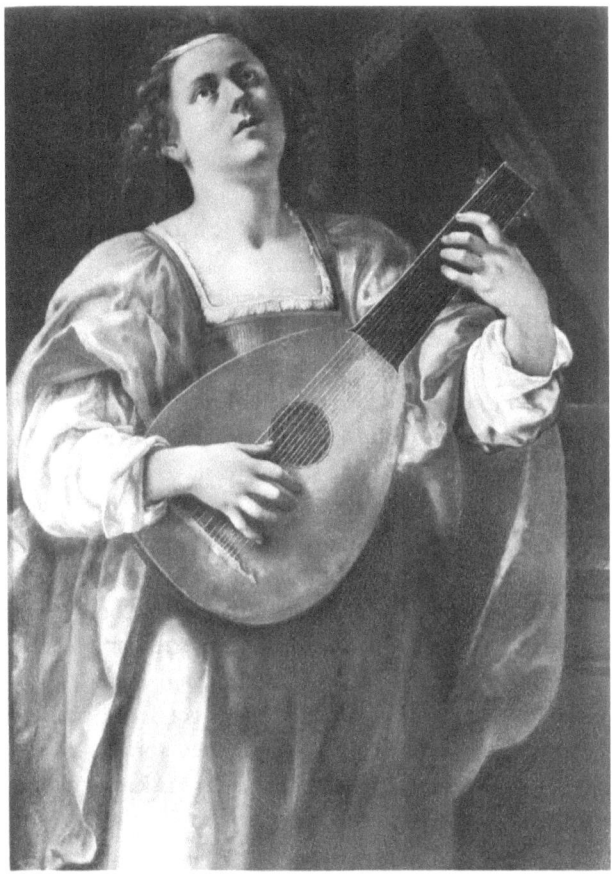

Figure 8. Artemisia Gentileschi, *Lute Player (Saint Cecilia)*, 1610s. Rome, Galleria Spada. (Photo credit: Alinari/Art Resource, New York.)

Artemisia's Galleria Spada *Lute Player* (fig. 8) is another matter. In the context of gendered norms, this woman's hands are extraordinary. Firmly modeled, with knuckles and jointed fingers, these agile hands credibly play the instrument. They seem almost more alive than the woman's face. Jointed hands and articulated knuckles link the Spada figure with the newly discovered Villa Medici *Lute Player* (fig. 2), which is identified in the Gentileschi exhibition catalogue as a self-portrait of the artist on the strength of its presumed identity with an Artemisian portrait of herself playing a lute mentioned in a Villa Medici inventory of 1638 (see Christiansen and Mann 2001, fig. 57). The hands of these two lute players are not identical in shape and coloration, yet they share the qualities of mobility and agility that are relatively rare in images of female hands—one indication that the painting could be by Artemisia.

More troubling for the Artemisia attribution is the lute player's eroticized decolletage, something rarely seen in Artemisia's clothed women. In the *Esther,* or the *Self-portrait as the Allegory of Painting* (see fig. 37), the neckline is as low, but the breasts do not heave out of it. Uniquely, the Naples and Uffizi *Judith*s (see figs. 22 and 24) display a sensuous, swelling curve in a single breast, yet this feature could refer to the seductive role the heroine assumed to snare Holofernes. The lute player's sensuality was emphasized in the wall label at the Metropolitan Museum's installation of the exhibition, where we read that the painting's erotic overtones were appropriate both to the traditional association of music and love and to Artemisia's reputation, "not simply as a painter," but as a beautiful and seductive woman. Here, again, a scopophilic bias interferes with good reasoning. Would the Artemisia who escaped from gossip-ridden Rome to the relative dignity of marriage and court status in Florence risk restigmatization as a seductive woman by presenting herself in this guise? It's certainly not impossible that Artemisia might have sexualized her own image, yet if we have to choose, it's much more probable that she did not. Conceivably, this is Artemisia's portrait of another woman, perhaps contextualized by some theatrical performance at the Florentine court (as Judith Mann suggests in the catalogue entry, though she proposes Artemisia in that role). Or, it might represent Artemisia herself, painted as another artist wished to present her, driven by the same eroticizing impulses that shaped the Metropolitan Museum wall label.

The latter possibility comes to mind when we consider the *Female Martyr* also newly identified as Artemisia and ascribed to her (fig. 1).

This woman slightly resembles the lute player, and also the Artemisia of Jerome David's portrait engraving, in the set of the eyes, nose, and mouth. Moreover, an inscription on the back of the panel identifies the work as by the hand of Artemisia, though we might question the accuracy of this inscription, considering that the inscriber also claimed that Artemisia was a "niece of Orazio" (Christiansen and Mann 2001).[2] A more reliable signifier than an inscription of uncertain vintage, it seems to me, is the telltale hand—for there is not so dainty and formless a hand in all of Artemisia's established oeuvre, no hand so relentlessly feminine, so lacking in structure.

In the exhibition catalogue, the *Martyr* is compared to Artemisia's Florentine *St. Catherine,* a painting that combines two of the artist's hand types in the same image. Yet the *Martyr*'s hand bears no resemblance to either of these hands. It displays neither the articulated knuckles of Catherine's right hand, nor what I once called the "dimpled knuckles" of her left hand. It is also inconceivable that the artist who painted that flabby hand with its wayward tapering fingers could have painting the strong, jointed, firmly structured hands of the Villa Medici *Lute Player* (fig. 2). This might be an image of Artemisia as a martyr, possibly even a copy of a painting by Artemisia, but it was surely painted by another artist. Given the stylistic divergence between the *Martyr* and the *Lute Player,* it seems to me that the echo of facial type from one to the other can only be explained by postulating that an ur-image of Artemisia's face lies behind the play with her identity in both pictures.

୬ఎ

When painting hands, Artemisia appears to think from inside her own body. It's not necessarily that she copies her own hands (though an artist always has this option), but that when she draws a female hand, she seems to experience it kinesthetically, feeling its capacity to move. Artemisia's male hands are much less anatomically convincing. In the Bologna *Gonfaloniere,* for example, one hand touches a table, yet without exerting pressure; the other hangs, graceful but lifeless, like an empty glove. Artemisia never painted a female figure who did not have at least one, and usually two, visible hands. In her pictorial world, where female protagonists succeed in their quests through manual dexterity and the hand is a synecdoche for female capability, women without hands would be disabled.

This is among the reasons why we should firmly reject the attribution to Artemisia of the Le Mans *Allegory of Painting* (fig. 9), an attribution sustained by the inclusion of the picture in the 2001–2 Orazio and Artemisia Gentileschi exhibition. In his catalogue raisonné of Artemisia's paintings, Ward Bissell has rightly protested this attribution, arguing that its "openly obscene" presentation of a reclining female nude from a viewpoint that emphasizes her buttocks would be unthinkable for Artemisia (Christiansen and Mann 2001; Bissell 1999, 299–301), especially because the figure represented is the Allegory of Painting, accompanied by the mask, brushes, and palette that are her attributes, an allegorical figure that was by the 1620s already identified with Artemisia herself.[3] Bissell claims that Artemisia would hardly invoke so compromising a self-reference and argues instead that the painter may have been Giovanni Baglioni, an earlier antagonist of Orazio who, as a man with an agenda, may have intended to wound Orazio by insulting his daughter.

If the painter of this objectified, debased, and disarmed Pittura did intend to evoke Artemisia in the image, as Bissell suggests and I think likely, then I would say the indignity was aimed not at her father but at Artemisia herself, for it clearly fantasizes the repression of her artistic agency, through figurative disempowerment and sinister sexualizing. The figure's arms are visually cut off at the elbow by objects or shadows—a form of castration in this context. Her visible body parts include long, inactive legs, a partially hidden but clearly reddened anus (as Bissell says, hinting at an intercourse that preceded the woman's sleep), and finally, diminished by the telescoping perspective, the truncated arms and a head that ostensibly rests on the lower strut of an easel, yet floats awkwardly like the organically disconnected elbow and knee. More truly obscene than the painting, and effectively more malicious than the artist's prob-

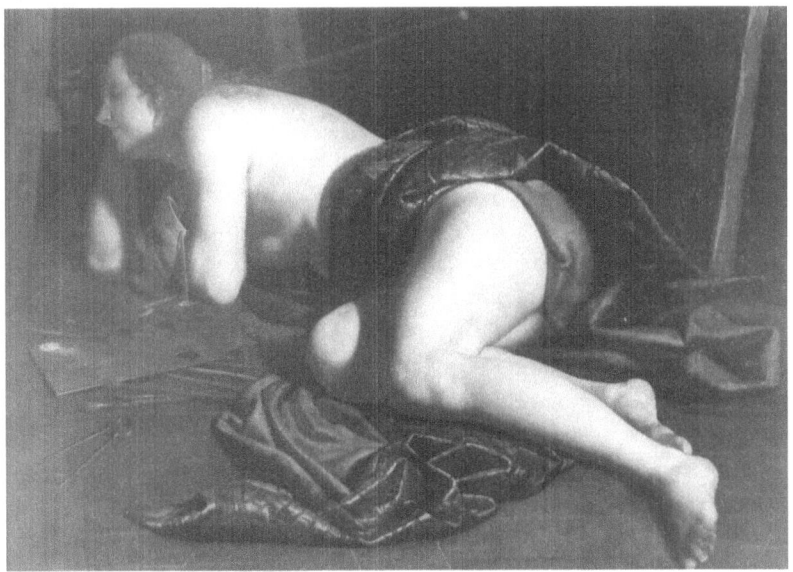

Figure 9. Attributed to Artemisia Gentileschi, *Allegory of Painting,* 1620s. Le Mans, Musée de Tessé.

able intent, is the notion still seriously entertained in the Gentileschi exhibition and its catalogue that Artemisia herself might have painted what would have been a deeply self-debasing picture.

What is gained by ascribing this painting to Artemisia? We might ask a similar question about the disputed *Cleopatra* (fig. 10) attribution—what is at stake in denying her authorship of this work? In both cases, though in reverse terms, the painter's artistic agency is compromised by the identification of the depicted body as her own. In both cases, as in that of the Villa Medici *Lute Player,* Artemisia the sex object supplants Artemisia the artist. Just for the record, the attribution of the *Cleopatra* to Orazio has been supported by an all-male cast of writers (Erich Schleier, Carlo Volpe, and, most recently, Ward Bissell and Keith Christiansen). Writers who support the attribution to Artemisia have been mostly, though not exclusively, female (the women include Ann Sutherland Harris,

Mina Gregori, myself, and, most recently, Judith Mann).[4] I hesitate
to invoke the specter of gendered scholarship, but gender-weighted
preference for experience over desire as a telling factor may have
led the women, but not the men, to reject the Orazio attribution on
the grounds of anatomical description. One has only to compare
Cleopatra's breasts, which are at least minimally flattened by gravity, with the perfect domical cupcakes that sit on the chests of
Orazio's Danae and other nudes to see radically divergent mentali-
ties about female anatomy at work here.

The attribution of the *Cleopatra* to Orazio is also fueled by the
woman-is-to-be-looked-at preconception, since some of its propo-
nents presume that Artemisia must have been the model for the
nude Cleopatra. Christiansen suggested this interpretation in the
Metropolitan wall labels; he was a bit more circumspect in his catalogue entry, yet he was quick to connect Cleopatra's portraitlike
face with the rumor that Artemisia sometimes posed nude for her
father (Christiansen and Mann 2001, fig. 17). Not so subtly, this
unsupported rumor, when combined with the identification of
Cleopatra as "really" Artemisia, renders seemingly credible the
slanderous hint, by one of Tassi's defenders in the rape trial, of unseemly behavior between father and daughter.[5] Missing is the consideration that if Orazio had been engaging in funny business with
his daughter, putting her face on a female nude would be incredibly
self-incriminating.

Of course, the *Cleopatra* is equally unseemly as a painting by
Artemisia, as long as we insist that the face of this nude woman
pinned to the bed and displayed for the gaze must be the artist's
own. Indeed, many feminists have expressed discomfort with the
attribution of the painting to Artemisia because of its repetition of
the pornographically flavored reclining female nude. I continue to
believe that its homely realism tends to subvert rather than reify the
eroticized type that may have been specified by her patron, and that
the painting is entirely comprehensible, and even complex, if interpreted in a straightforward way as an image of Cleopatra, queen of

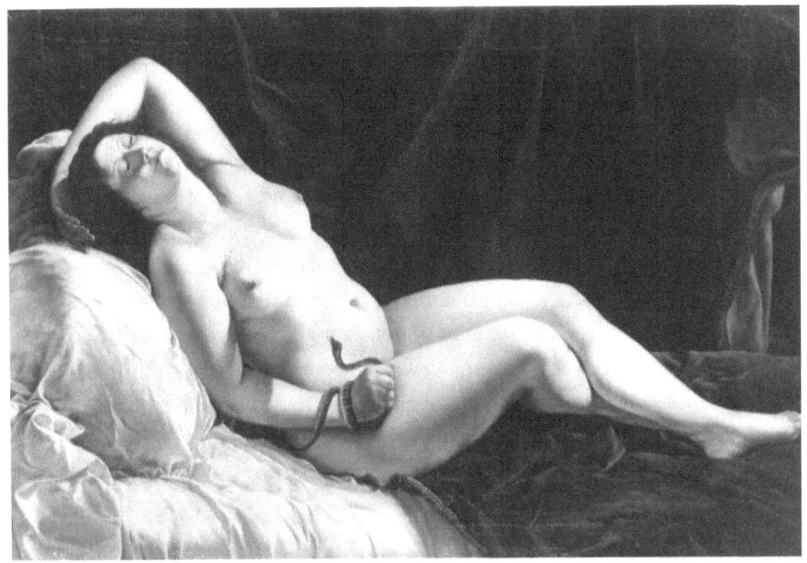

Figure 10. Artemisia Gentileschi, *Cleopatra*, ca. 1621–22 (or, Orazio Gentileschi, ca. 1610–12?). Detail. Milan, Amedeo Morandotti.

Egypt, directing her own suicide (see Garrard 1989, 244 ff.). In further support of the Artemisia attribution, I would emphasize one neglected consideration: agency in this painting is expressed in the steady fist that grips the asp and controls the narrative.

The hand test alone would place this disputed picture firmly in Artemisia's oeuvre, for there are no Cleopatras in art who clutch the asp so forcefully, as Mann notes in the Gentileschi catalogue (Christiansen and Mann 2001, 304). And there is no female hand in Orazio's art comparable to Cleopatra's tightly gripping fist, whose intensity is punctuated by a protruding thumb. I count two fists in his entire oeuvre, neither with a visible thumb, and both of these belong to figures for which Artemisia may have posed (the Detroit *Violinist* and the Houston *Sibyl*). To find this hand in Artemisia's work, however, we have only to look to the Naples, Pitti, Uffizi, and Detroit *Judith*s (figs. 22, 29, 24, and 5, respectively). The fact that

Orazio never used the gesture, while Artemisia made it a virtual trademark, joins many other considerations to support the probability that it was she who painted the *Cleopatra.*

The prominence of female fists in Artemisia's oeuvre runs considerably against the cultural grain for, according to representational norms, a fist is masculine, an open hand feminine. He who brandishes a fist threatens, asserts force or, in the gestural world of modern sport, asserts victory as an achievement specifically linked to his manhood. At Wimbledon in the summer of 2002, Lleyton Hewitt and Serena Williams frequently made the victory fist when they won a point or a game. Nevertheless, the championship photographs gave us gender-appropriate gestures for each: he pumped, she waved.

ᨪ

Artemisia knew quite well what female hands are supposed to do. She could produce the pampered hand or the graceful hand with the best of them, especially in the Casa Buonarroti *Inclination* and the Pitti *Magdalen* (see fig. 31), paintings in which grace distinctly overtakes dexterity. But hands are shaped by class as well as gender. Artemisia's Florentine characters, echoing the lifestyles of their courtly patrons, sustain the Petrarchan ideal of feminine beauty quite late into an age that had in Rome been radically disarranged by the new working-class aesthetic of Caravaggism. A trace memory of her Roman origins may explain the fact that Artemisia attaches even comely hands to rather muscular forearms, which she usually contrives to expose. The strange awkwardness of the *Magdalen*'s left hand may have resulted from a head-on collision between the Florentine beauty convention that called for long tapered fingers and Artemisia's naturalist impulse to articulate the joints of a moving hand. Yet its exaggerated jointing borders on parody, hinting at a resistance to the conventions of gender and class.

Later, in Naples, Artemisia joined women of different classes in the same painting. The servant at lower left in the Columbus *Bathsheba* is a reprise of a figure in the *Birth of St. John the Baptist* (fig. 4), both assertively defined as working-class by their rolled-up sleeves, muscular forearms, and reddened skin. Similar servant women discover the dead queen in the Roman *Cleopatra.* In the *Bathsheba,* the prominently positioned working woman is strongly contrasted in type with the beautiful and opulent, white-skinned heroine—a juxtaposition that is highly unusual in Neapolitan painting of this period. It is a form of *contrapposto,* to be sure, a pleasing contrasting of opposites, which might have been encouraged by her patron. Yet one wonders whether the artist's own sympathies might have intruded. Positioned by her liminality as an artist to know the worlds of both workers and aristocrats, Artemisia could present both from experienced knowledge. We might surmise that in those pictures that increasingly present glamorous and passive heroines, she included the working women, voluntarily, as displaced models of female agency.

※

In a broader sense, even when detached from specific gestures, the hand functions as a gendered signifier of cultural prowess. From antiquity through the Renaissance, hands were considered to represent the brain, an organ that was effectively masculine. As we learn from Claire Sherman's recent exhibition and catalogue devoted to the hand, terms like "to grasp" or "to apprehend" show how persistently the intellectual is expressed through the manual. "Taking hold" means "understanding new ideas." For Aristotle, man's hand distinguished him from animals: "The hand is for the body as the intellect is for the soul" (Kemp 2000, 22). In the art of painting, the hand is the visual voice of the intellect; Leonardo da Vinci famously avowed that the motions of the mind must be expressed by the motions of the body. The Renaissance artist's hand was both agent and sign of his creative ability. Giotto, for example, was celebrated for his *manus et ingenium,* skill and talent (Baxandall 1971, 15–16). Two centuries later, when the craftsman's talent had been magnified into the artist's genius, Dürer was praised for his "divine hand." As Richard Spear has pointed out, this figure of speech and its counterparts—divine brush,

divine art, or the learned hand, *dotta mano*—were all used to refer to a nexus of artistic genius, divinity, and imagination only
found in the greatest artists: Raphael, Michelangelo, and Titian
(Spear 1985, 259–65).

What of the hand of the woman artist? Artemisia's younger
contemporary Elisabetta Sirani was praised by a contemporary
Bolognese poet in masculine terms, as Babette Bohn has recently
pointed out (Bohn 2002, 57–79). He called her "*pittore*," not "*pittrice*" (male, not female painter), and described her as empowered
by a *destra armata,* her strong right arm. Sirani's heroic images of
Judith and Timoclea exhibit a commanding dexterity that may
have been inspired by Artemisia's strong-handed women, yet the
Bolognese painter received different critical treatment. The viril-
izing of Sirani distinctly differs from Artemisia's positioning by an
anonymous Venetian poet, who juxtaposed Artemisia *pittrice* with
a hypothetical *pittore,* to contrast their depictions of an *amoretto.*
The imaginary male painter is fortified with a *dotta man virile,* a
learned masculine hand; Artemisia, by contrast, has the (more
limited) power to create a lifelike image, an unsurprising achievement for a woman, who can, after all, give birth to a real child—
that is to say, whose natural sphere is not artistic creation but maternal procreation.[6]

We see Artemisia's unlearned hand holding a paintbrush in
the well-known drawing by her contemporary Pierre Dumonstier
le Neveu (fig. 11). In an accompanying text, the draughtsman tells
us that Artemisia's hand stands for her ability to create ravishing
images for discerning eyes (Garrard 1989, 63–64; Bissell 1999,
221–22). There is a hint of Petrarchan fetishizing here, since male
artists blessed with divine hands were rarely if ever represented by
their hands *per se.* In the early modern period, when artists were
engaged in a campaign to elevate the intellectual status of their
practice, this would have been a reminder of the very thing up-
wardly mobile artists were trying to make people forget—that
great art might be generated in the mind but had to be executed
by the lowly hand. If the highest praise possible for a woman artist

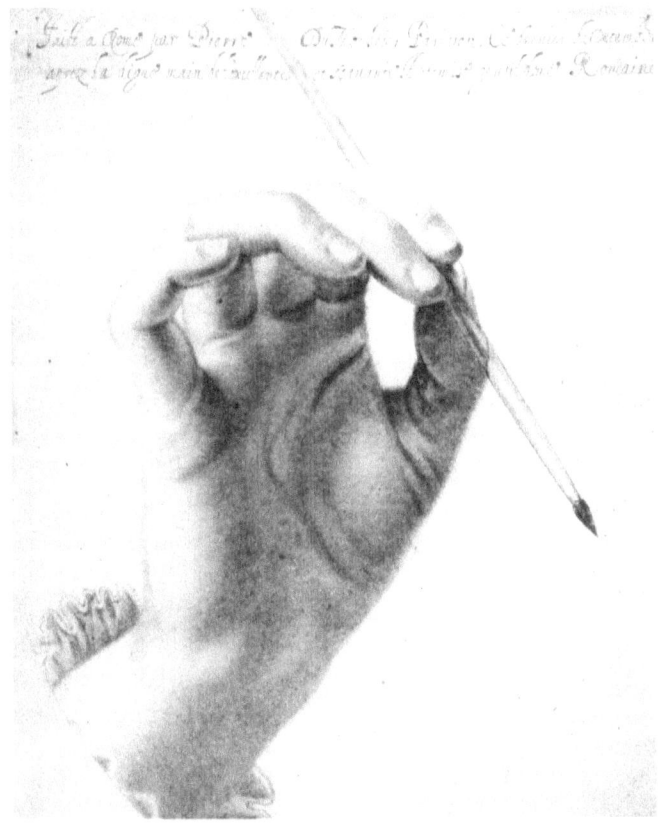

Figure 11. Pierre Dumonstier le Neveu, *Drawing of the Hand of Artemisia Gentileschi,* 1625. London, British Museum.

is honorary masculinity, something that Elisabetta Sirani received fully in the poetic tribute to her *destra armata,* in the case of the more threatening Artemisia Gentileschi, the homage is qualified by gender, both in the anonymous Venetian poem and in Dumonstier's drawing.

Dumonstier associates Artemisia with the idea of beauty, not only in his image of her hand alone but also in his text, which links Artemisia's right hand with the much-praised beauty of the hands of Aurora. This might be a conventional allusion to Homer's "rosy-fingered dawn," but it must also indirectly refer to Artemisia's own painting of Aurora, known from its description by the seventeenth-century Florentine writer Filippo Baldinucci, which Bissell has recently identified with a painting in a Roman private collection (fig. 12).[7] I would accept the *Aurora* attribution (with some reservations about the handling of the *putto* and the landscape), because what is most persuasively Artemisian about this image is the pair of prominent and active hands. In significant contrast to contemporary images of Aurora—such as Guido Reni's version at the Casino Rospigliosi, which presents the goddess of dawn floating like a ship's figurehead, with floral wreaths in her arms, or Guercino's Casino Ludovisi goddess, who is seated in a chariot strewing flowers—Artemisia's Aurora steps free of her chariot, a full-bodied, striding personification. Again, her agency is emphasized: the muscular goddess physically parts the sky with her hands, her flattened palms pressing firmly against the dark walls of night, just as Baldinucci describes. Unusually, Baldinucci praises both the *ingegno* and *mano* of Artemisia, an even-handed gesture that differentiates him from Dumonstier and the Venetian poet, who qualify Artemisia's artistic hand by its gender, subtly repressing memory of the virile hands she actually painted.

❧

I have written before about the interactive dynamic that seems invariably to develop between Artemisia Gentileschi's art and its reception, both in her time and ours (Garrard 2001, 118–23). Writers, then and now, have reacted to her strong women and their aggressive deeds with praise for the beauty of the artist and her ravishing imagery, and with innuendoes about her eroticized reputation. So it is not surprising that in the Gentileschi exhibition of 2001–2, the largest and most widely viewed display of Artemisia's art ever mounted, and at the symposium in St. Louis that was the climax of the Gentileschi year, once again Artemisia's artistic assertion—claiming power for her female heroes and artistic identity for her-

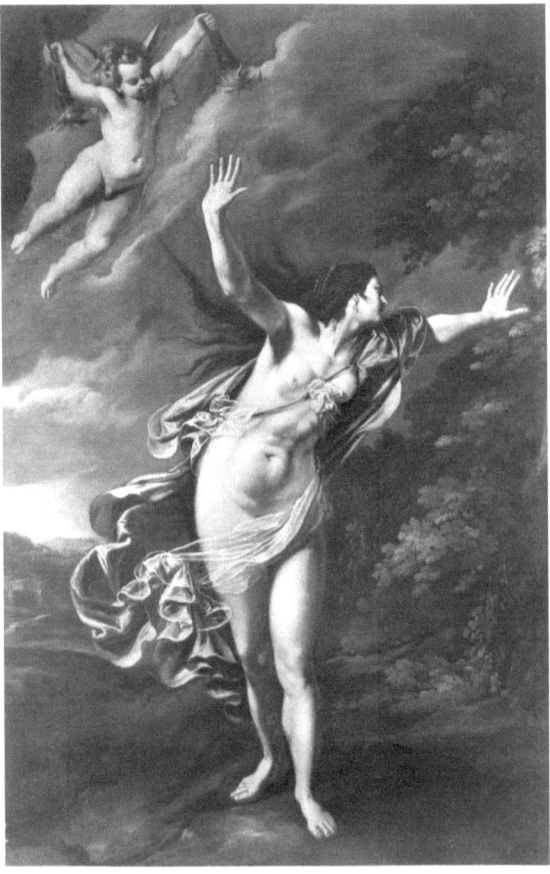

Figure 12. Artemisia Gentileschi, *Aurora*, ca. 1625–27. Rome, private collection.

self—met cultural repression. Nobody meant to do her harm, but many are complicit in undermining Artemisia's artistic agency. It is not only those who enthusiastically support dubious attributions to Artemisia who would demean and belittle her as an artist. Nor is it only Keith Christiansen, who produced the dismissive and defamatory wall labels at the Met (yet in his paper at the Artemisia symposium in St. Louis tacked surprisingly to offer readings of Artemisia's paintings that fully credited her with intention and purpose), nor

Ward Bissell, who decided to reattribute at the symposium virtually all of Artemisia's early paintings to Orazio, to the mystification of symposium participants and audience alike. It is also that, throughout the catalogue essays, one finds a systematic denial of independent artistic agency to Artemisia, a habit of looking at her as always reactive—to other artists such as Orazio, Reni, Vouet, or Guercino, or to her patrons' demands—but rarely as proactive. The first English-language exhibition catalogue devoted to Artemisia's art is an impressive and useful volume in many respects, yet it is disappointing to see so little attention given to her creative originality.

This brings me again to Artemisia's depiction of hands, for it is here especially that she talks back to her critics, speaking the agency of women in a gestural voice that cannot be repressed. As Artemisia promised her patron Don Antonio Ruffo in March, 1649, "The works will speak for themselves" (Garrard 1989, 391–92). To facilitate their doing so, I offer several examples of Artemisia's manual telegraphy, instances in which she expresses identity or undermines convention through coded gestures of hand and arm. One that I have previously noted is the protagonist of the Seville *Magdalen,* whose head is supported by an awkwardly bent wrist. I have recently argued that this is an intentional allusion to artistic melancholy, on the model of Michelangelo, who is seen in this pose in a sixteenth-century engraving, following his own use of the pose to signify the melancholic temperament. With a single gesture, I proposed, Artemisia brought the concept of creative melancolia to her *Magdalen* in order to convey something about her own creative powers as an artist (Garrard 2001, chap. 1).

If the turn of a hand could carry private meaning for Artemisia, then perhaps significance is also to be found in a half-hidden gesture in the painting of *Clio* (fig. 13). Artemisia inserts herself into this image of the muse of history, for by placing her signature on the page of history, along with the name of her patron, she intertwines the agenda of her patron's fame with her own. I doubt that the face of Clio should be interpreted as an Artemisian self-portrait, yet the figure's akimbo left arm and bent wrist might have been an imprint

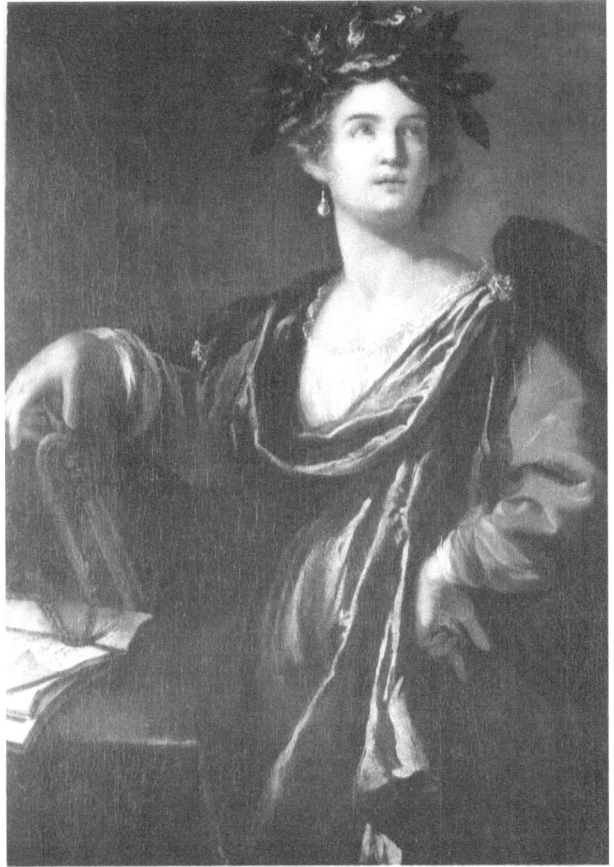

Figure 13. Artemisia Gentileschi, *Clio, Muse of History*, 1632. Private collection.

of self as legible (to those in the know) as the artist's signature on
the page. For is there not the ghost of a familiar image of Artemisia
embedded in Clio's pose? A number of writers have identified
Artemisia's face in the woman holding a fan who looks down at us
in Orazio's fresco at the Casino of the Muses (fig. 14). We can't be
sure about the face, but I do think that we may see Artemisia's own
body language here. As Joaneath Spicer has pointed out, the hand-

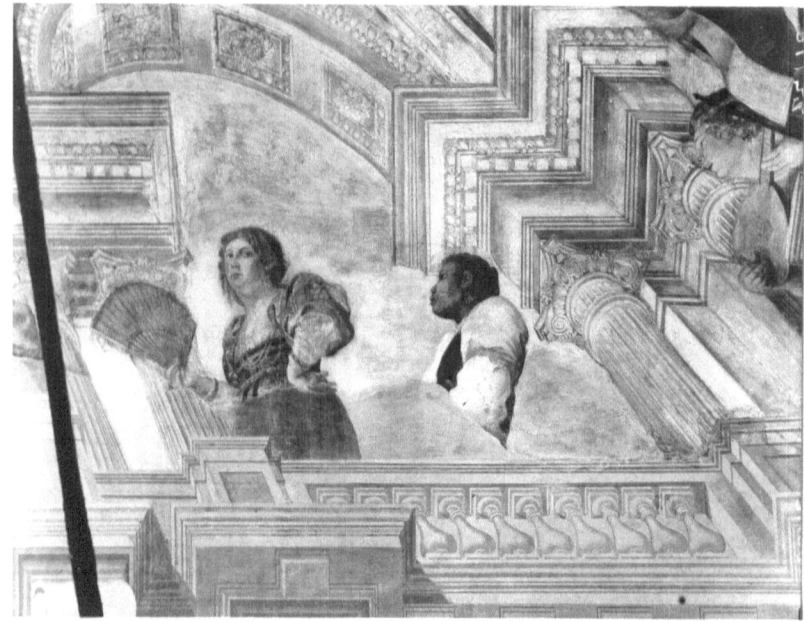

Figure 14. Orazio Gentileschi and Agostino Tassi, *A Musical Concert with Apollo and the Muses,* 1611. Detail of woman holding fan. Fresco. Rome, Palazzo Pallavicini-Rospigliosi, Casino delle Muse.

on-hip, jutting elbow stance is a very unusual pose for a woman to strike in art. By contrast, male figures often display themselves in this pose (think of Donatello's bronze *David*), which connotes self-assertion, cocky confidence, or elegant showing off (Spicer 1991).

The rare assumption of such a posture by two female figures linked with Artemisia suggests her presence in both instances. Though not a self-portrait, the *Clio* bears a clear conceptual relationship to Artemisia's identity. Here as elsewhere, the artist's sense of herself invades the female characters she invents. The figure in the Casino of the Muses is unlikely to "represent" the eighteen-year-old Artemisia, but perhaps she served as Orazio's model (a very different thing from posing in the nude). And if so, why not imagine that she struck her own pose? She was, after all, not a professional model, but by all accounts a feisty and self-assertive young woman. It seems to me entirely possible that the woman in the fresco, only subtextually Artemisia when painted, might have later been claimed by the artist herself as a signature posture.

Another work that has been persistently connected with Artemisia is the *Allegory of Painting* in the Palazzo Barberini (fig. 15).

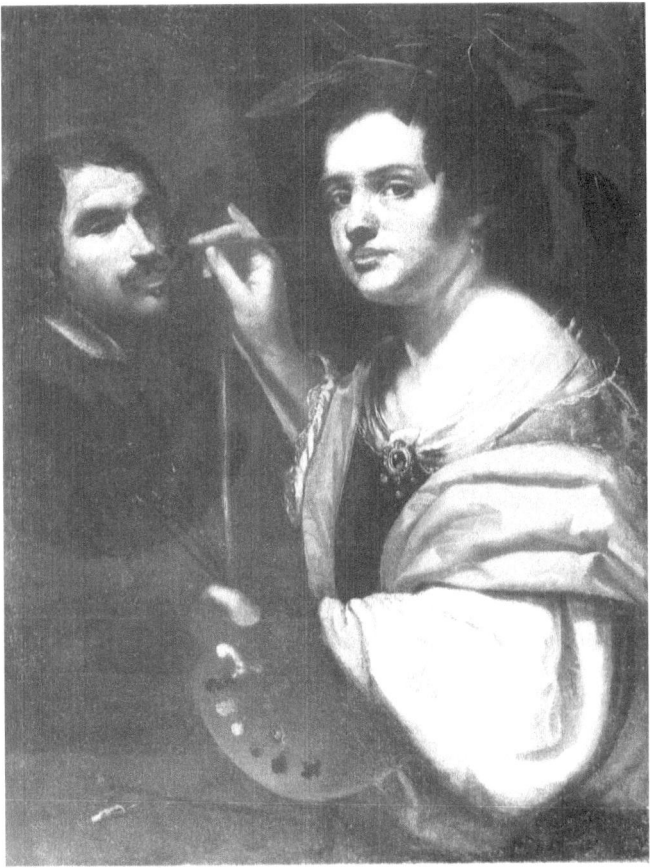

Figure 15. Attributed to Artemisia Gentileschi, *Portrait of a Woman Artist as the Allegory of Painting,* ca. 1630? Rome, Galleria Nazionale d'Arte Antica, Palazzo Barberini.

There is general consensus that the picture may represent Artemisia as Pittura, though some writers, including myself, have doubted that she painted the portrait (e.g., Strinati and Vodret 1998). But look at this figure's painting hand, and its lifted little finger—the ear-finger, as it was called in Artemisia's time. According to John Bulwer's *Chirologia,* a seventeenth-century vocabulary of gestures based on common usage in gestural discourse, the raised ear-finger (in Bulwer's illustration, it is raised as high as in the *Allegory*) represents contemptuous provocation, a dare or challenge advanced by those confident in the strength of their abilities (Bulwer 1974, 136). Once we realize that this Allegory of Painting is challenging the viewer, our understanding of the picture is changed. If painted by Artemisia, this would be an allegorized self-image of an aggressively competitive artist who challenges her male peers—an image that corresponds both to her known ambition and her reception. More likely, it was another painter who fixed Artemisia's image as a competitor in the world of art. But, either way, the picture is *about* her artistic ambition. It is not farfetched to imagine that it was Artemisia the model who initiated the gestural challenge preserved by the artist who painted her.

Finally, even *Corisca and the Satyr* (fig. 16) may subtend a coded gesture. In this painting, Artemisia presents a scene from Battista Guarini's *Il Pastor Fido,* in which a nymph cleverly escapes a lecherous satyr. The beautiful hair that attracted him turns out to be a wig, Corisca makes her getaway, and the joke is on the satyr. Artemisia's very choice of this rarely depicted episode reveals her feminist sensibilities (Garrard 1993). But take a good look at Corisca's left hand. The play of shadow blurs the fingers so that only three are clearly visible, but two of these, the index and ear-finger, are prominent and slightly advanced. Bulwer explains the meaning of this gesture in its more obvious form: "To present the index and ear-finger wagging," he says, is a sign of folly on the part of its recipient. "It implies such men to be asses," to have wagging asses' ears. (It is also, of course, a sign of cuckoldry, as Bulwer notes.)

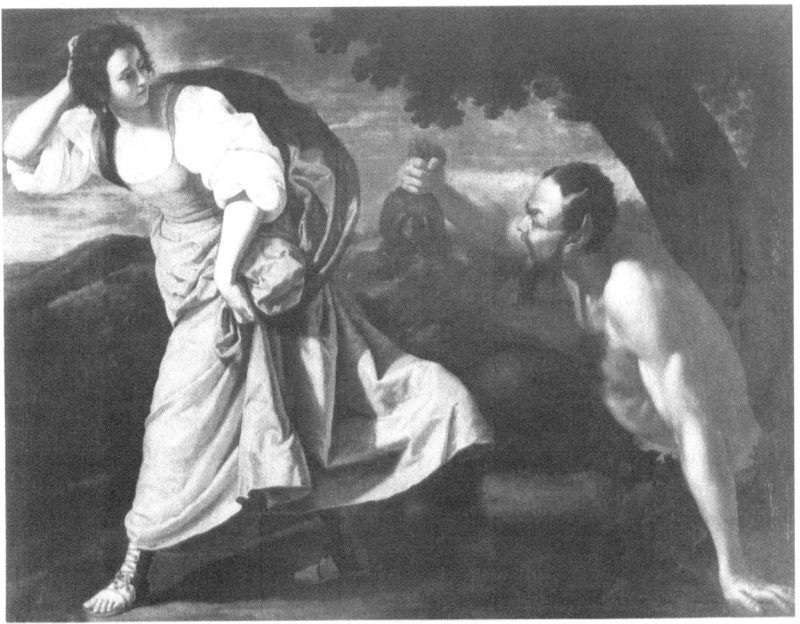

Figure 16. Artemisia Gentileschi, *Corisca and the Satyr,* 1630s or 1640s. Private collection.

Now, Artemisia did not go so far as to have Corisca wag her fingers at the lecherous satyr, for that would distort the narrative. But a visually literate Italian would surely pick up on this hint of the ass-eared insult, especially the wit of its relevance to the goat-eared satyr. Those who imagine the satyr to be the hero of this painting and Corisca the wicked villain—this has been insisted on by certain modern art historians—might not have noticed this subtle detail. However, contemporaries of Artemisia such as Isabella Andreini and Valeria Miani, women who wrote pastoral dramas that relish the topos of nymphs outwitting and humiliating satyrs, would surely have shared the painter's glee in showing us what Corisca thought of the satyr, and whose story this really is (see Andreini 1995; Cox 2000, 55).

᪐

In the wake of the Gentileschi exhibition, our ongoing project of defining Artemisia's oeuvre has become increasingly problematic and has therefore acquired growing urgency. As with other artists whose oeuvres are known insufficiently, it is a chicken-and-egg situation: in deciding what paintings are by her hand, we must be guided by our sense of her artistic identity, yet that identity can only be created out of the aggregate of her known works. At present, there is no consensus about Artemisia's identity, and recent writers sharply disagree, perhaps most notably about the relevance of gender considerations for her work. As I have long argued, gender issues and even feminism, understood in its broadest definition, are not extrinsic to Artemisia's art, but are manifestly at its heart. Those who perceive in this a feminist bias should also recognize the more pernicious forms of gender bias that go unacknowledged. For, as the examples discussed in this essay show, gender stereotypes can be used to diminish Artemisia and deny her cultural agency, sometimes by the same writers who deny gender's relevance for her art.

Because connoisseurship is not a socially neutral practice, it is necessary to question attributions that seem suspicious or ill-founded—certainly those that are incompatible with what we know of Artemisia's style, but also those that are inconsistent with her conceptualization of female characters and their action in the narrative world. Part of the questioning is deconstructive: *cui bono?* what's at stake? From what definition of the artist, we must ask, does a particular attribution derive?

Yet our work must also be constructive, for if we believe that Artemisia's art is more important for art history than the issues of her putative personal beauty presently being exploited and the cultural sexualization presently being imposed on her, then it is time to shift attention back to the paintings and their participation— perhaps better here is Griselda Pollock's favored term, their *intervention*—in the discourses of art and art history. As we see especially in her gestural rhetoric, Artemisia was an artist of great expressive subtlety and visual wit, and she disrupted the art-world dialogue by presenting an exemplum of female agency that upset gender expectations, both in her own time and ours. Artemisia's intervention sparked an intense critical debate that has not ceased, and we owe it to her to keep this debate on track.

JUDGING ARTEMISIA
A Baroque Woman in Modern Art History

Nanette Salomon

On Judgment and Art/History

The 2001–2 exhibition Orazio and Artemisia Gentileschi: Father and Daughter Painters in Baroque Italy, was organized around the unusual idea of presenting the work of two artistic personalities. More unusual was the fact that the two were related as father and daughter. And even more unusual was the fact that the woman of the pair was better known than the man. The exhibition and its catalogue, then, produced an occasion rich with the possibilities for various kinds of analysis. This opportunity was not lost to the multifarious communities that feed on such events, from the very popular to the very scholarly.[1]

Throughout there seemed to be an irresistible desire to assess which of the two artists had come off better. For example, we saw statements such as "The direct comparison suggests . . . that the father's sporadic but undoubted mastery overshadowed the capacities of his daughter" in the *Times Literary Supplement* (Rabb 2002). On the other hand, *Time Out New York* magazine proclaimed, "A daughter's legacy continues to outshine her father's at the Met" (Valdez 2002). Less certifiable but certainly as endemic were the discussions of, again, a wide range of people—from the average museum-goer to the graduate student and the established scholar—in the exhibition itself (at least at the Metropolitan Museum of Art and in St. Louis where I observed them), all pontificating on the comparative talents of the two artists.

The two-artist structure clearly created a binary opposition that inevitably summons the art-history trope of "compare and contrast," which triggers value judgments through the practice of comparative analysis. My intent in this chapter is to look at the workings of this trope in the past and in the present. In this sense the chapter continues a project that has occupied my thoughts and publications for some time (e.g., Salomon 1998). And as feminists, particularly the women writing in this volume, have been arguing for decades, such comparative judgments are particularly deleterious to the critical fortunes of noncanonical—that is to say, those artists who are not Euro/American white, male, and upper class. I want to use this occasion to shed some light on the historical and ideological frames of artistic judgment per se by looking at the judgment of Artemisia Gentileschi.

The current formulation of the "comparison," that is, the conventional device of "compare and contrast," has been the staple of art-historical analysis since the days of Heinrich Wölfflin, and its invitation to put a "versus" between two artists insists that one side be master, the other side pupil; one major, the other minor. In fact, the idea of comparative judgment is much older than Wölfflin, at least as old as the devaluation of women and other minorities within the construction of the art-history canon.

Historicizing Judgment

The motives for the merely stated, unexplained, or undefended artistic judgments run deep. Of these, the most significant, is seems to me, is the desire to define oneself through the expression of a personal opinion and further, to situate oneself in relation to others through the exercise of passing judgment on the quality of art. And as naturalized an act as that may have become, it is learned social behavior.

It has a history, not only with a starting point but also, like all histories, with changing terms of value.[2] With the desire to understand why and especially how we employ the terms of value with which we judge art, artists, and particularly Artemisia Gentileschi, I consider two crucial moments in this history. The first is the Vasarian one in the late sixteenth and early seventeenth centuries—the "age of criticism" when these ideas were first formulated—which, significantly, coincide with the life of Artemisia Gentileschi. The second moment is the feminist moment in the late twentieth and early twenty-first centuries, which is to say our own age, when the critical fortune of Artemisia has reached celebrity status. The former finds its earliest articulation in the written work of Giorgio Vasari, a Florentine contemporary and friend of Michelangelo. His sixteenth-century book, *The Lives of the Most Excellent Italian Architects, Painters and Sculptors,* first published in 1550 and reissued in a much enlarged edition in 1568, is generally credited as being no less than the first "modern" exposition of the history of Western European art, a claim that acknowledges its tremendous influence. In his *Lives* Vasari writes, "It was not my intention . . . to make (merely) a record of artists and a catalogue, as it were, of their works." The real historian, Vasari claims, will do more, "he will pronounce judgments which are the soul of history; he will discriminate the good from the better and the better from the best, and most of all, he will investigate the causes and roots of styles" (quoted in Gombrich 1978, 109–10).

Vasari's work is a liminal one, traversing the world of the artist and the world of the connoisseur. Because he was himself an artist, addressing other artists as well as art lovers, Vasari's notion of the exercise of aesthetic judgment in its various meanings was meant to influence the quality of art at the level of its production—that is in the studios of artists themselves. Significantly, however, many writers on art of the next generation who promulgated Vasari's ideas emerged not from the pool of artists but from that of humanists and clerics. As Moshe Barasch put it, "They worked in chancelleries and libraries or were dignitaries of the Church, but they never held a brush or chisel in their hand" (1985, 206). It was their project to equip the emerging dilettante with a way to demonstrate an understanding, one might say mastery, of matters of culture—not unlike the "mastery" demonstrated by visitors to the Gentileschi exhibitions.

Just as the writers on art in the Renaissance were less and less practicing artists, so too were the new Renaissance readers, who were styled as educated members of the general public who were able to appreciate art and culture—and, indeed, needed to. This newly fashioned social group was defined as the artists were, as white, male, and upper class. This expanded the group through "natural" empathy. It was thought that though these "gentlemen" did not actually make art, they were, nevertheless, entitled to judge it. Indeed, Vincenzo Borghini early on made the claim that the judgment of art was actually better left to the critic, and not to those who practice art, a dispute that continues to this day (Barasch 1985, 206). Although these ideas began with Vasari, it was his immediate follower, Raffaello Borghini, in his book *Il Riposo,* published in 1584, who emphatically states that he writes his biographies of artists for those who, though not artists, wish to be in a position to judge works of art (see Blunt 1940, 101). This is the historical moment when a privileged segment of the newly formulated, so-called public is first given the critical means to judge the quality of works of art. It is also the moment when, in a related coincidence, Italian art theory becomes especially overexcited and intensely abstruse.[3]

The changing evaluation of the modes or styles in late sixteenth-century Italian art theory has a bearing on the "judgment" of Artemisia—in her own day as in ours. Vasari, like others writing on art during Artemisia's lifetime, assigns to the word *judgment* the general meaning for which we sometimes use the word "taste," signifying an evaluation of or discrimination about a work against some standard of excellence. Part of the modern mechanism by which styles in the service of constructed taste or personal opinions obtain social value is their paradoxical nature as absolute (classic) and therefore unchanging and as constantly needing to be supplanted or superseded.[4] Consequently it makes sense that in Artemisia's day, as in ours, this "standard" was in flux. Although differing modes or pictorial strategies (sometimes called "styles") can and do coexist, the judgmental imposition of a particular standard in a particular historical moment would cause one to rise and another to fall in the sphere of public opinion or value. This was precisely the case at the end of the sixteenth century and beginning of the seventeenth century when tides were shifting from one visual mode, sometimes called mannerism, to another, usually called baroque. Although these different modes are generally couched in art history as formal or stylistic ones, we have learned that changes in style and presentation incur deeper changes in meaning than the notion of mere aesthetics would imply.[5]

Three Ways of Picturing Susanna

Analyses of Artemisia Gentileschi's three versions of the biblical subject of Susanna and the Elders, painted at three distinct periods of her life and of the seventeenth century, 1610, 1622, and 1649, clarify these shifting priorities and what was and is at stake in judging Artemisia. This exercise makes clear how much deeper, richer, and more complex is the shift in visual language from one example of Susanna to the next, than the simple and simple-minded explanation of them as a move from mannerism to baroque could ever suggest. My analysis is also offered as an alternative to comparative analysis in the "versus" mode—as a way to understand paintings on their own terms. All three are bound to the apocryphal story of Susanna, a beautiful young matron, who is spied upon at her bath by two elders who come upon her at the moment when her maidservants have gone to fetch oil and balsam. Taking advantage of her vulnerability at that moment, they proposition her, threatening to accuse her of adulterous acts with a young man if she does not comply. In virtue and chastity she refuses them even with the threat of being stoned to death as her punishment. At her trial the young Daniel separates the elders and finds their testimonies to differ in details. They, rather than Susanna, are stoned to death for bearing false witness. The narrative in the Bible is relatively long and de-

tailed, much longer indeed than my summary suggests. It is a literary narrative that marks its progress through time and place; first
this happened here, then that happened there, and so on. Significantly, Western European paintings since at least the Renaissance have developed various strategies for making visual in a still
image the time and place function of literary narrative. And it is
clear that these three paintings of 1610, 1622, and 1649 are bound to
the apocryphal Susanna story in radically different ways.[6]

Nevertheless, general discussions of these paintings seem to
pit them against one another, with the earliest used as both the
standard to which the last two must measure up and, paradoxically,
the work whose "untraditional" and "innovational" composition is
somehow "corrected" in the last two. It seems to be difficult to be
one person and love all three. Implicit judgment of these works
comes also in the popular condition of value, that is, attribution.
This activity was codified by Vasari and is of ultimate importance
for a market-driven formulation of artistic value in our own times.
Although all three are signed and dated, a great deal of thought and
energy has gone into the question of who else may have painted
them. In the end the issue is usually resolved by the compromise
that Artemisia was guided by, collaborated with, or painted in the
style of another artist (Christiansen and Mann 2001, passim).

Three Stories of Susanna

Despite the usual assertion that the 1610 version of Susanna is naturalistic, it seems to me to be the most mannerist, the most—dare
I say it—abstract (fig. 17). Abstraction as a visual strategy that re-
moves the event from the lived human experience of a particular
time and a specific place seems, indeed, to be this painting's point.
Specifically, it is abstract in the extreme compression of three-
dimensional space, pressing everything forward yet tellingly not
out of the pictorial space; abstract in the heightened formal division of a stark, stagelike foreground affected by the stone parapet
that stretches relentlessly from one side of the frame to the other, a

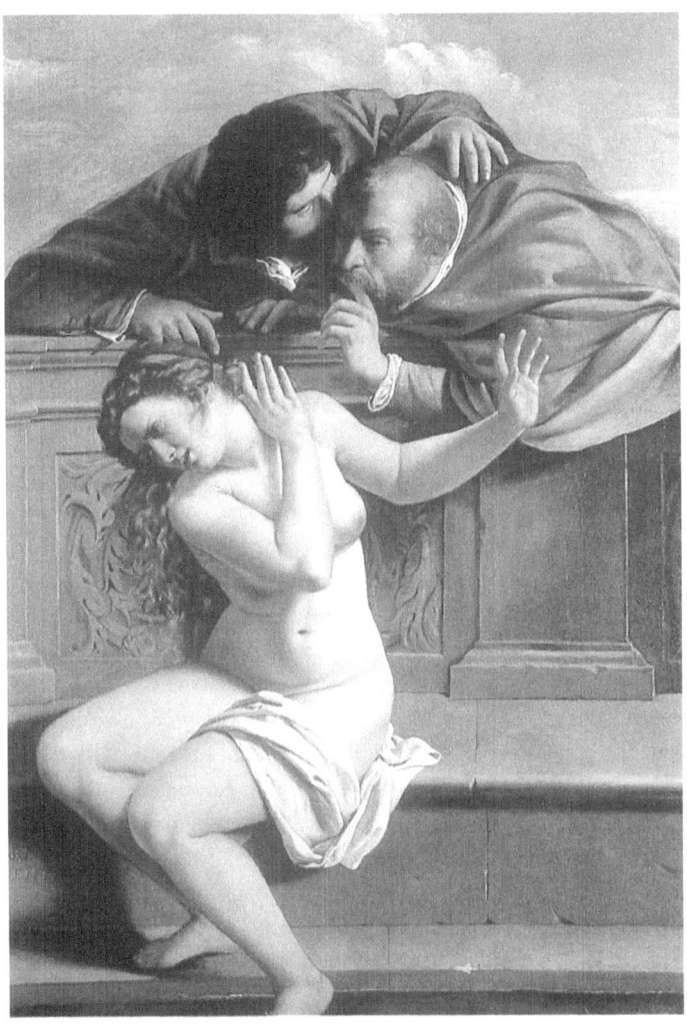

Figure 17. Artemisia Gentileschi, *Susanna and the Elders,* 1610. Oil on canvas, 66 7/8 × 46 7/8 in. (170 × 119 cm). Pommersfelden, Collection Graf von Schönborn.

division that bounds Susanna but does not keep the elders out. It is abstract for its pointed absence of any gardenlike foliage, transposing instead organic, leaflike forms into the stony relief panel just behind Susanna's torso; abstract with only the most minimal indication of water for her bath; abstract in the collusive unity of the form of the two elders as one, portrayed in a Leonardesque darkness and secretive evilness that also expands from one side of the frame to the other without a break and contrasts with the light-filled single figure of Susanna; abstract in the body language of Susanna whose torqued body and rhetorical gestures neither protect nor defend her. The painting belongs more comfortably in the realm of metaphor than narrative; its effect is more symbolic than naturalistic.

In all these aspects the painting sits well within Vasari's prescribed value system and may thus be seen as responding to the tastes of the late sixteenth century. For Vasari, an artist's contribution was valuable insofar as it advanced the progress of art toward "perfection" especially with regard to the conceptualization through *disegno*. This, in turn, he linked to the workings of the intellect as opposed to those of the senses. *Disegno* on some important level operates as an apology for images that did not obey strictly rational rules that would result in anatomically and perspectively "naturalistic" and "correct" images. Mostly, it is a catchword for a mode of painting associated with central Italy, especially in opposition to North Italian, Venetian, painterly colorism. This is of some consequence for my analysis, as it is precisely Venetian painting of the sixteenth century that developed and popularized the images of the female nude posed in the same frame with a dressed male. The depiction of *Susanna and the Elders,* specifically, as in the paintings by Veronese and Tintoretto, was first popularized in northern Italy.

The visual mode of Artemisia's 1610 *Susanna* is strongly vested in the *disegno* of central Italian painting with its cool palette, its smooth application of paint, and its strong, expressive use of outline. The texture of the paint itself is evident in only limited areas of the elder's undergarments. The cool palette and glazed surface afford the viewer—as the viewed—a shield: not so much a distance,

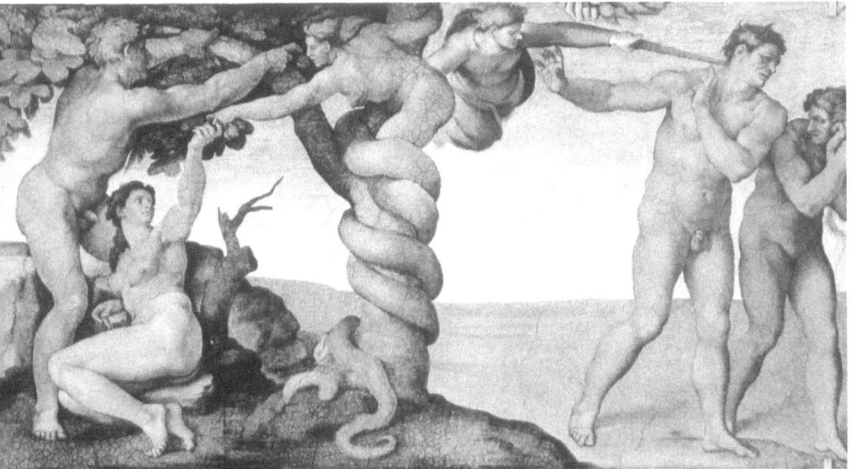

Figure 18. Michelangelo, *The Fall and Banishment,* 1509/10. Fresco. Vatican City, Sistine Chapel.

as a separation between one another. They provide a safe, if invisible, partition that mitigates the stark presentation of the body. They make the vision bearable. It is not surprising that a comparison can be made between this image and one by Vasari's hero, Michelangelo. Michelangelo was a daunting presence for any artist in the seventeenth century, and Artemisia was no exception. Her depiction of Susanna has been compared with Michelangelo's banished Adam from the Sistine ceiling, but I find it even more comparable to the seated female body of Eve in *The Fall and Banishment* (fig. 18). This comparison is not only formally satisfying but also works well on the level of meaning, since with Eve we have the same tropes of a woman in a garden pressured to make a (sexual) decision that will be pressed into the service of Christian morality.[7]

Still another painting by Michelangelo may bring us even closer to an appreciation of the distinctive way Artemisia's painting makes its meaning. The *Doni Tondo* (fig. 19) by Michelangelo has been proposed as a source for Artemisia in the literature. Mary Garrard in her groundbreaking monograph of 1989 noticed the similarities of Su-

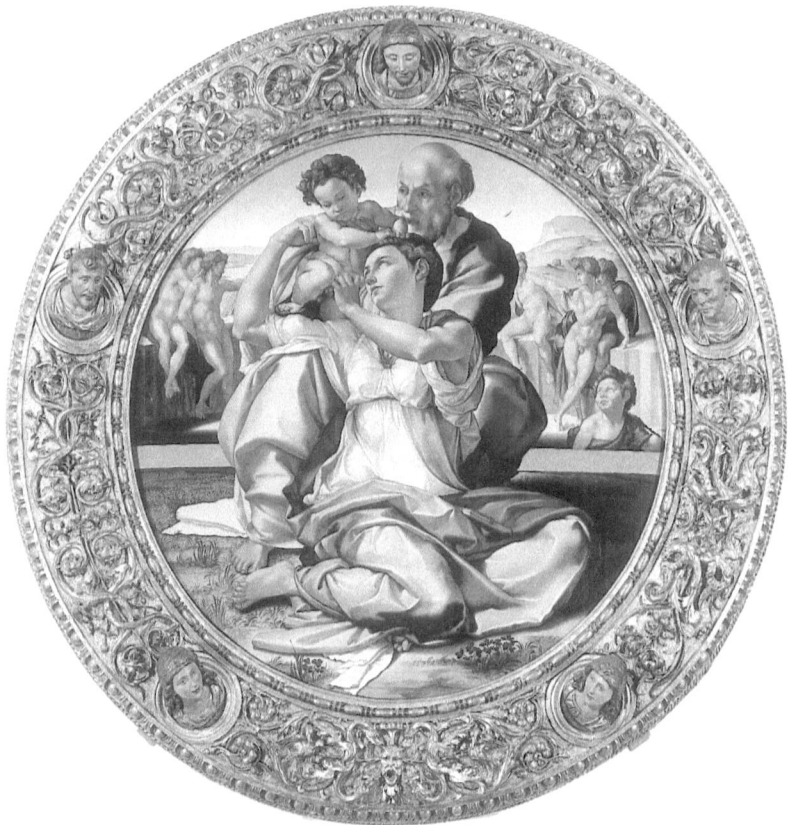

Figure 19. Michelangelo, *Doni Tondo* (The Holy Family with St. John), ca. 1504–1506. Oil and tempera on panel, diameter 120 cm. Florence, Galleria degli Uffizi. (Photo credit: Scala/Art Resource, New York.)

sanna's position to Mary's, and the way the patriarchal, balding, aged man surmounts the scene in both (198). I concur, but what I want to emphasize here is the comprehensive premise of Michelangelo's painting as well as Artemisia's. One quick way to get to that is to compare the *Doni Tondo* with another Renaissance painting, Raphael's *Holy Family* of around the same period. The difference is manifest in, but not limited to, their landscape background, which has a normative "realistic" effect in the Raphael, but is abstractly conceived by Michelangelo, who fills it with posing male nude youths.

Upon looking more closely, several fundamental structural similarities appear between the *Doni Tondo* and the 1610 *Susanna*. The most obvious one is the stone wall that separates realms, front and back. In the *Doni Tondo* the division has been interpreted as the contrast of different systems of belief: pagan antiquity represented by the nude youths and Christianity represented by the Holy Family. In *Susanna* the division separates an abstractly conceived, menacing, and elderly male lust from innocence and youthful female chastity. In the seventeenth-century, abstracting, iconic qualities of this compositional structure abound. It can be seen as a Gentileschian predilection in general, as in, for example Orazio's *Rest on the Flight into Egypt*. Here too, a subject that almost demands a landscape setting is transformed in meaning and effect through the use of a stark, inorganic, horizontal wall that separates the donkey as a sign of the mundane from the Holy Family.

For my comparison of the three *Susanna* paintings, it is noticeable that the abstracting qualities of the 1610 painting shift its concept from one form of story presentation to another kind of narrativizing. The abstract form of storytelling serves the purpose of finding the visual equivalent of a deafening silence, a dreamlike experience of the internal need to scream a scream that cannot be screamed. Silence and whispering are, of course, more literally developed in the elders; the younger buries his face into the ear of the other to whisper and conspire, and the older presses a finger to his lips to silence Susanna's crying out. But the true silence of the scene comes from its formal abstractions, its utter absence of space as air and time as sound. It moves the narrative to the viewer's own discomfort through empathy and moves us to a kind of gasping for air.

The superficially similar *Susanna and the Elders* of 1622, newly restored to Artemisia, speaks an entirely different language (fig. 20). Before going into an analysis of that painting, I wish to remark that its own history in the literature on Artemisia underscores how pre-

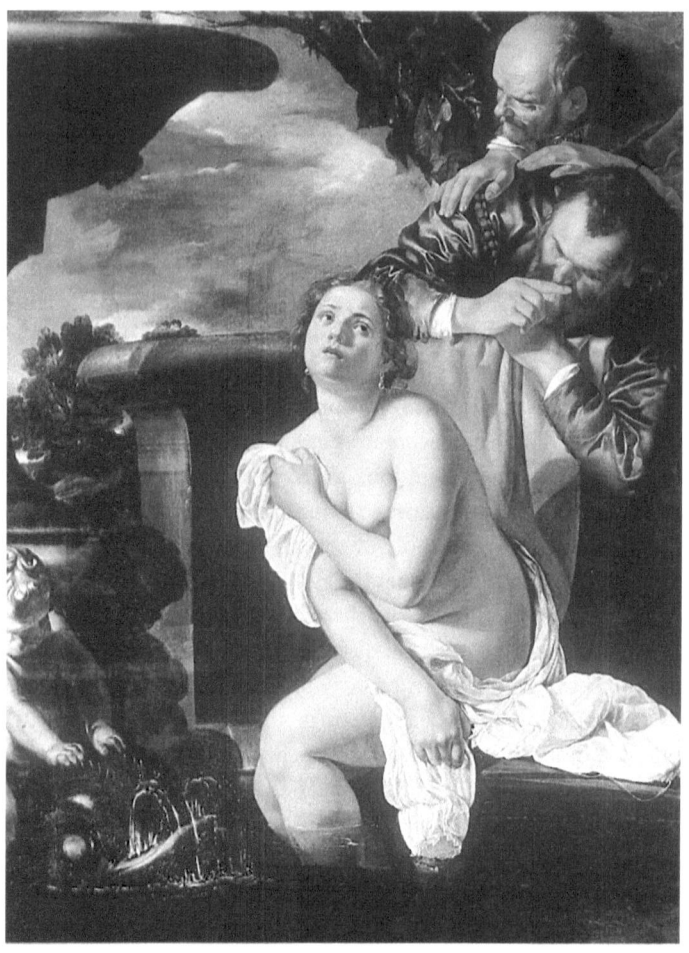

Figure 20. Artemisia Gentileschi, *Susanna and the Elders,* 1622. Oil on canvas, 63 5/8 × 48 3/8 in. (161.5 × 123 cm). Stamford, Lincolnshire, Collection of the Marquess of Exeter, Burghley House.

carious and subjective is our description of what we see. Garrard initially felt that Artemisia could not have painted this *Susanna* because she saw the figure as too seductive (Garrard 1989, 204). The catalogue authors saw the same figure as spiritual in her appeal to God (Christiansen and Mann 2001, 356). Each reading has some validity. Together they are a sobering reminder of how personal vision is and of what we are doing when we "do" art history. This may be one of the most important lessons of feminist art history.

Before taking on the crucial issue of gender as regards either the artist or the viewer, I want to characterize the painting's mode of storytelling. In distinction from the earlier work, here, indeed, one may speak of a "naturalism." This mode is constructed through the landscape details of the background, seen to the left of the wall, which significantly now stops about two-thirds through the painting. This gives us access to the depth of the scene. Another manifestation of naturalism can be seen in the way the figure of Susanna is developed in greater plastic form through an intensified modeling in dark and light. Moreover, the identifiable details of Susanna's chemise are made visible through the stitched sleeve and laced cuff articulated in the kind of detail Roland Barthes credited with producing the so-called "reality affect." This effect occurs through small realistic details whose primary function is not to advance the plot or story but to establish the believable premise of realism of the whole (Barthes 1991, 11–17). The approach of the elders is from the right, not directly and threateningly from above her outstretched neck. The painting further partakes of the strategies of storytelling by the description of the elders' more attenuated approach and response. The elders are still physically, collusively joined by a single drawn outline but now their heads at least are separated.

Compared to the abstracting form of story-telling in the 1610 painting, here the opposite seems to occur. If the garden setting in the 1610 work had been relegated to a stony relief, as if to hold the memory of a real garden in an abstract world, here it is, conversely, the presence of an abstracted ominous evil that has been transposed and supplemented through detail. This is represented in the

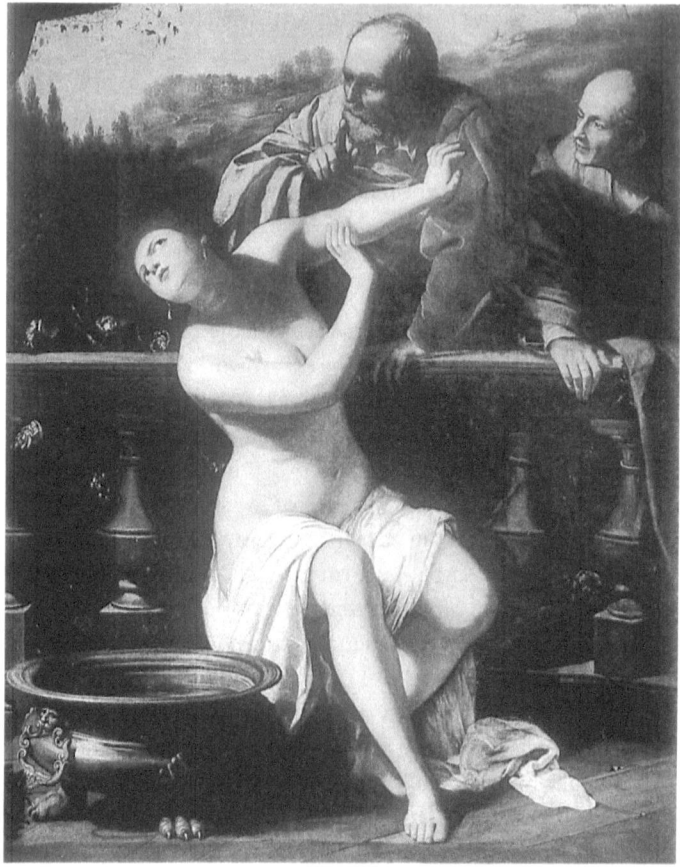

Figure 21. Artemisia Gentileschi, *Susanna and the Elders,* 1649. Oil on canvas, 80 3/4 × 66 1/8 in. (205 × 168 cm). Brno, Moravská Galerie.

dark, stormy clouds and, especially, in the dark, shadowy figure that plays off of the fountain sculpture of cupid. Here the god of love's dark other side, not Eros but anti-Eros, forebodes the lusty intentions of the elders. Naturalistic depiction, thus, still conserves an intellectualized representation of evil.

Many of the same pictorial strategies are heightened in the language of Artemisia's 1649 interpretation of the subject (fig. 21).

Landscape fills the background above and beyond the balustrade that is no longer a solid, impenetrable mass. Land and air are available through its regularly spaced supports. The female body is volumetric, now not only by dint of light and shade modeling but also by posture, especially evident in the space between her arms and torso and between her legs. This spacing attracts attention to time, that key of narrativity.

Time is measured out as tempo by the spaces between the figures; the two elders are now clearly separated and conceived as if in sequential approach, first one then the other. Again, good and evil as abstract concepts are metamorphosed in their expression as seemingly ancillary details. Their contrast is now transposed onto the feet that run across the lowest horizontal strip of the painting. Here the feet of the basin reveal hideous and menacing claws, with their threatening, long, steely nails—which are visually contrasted to the sweet, regular toes of Susanna's right foot.

Making Sense of Change

With these three paintings we have traversed a series of alternative visual possibilities and their semantic potential. There are different ways to make sense of the changes in Artemisia's three *Susanna*s. One argument might be that her work shows a progressive realism or naturalism that could be attributed to Artemisia's "development" as an artist. This we will presently see to be untenable. Another, more plausible argument might be that the changes were professional adjustments made to accord with the traditions and tastes of the different cities in which the various paintings were painted. In an entirely different realm, one may view this change as evidence of increasing distance from the biographical event that initially facilitated Artemisia Gentileschi's entry into the canon and sensationalized her art—her multiple rapes by Agostino Tassi, the artist to whom her father, Orazio, gave her as an apprentice. Of the three, the painting of 1610 has most particularly been related to this event, even though technically it is dated before the rapes took place. Nor is the story of Susanna and the elders exactly a rape story. In the narrative, she is propositioned, she is given a choice, albeit under a death threat, and she declines. She decides to suffer the awful consequences of that decision, but it is her decision. That is what is recalled in the gestures of Susanna in the first and the last of Artemisia's renditions. The literary story allows for time to intervene between the heinous approach and the threat of death, a space of time that allows the event to be rectified. With rape, it is precisely that lack of time that enables the act.

In the end, the effect that the real and detestable assault on her body had on her art must have had much more complex psychoanalytical manifestations, filtered, as all traumas are, through internal defense mechanisms and external social practices and ideologies. For the latter, a deep, abiding sense that woman cannot be heard is signified in feminist discourse by the word *subaltern*.[8] The formulation of this ineffectual position is one of "voicelessness." In contrast to this voicelessness, the socially sanctioned collusive secrecy of male assaults on women is articulated even in the apocryphal text. If the first painting is most eloquently silent, the last one tells the story as one in which time is key. Earlier I intimated that the evolutionist argument is untenable. These issues can be further extricated in an analysis of the other subject that is so closely identified with the life and work of Artemisia Gentileschi, Judith beheading Holofernes. More strongly than the *Susanna*s, the paintings Artemisia Gentileschi made of this subject are inexorably connected to the judgment of Artemisia, especially in current art history. Since the earliest one is contemporary to the earliest *Susanna,* while it is so dramatically opposed in mood, the argument that the *Susannas* show a development toward great naturalism is clearly untenable.

Susanna and Judith

Artemisia's first version of *Judith Beheading Holofernes* (fig. 22) hung next to the 1610 *Susanna and the Elders* in the Metropolitan Museum of Art venue of the exhibition. This juxtaposition gave a

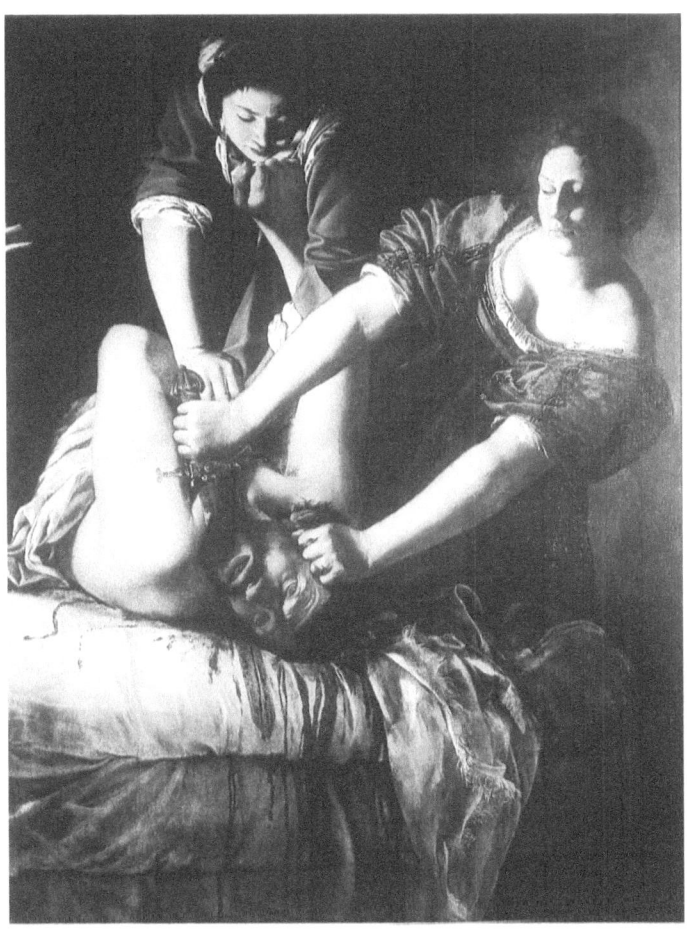

Figure 22. Artemisia Gentileschi, *Judith Beheading Holofernes,* 1612–13. Oil on canvas, 62 1/2 × 49 3/8 in. (158.8 × 125.5 cm). Naples, Museo di Capodimonte. (Photo credit: Alinari/Art Resource, New York.)

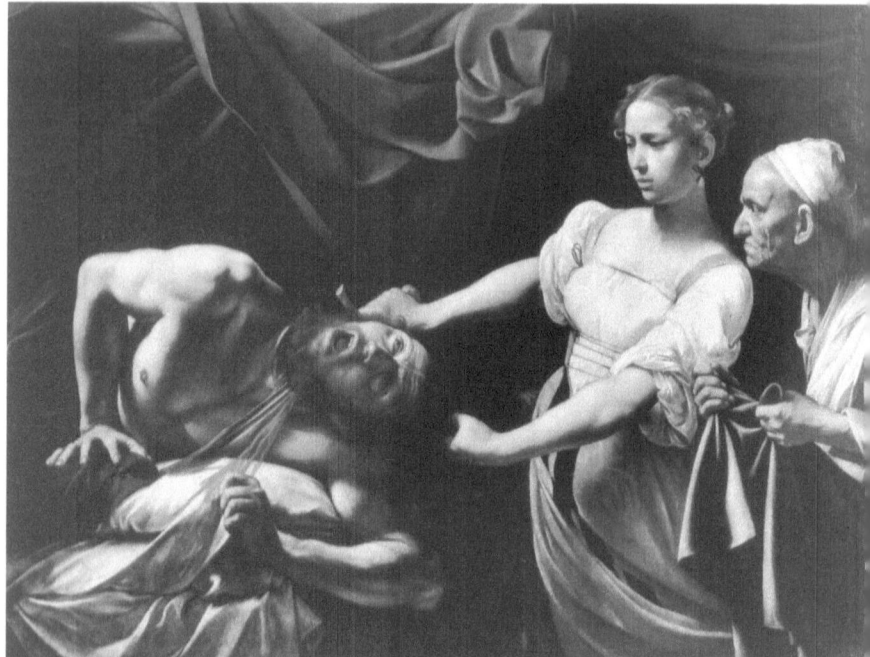

Figure 23. Caravaggio, *Judith Beheading Holofernes,* ca. 1600. Oil on canvas, 145 × 195 cm. Rome, Galleria Nazionale d'Arte Antica. (Photo credit: Art Resource, New York.)

dramatic impression of her artistic range. As an action-packed narrative depiction of the quintessential dramatic, adrenalized moment of the story of Judith, further discussed in the next chapter by Elena Ciletti, it contrasts with the most abstract of the *Susannas*. Together they belie any attempt to see either a personal or social development in the movement from icon to narrative.

The story of Judith also comes from the Old Testament Apocrypha. Judith, a Jewish woman, seizes the opportunity to liberate her people by decapitating Holofernes, the Assyrian general menacing them. When he falls asleep after drinking too much at a banquet to which he has invited her, Judith grabs his sword and with two blows cuts off his head. She then hands his head to her maidservant and brings it before her people, where she brandishes it as evidence of God's deliverance. Once again the story is fairly long and detailed, and once again it is the artist's choice of a moment among many possible moments that is telling. In 1608–9, that is three or four years before Artemisia's painting, Orazio had, as had most artists of the period, depicted the moment after the decapitation when Judith and her maidservant, holding Holofernes's head in a basket, furtively look back to what is assumed to be the general's body. Orazio's work is indebted to Michelangelo's interpretation of the subject and especially to Vasari's description of it, to which I return below.

In this instance and its close variant of 1620, Artemisia had, by contrast, chosen the so-called baroque moment, that is the moment of greatest dramatic impact, the "make or break" moment of the story—would she or would she not be able to kill him before he came to his senses enough to kill her? In choosing this moment and, in relation to it, the composition, Artemisia provided history with one of its most useful and used comparisons—that between her painting and Caravaggio's depiction of the same subject painted about ten years before (fig. 23).

It would not be a daring claim to state that art historians consider Caravaggio as the great master founder of baroque naturalism and the well-spring from which all subsequent baroque realism draws. A comparison between his constructed relationship with Orazio as opposed to Artemisia yields useful insight into how stereotypes about male and female artists are still unwittingly being perpetuated. In our present context of an analysis of judgment, it is relevant to probe the various ways Caravaggio is invoked. For Orazio, the encounter with Caravaggio is used as evidence of Orazio's flexibility as an artist, since he was around forty and therefore an already fully mature artist when Caravaggism became the style du jour. Artemisia's relationship with Caravaggio has been conceived as more contentious, providing an opportunity to judge one against the other, with Caravaggio inevitably coming out the better of the two.

Among the criteria for judgment in this comparison is a desire

to see the artists' different interpretations of the subject as a function of their gender difference. This commonly takes the form of
the academic question "Can you tell which of the two was made by
a woman and which by a man?" Aside from reverting to highly re-
ductive and essentialist stereotypes about men and women, such a
question requires us to see these two paintings in a sort of vacuum,
outside the general taste for this subject in baroque culture. It was
not only a particularly popular subject for artists, but also appeared
as the subject of an unprecedented number of poems, plays, and
operas in Italy at this time.

The question also implicitly takes into account biographical
knowledge in a selective, unequal way. For example, it counts on
some knowledge that this particular woman was raped by 1612/13,
before the painting is generally dated. But the question dare not
take into account the particular biographical knowledge that this
particular man, Caravaggio, had actually killed a man and so had
the life experience of stabbing someone to death. Scholars are in
general agreement that Artemisia used her features for the face of
Judith. But then what to do with the idea that Caravaggio may have
painted his features as the beheaded Holofernes?

Moreover, there is no telling what happens when other *Judith*s
by other artists of the period enter into the equation. How does the
general popularity of this theme and the related decapitation
themes of *Medusa, David Beheading Goliath,* or *The Beheading of
St. John the Baptist* destabilize the question and its predetermined
answer? Delving a little deeper, we may wonder why looking for
gender difference is such a comfort zone for us, and how the search
itself is complicitous with the centuries-old agenda of Western
culture to define the difference between men and women as the
most compelling and overriding aspect of human relationships.

Another way to frame an analysis of this comparison could be the
issue of what I have discussed as social collusion gathered around
gender in the 1610 *Susanna and the Elders,* which hung beside *Judith
Beheading Holofernes.* Just as two elderly men conspire to attack a
young woman in the *Susanna,* here two young women perpetrate

the act in accord with one another against a single man. How many Judiths does it take to kill a Holofernes? This issue becomes particularly pointed in comparison with Caravaggio's painting of the same subject, in which Judith acts alone (Pollock 1999, 110–15).

Many authors have noted the important difference between Caravaggio's painting and Artemisia's, where in the former the handmaiden is portrayed as aged, recalling the pictorial conventions of a procuress or, alternately, a chaperon. She stands at the ready to receive the head. In Artemisia's painting, in contrast, the maidservant is a doppelgänger for Judith herself and is very much in the mix, holding Holofernes down with her body weight while Judith cuts into his neck. Excitement and danger are conveyed in the confusion of the three figures' arms that cross and criss-cross; just as Judith's arms and hands grapple with Holofernes's head, so his massive right arm and hand grapple with the head of the servant. His fist is nearly the same size as her head. Holofernes's raised arm was already figured as a threat in Michelangelo's rendition of the subject, an aspect to which Vasari is particularly sensitive. In his description of Michelangelo's Judith, he writes that the general was killed "while raising an arm and a leg and making a noise in the tent." Of Judith he writes, "She shows by her attitude fear of the camp and terror at the sight of the dead body." This is a psychologically nuanced description that will have greater relevance for some later paintings by Artemisia.

Vasari's mention of Holofernes's noise in Michelangelo's painting is rather odd, since he is already decapitated in that scene. It is, however, an aspect that is not lost on Caravaggio, who shows him in the process of a startlingly realistic, open-mouthed scream that is made all the more haunting as it emanates from a face that is lit from below. Screaming was fascinating to Caravaggio, as can be seen in his painting of the decapitated Medusa. Caravaggio's ability to depict sound so realistically is noted by several art critics in the seventeenth century. Baglioni in 1642 writes: "[Caravaggio] painted a boy bitten by a lizard; . . . you could almost hear the boy scream, and it was all done meticulously." Joachim van Sandrart, writing a few decades later, wrote that Caravaggio painted "a child with a basket full of flowers and fruit, out of which a lizard bites him on the hand, making him seem to cry out bitterly, which is wonderful to see, and made his reputation grow notably all over Rome" (both cited in Spear 1971, 22).

Artemisia's Holofernes takes on many of the same expressive devices. They may seem even more immediate and compelling to us today than they originally were, since by all evidence the composition has been cut down on several sides. The end effect brings the viewer closer into the scene and compels greater participation on our part. We don't know exactly when the changes were made to the canvas, but the original probably looked more like Artemisia's later version of the painting executed about eight years later around 1620.

Judith as "Artemisia" and the Feminization of Artemisia

The Uffizi painting of 1620 is the most highly touted and reproduced work by Artemisia Gentileschi (fig. 24). It is the piece that holds her place in the art-history canon as an infinitely useful example of baroque art and woman's art in the recently more inclusive Janson-like survey books for Art 101, although tellingly not in Janson.[9] So much, in fact, needs to be and can be pushed through this painting that it becomes an ideal vehicle for an assessment of the current state of judging Artemisia. As with the earlier version of the subject, it seems irresistible to talk about Artemisia's rape in connection with it, even if only to say that the painting cannot be directly related to the rape. This compulsive biographism immediately sexualizes the subject and the artist to a degree that no longer allows us to see the painting as a work of "art" in canonical terms. Having said that, let's try to have a closer look. To aid this endeavor, we can ask why has *this* painting been judged to be the one that represents Artemisia over the earlier work, of which it is a variant and which is, indeed, closer to the date of her rape and trial? The mere *fact* that the earlier work was cut down would not affect this decision, since other famous paintings have been even more severely

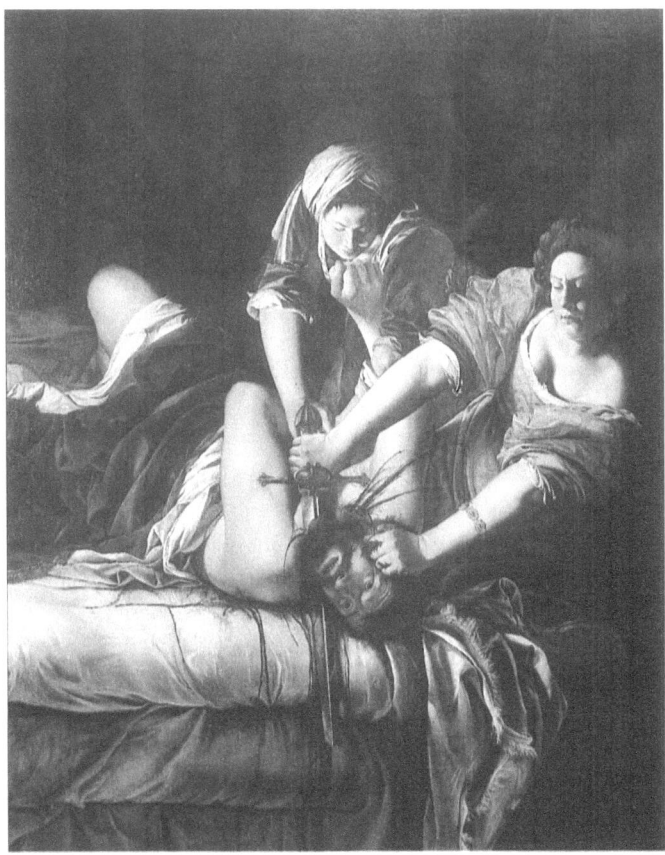

Figure 24. Artemisia Gentileschi, *Judith Beheading Holofernes*, ca. 1620. Oil on canvas, 39 3/8 × 64 in. (100 × 162.5 cm). Florence, Galleria degli Uffizi. (Photo credit: Scala/Art Resource, New York.)

cut, such as Rembrandt's *Nightwatch*. But the visual consequence of that fact might have informed the judgment. Nor do I believe that the *fact* of the possible patron for this later work, the Grand Duke Cosimo II de' Medici, would make a difference, but again the visual consequences of that patronage might have done so.

How do the two works as we now have them, compare? The

larger view of the scene renders it, by definition, more distant. It has also been called more balanced because it centers the figures of Abra, the servant, and Holofernes. To the left is the extension of Holofernes's body, and to the right is Judith. The more balanced composition is enhanced by a color change: Judith's dress is blue in the earlier version, and it is a more sumptuous gold damask in the later one. Judith's hair is tighter and more elegantly bound. The painting, in general is more refined. Together, these details, with the greater distance afforded the viewer, allow the image to be apprehended as a more aesthetic, artistic object. The shock and horror engendered in viewing such a realistically presented scene are muted by the possibility of putting it back into its frame so to speak, of muting its outcry.

Just as the details of Artemisia's various images of Susanna allowed us to appreciate the diverse visual modes of storytelling at work in them, the details of her depiction of Judith can be enlisted to do the same. The change in costume and especially in jewelry has for me significant dimensions that go beyond but do not exclude the formal ones. The bracelet is particularly visible because of the way it breaks the flesh-colored expanse of her outstretched arm. It demands to be seen and interrogated. In fact, various interpretations have been offered for the intriguing figures readable in the little vignettes around it. Some have seen an ironic reference to Mars, the god of war, rendered helpless here at the hands of a woman. Others have seen references to Diana, the goddess of the hunt, whose Greek name was Artemis, from which Artemisia's own name was derived.

I am not sure that we can see enough to be that specific about the identification of the figures. I am more interested in the meaning of a bracelet as such. It is, indeed, part of the apocryphal text that, in preparation for her rendezvous with Holofernes, Judith "dressed up," putting on fine clothes and jewelry. This text was, however, as available to her in 1612 as it was in 1620. The bracelet's inclusion, like the figure's more refined hairdo and dress in the later work, strike a chord of femininity, a certain kind of femininity that is put on, in both meanings of that phrase. It is applied to the body of the

woman as a conscious act of dressing up and, perhaps, an unconscious act of masquerade or disguise. This second meaning was
developed in the early history of psychoanalysis by Joan Riviere's
important paper entitled "Womanliness as a Masquerade" (Riviere
1986, 35–44).

According to Riviere's theory the practice of a cultivated, feminine self-presentation is affected by women to allay their anxieties
for having achieved success in a man's world. Further, the accentu-
ation, if not exaggeration, of femininity may be seen as a strategy
to disarm the threatened male. Both Judith and Artemisia might
be seen as prime examples of women who take on positions (literally
for Judith) and activities that social stereotyping reserved for men
only. By heightening the gender definition, Artemisia underscores
the issue of difference itself, whereby the narrative solicits an explanation, just as the small and youthful David needs to contrast with
the great size and age of Goliath. In each case the explanation comes
from the necessity for a miracle through the intervention of God,
not something on which the common person can count.

In a similar vein, the fine quality of Judith's clothes and jewels
provides a class distinction for her that allows the narrative to be
read as a moral. That is to say, precisely because she was a woman
of the upper class, her act is one that goes against all expectations of
her as a lady. She contrasts with the somewhat ambiguous class of
the more disheveled Judith in the earlier version. So compelling
and necessary, and for godly reasons, is this horrific act, that she ex-
ecutes it despite her social status and in deference to her moral up-
bringing. This storytelling by means of contrast leads us to the
other important realistic detail, the blood that spurts from Holofernes and spots her dress and breast.

Among the most dramatic details is the spurt of blood that results from Judith's cutting into some artery or vein in Holofernes's
neck. This spurt is also prominent in Caravaggio's painting, but not
in Artemisia's earlier one. It pinpoints the moment of the narrative
in a horrifying way, communicating that Holofernes's heart is still
forcefully pumping blood and that Judith's blow to his neck has

rerouted the course of that blood. The moment captured is precisely the moment between life and death. Perhaps this is the most terrifying moment of all, the moment when a person is still alive enough to know that he or she is dying and there is nothing that can be done about it. And with his last breath, he utters his last groan.

The aestheticized composition of 1620, then, allows Artemisia to go further on the level of the narrative details. She has traded off a dramatic, visually immediate, and gut-wrenching grip on the viewer for the more narrative telling of immediacy and gut-wrenchingness. The latter is, clearly, much more demure and agreeable for the survey texts.

Ever Greater Distance, Ever Greater Refinement, Ever Greater Art

Moving even further in that direction, survey books, most notably the many editions of Janson, have begun to replace the 1620 *Judith Beheading Holofernes* with Artemisia's 1625–27 painting of *Judith and Her Maidservant* leaving the tent of Holofernes (see fig. 5). While based on of the same apocryphal text, this painting takes an entirely different moment as its subject. The subject here is more in keeping with Orazio's paintings of 1608–9 in Oslo (fig. 27) and of 1621–24 in Hartford, and with Artemisia's own previous painting of 1612–18 in the Pitti Palace in Florence. In all, the paintings are far more decorous, as Holofernes has already been decapitated and, as in Michelangelo's formulation, his head is carried in a basket by one or both of the young women. We are not asked to bear witness to the physical acts that brought us to this point in time.

The Detroit painting (fig. 5) shares with these paintings the emphasis on the women's furtive looks, an aspect already noted by Vasari as remarkable in Michelangelo. Of his Judith he writes, "She shows by her attitude fear of the camp and terror at the sight of the dead body." True to baroque principles and unlike Michelangelo, who includes the body of Holofernes as the recipient of the women's gaze, the Gentileschi paintings depict the women looking offstage so to speak, constructing the danger as an unseeable unknown to be found in the preserves of the real viewer rather than the realm of the fictive image. In these hushed scenes, all sense of the figures' volition is directed inward. To this end, the darkened, unarticulated spaces of the Caravaggesque backgrounds prove to be very effective, as they are in suggesting the socially induced danger that women feel when they are out alone at night, especially in strange places.

While the Detroit *Judith* by Artemisia shares all of this with the others, it is in many ways a unique formulation of the subject. This is significant and worth pausing over, since the painting is judged as being Artemisia's "finest work" (Christiansen and Mann 2001, 368). Compositionally, this painting is a full-length format, unlike the three-quarter-length format of its predecessors. This by definition puts ever greater distance between the scene and the viewer. Moreover, the physical bond between the two women is broken, for despite the fact that their attention is unified, turned as they are in the same direction, Judith stands erect, while the servant Abra kneels to wrap up the head of Holofernes. This visually sets up a social hierarchy that is elsewhere also manifest, most clearly in the heads of the two women. Judith is essentially bareheaded, wearing a tiara of sorts on top of her braided hairdo. Her maid wears, instead, a modest white headdress, which is visually akin to the white material she wraps around the barely visible head of Holofernes. Her gesture is a self-referential one for Artemisia, since it is so similar to the one Abra makes in other pictures where she holds him down for Judith to cut off his head. Of greatest importance, here, is that Judith is physically and definitively separated from that gruesome and unladylike act.

The most dramatic aspect of this painting is surely the treatment of light. More than the merely darkened background of the other Gentileschi *Judith*s the treatment of light in this picture tracks its effects on the figures and objects within it. One can see this as a part of the larger desire to articulate the space of an interior lit by candlelight, one of the most immediate consequences of including the light source within the painting. Other elements that work towards this end are the red draped curtain in the upper right corner and the table to the left that holds the candle as well as other still life details such as the gauntlet and scabbard.

The implications of candlelit scenes are multiple. They include the kind of dramatic intimacy, here between the two women and the viewers, that is essential in holding the scene together and is a trade-off for the loss of their intimacy in physical proximity. Moreover, the candlelit room substitutes the condition of the setting for the positions of the figures as the cause that makes them hard to see. What I mean by this is that since Michelangelo's interpretation, the furtive and fearful look of the women was communicated by the way they turned their faces from the viewer. In some of the most beautiful examples of the profile, Judith and Abra not only look off the scene but into it. In the Detroit painting they definitely look off the scene, but the difficulty in seeing their faces is the pointed work of the large shadows created by the light conditions.

The painting balances its appeal to the viewer between representing an action that is packed, a realistic narrative, and exhibiting artistic virtuosity in self-reflexive display. The latter is particularly noticeable in the presentational curtain, the meticulous still life, and the dramatic light effects. It may thus be seen as the ultimate negotiation of divergent motives abetted by changing values and tastes in Italy by the end of the 1620s, when the more extrovert aspects of Caravaggism were already becoming progressively less popular. At the same time, this painting is also negotiating an "Artemisia" for changing values and tastes in American academic circles of the late twentieth and early twenty-first centuries, where the inclusion of women artists is by now socially mandatory, while the examples chosen from within that corpus and from the individual oeuvre of each artist to represent the category are decidedly less shocking, more "civilized."

Judging Artemisia is, then, a practice that has been going on for many years. It may be said to have begun with artistic value judgment itself, back in the time of Vasari and the late sixteenth century. I have not intended to plot the critical fortunes of Artemisia Gentileschi for each generation from that point in time to ours; rather, I mean to underscore the connection of our own practices and the social needs those practices satisfy to the practices of her time. At each turn the judgment of Artemisia reveals more, as a practice, about those who are doing the judging than it does about Artemisia herself, who will forever remain, like all historical figures, a mythic unknown.

"GRAN MACCHINA È BELLEZZA"
Looking at the Gentileschi *Judiths*

Elena Ciletti

What motivates reading and interpretation is desire, and . . .
we are responsible for recognizing such desire.

—Griselda Pollock

Postmodernism and genealogical method have taught us to
read representation for what it is, to acknowledge that any
access to meaning is mediated by representation, to respect
surface and exteriority.

—Biman Basu

The timing of the epochal Orazio and Artemisia Gentileschi exhibition at the Metropolitan Museum of Art in 2002 could not have
been more fortuitous for me. I happened to be on sabbatical leave,
my version of "summer afternoon," Henry James's famous candi-
dates for the two most beautiful words in the English language.
After twenty years of starts and stops and detours, I was finally im-
mersed whole-mindedly in a project on Artemisia. The topic was
the iconography of her four major paintings of the biblical heroine
Judith. Normally residing in museums in Florence, Naples, and Detroit, they were gathered together in New York for the first—and perhaps the last—time in history, along with works on the same subject

from Oslo and Hartford by her father, Orazio. Here was an unrepeatable chance to test and refine my long-simmering ideas against the ultimate adjudicating court, the material reality of the paintings themselves. It was a chance for extended reveling in their sheer physicality and visuality, thereby attending to the source rather than the cloud of dense scholarly "air" that has come to envelop them. A chance to let the much talked-about paintings talk back. To eavesdrop on their silent conversations with each other. This article is about what I heard and saw.[1]

There is of course no such thing as unmediated looking, a truth intensified by the plenitude of the Gentileschi literature in recent years.[2] It is well known that Artemisia Gentileschi has become the object of an industry or cult of late, which has generated not only scholarly work but also numerous fictional, theatrical, and cinematic treatments of her life and art, some of which are scrutinized by Griselda Pollock in this book. Central to all of these has been the recalcitrant question of the extent and the nature of the stylistic and iconographic relationships between father and daughter, a question richly explored by the exhibition. These relationships impinge with particular stubbornness on the images with which Artemisia is most popularly associated, her paintings of the biblical heroine Judith, the courageous and chaste widow who saved the Jewish people from annihilation by beheading an enemy general, Holofernes.

The subject of the text of the Book of Judith itself, part of the so-called Old Testament Apocrypha, its complicated heroine, and its long cultural *Nachleben* (afterlife), is vast and controversial, and has inevitably colored the attention to Artemisia's paintings.[3] They have become the site of a large and fractious literature involving and transcending art-historical issues. A paucity of documentation has exacerbated the situation, and much that is fundamental remains to be discovered about these works. Beyond the shifting borders of Artemisia's artistic relationship to her father and to the wider currents of Caravaggesque style, her *Judith* paintings have been tied to contemporary Counter-Reformation theology, history, literature and politics; to the patriarchal social norms of her time and the protofeminist resistance thereto; and to the artist's own psychobiography. Predictably, the most commonly met inference is that Artemisia's images of this theme are autobiographical psychodramas enacting either her own well-documented experience of sexual violence, perpetrated by Agostino Tassi, or its traumatic aftereffects, the cathartic expression of explicit revenge or repressed rage. As Pollock has noted, Artemisia Gentileschi's *Judith*s are a space in which possible contrary meanings can vie with each other (1999, 112). In this regard, they are very like the scriptural book on which they are based.

The artist would certainly have assumed her audience's familiarity with the essentials of the plot of the biblical tale of Judith and Holofernes, discussed by others in this volume. Long a popular figure for her larger-than-life character and the irresistible drama of her story, Judith was a traditional symbol of a wide range of emblematic virtues with both religious and civic dimensions—chastity, humility, fortitude, and justice, for instance—and thus of victory over the equally iconic vices associated with her adversary Holofernes: lust, arrogance, and pride. She acquired renewed currency in the religious turmoil of the sixteenth and seventeenth centuries, wherein these polar identities were easily adaptable to the contemporary situation. As an idolatrous Assyrian, Holofernes was inevitably cast in the role of arch-heretic, and the virtuous Jewish widow who undid him by her beauty and her courage was available for appropriation by everyone in need of a brave defender. The fact that Judith had prevailed over an enemy of superior force was particularly appealing. Catholics and Protestants alike embraced her ancient identity as a personification of the biblical moral of strength in weakness; the widow Judith, a "mere" woman, overcomes the enemy of her people with power that is miraculous, divine, and that is the sign of her righteousness. The scriptural text makes it clear that the gender reversal at the center of the story, the independence and ruthlessness which are transgressive for a female, is but a temporary inversion of the natural order, as Judith goes on to live out her days in exemplary celibate seclusion. But it is also a significant episode in the ongoing biblical saga of God's paternal protection of his Covenant People.

The Naples *Judith*

Any consideration of Gentileschi's *Judith* paintings must begin with her first treatment of the subject, the *Judith Beheading Holofernes* from the Capodimonte Museum in Naples (see fig. 22).[4] The painting in Naples is dated by almost all recent Gentileschi scholars to around 1612, a rare case of critical agreement in the modern scholarship. Chronology is a particularly knotted issue in her oeuvre, one that I am bypassing throughout this essay in favor of the dating proposed by Christiansen and Mann in the exhibition catalogue, which sometimes conforms to and sometimes diverges from the monographs of Garrard (1989) and Bissell (1999). Beyond the dating, most aspects of the work are shrouded in either mystery or controversy or both. Most notably, it is the only one of the four major *Judiths* to have its attribution to Artemisia challenged in current scholarship, although this claim is not accepted by either the exhibition catalogue or the major monographs.[5]

In addition, this painting shares with other representations of Judith beheading Holofernes a tradition of erroneous terminology. Both the deed and the images devoted to it are often referred to as the *murder* of Holofernes, a judgment in violation of the story's biblical source. The Book of Judith's point of view is that the killing of general Holofernes is a legitimate act of war, not a crime, and the spirit in which both Jews and Christians interpret the triumphant, sanguinary episodes of their holy writ is celebratory, not accusatory. This was certainly the position of Counter-Reformation Catholic culture during Artemisia's and Orazio's lifetimes.

At the Metropolitan exhibition, the Naples *Judith* was hemmed in on a crowded wall, guaranteeing a perpetual traffic jam of viewers, and its simple frame seemed to confer on it an undeserved modesty with respect to its neighbors. But even without these impediments, this notorious and controversial painting is literally hard to see. It thwarts even the most basic visual analysis, for two reasons. First of all, its deteriorated surface condition impedes assessment of its intended textures. There are holes, blisters, *pentimenti*, repainting, and large areas of abrasion, and the dark shadows have blackened considerably. Equally frustrating, its current size (slightly over 62 by 49 inches) is problematic. While there is agreement that the canvas has been cut down on the left side, there is confusion about the extent of its alterations and therefore about the original size, format, and composition, which may have included a candle in the lower left corner. Diverse surviving seventeenth-century replicas, not to mention Artemisia's own celebrated "revision" in the Uffizi, complicate rather than clarify these fundamental issues. Nevertheless, it is, of course, an intensely dramatic painting of a blatantly gruesome event, a tour de force of chiaroscuro and compositional effects, a sensational claim to mastery for a painter not yet twenty years old.

When I had first seen it in person, in the exhibition Painting in Naples, 1606–1705, at the Royal Academy in London in 1982, I recorded in a journal that I thought it too terrifying to look at. This was no doubt a naive position, but it had been reconfirmed for me repeatedly since then in the darkness of the art-history classroom, where in the artificial illumination of slide technology, the painting projects from the screen with jolting effect. I have given many a lecture about it to audiences discomfited by the frontal view that I myself was avoiding in favor of furtive peripheral glances. Bolstered further by the constant testimonials to its brutality in the Gentileschi literature, I was prepared at the exhibition in New York to be shocked once again. This is, after all, a painting that has been often referred to, in both the Met's accompanying label and Mann's catalogue entry, as a "bloodbath." But the painting did not behave as I had anticipated.

Gradually, I came to feel that visually the interest and therefore the drama in this work lie not in the explicit horror of the struggling Holofernes and the famous foregrounded composition of radiating arms, but in the mysterious light and shadow which envelop the maid who assists Judith and the head and shoulders of the heroine herself. Its source may plausibly be the hypothesized candle (now eliminated, beyond the frame) on the lower left. In any case, on the side facing Judith, the maid's foreshortened head is so inventively shaded and so artfully related to and set off against the surrounding areas that it may be the focal point of the whole work. It occurred to me that the sheer presence exerted by this maid reinforces the inclination to personalize her by granting her a name.

Indeed, the Gentileschi literature participates in a long, but technically incorrect, literary tradition that names her "Abra." As biblical scholarship indicates, Judith's assistant is nameless in the Book of Judith.[6] In its most complete form, which is the version in the Greek Septuagint Bible, she is referred to by several terms that are descriptive rather than nominative, one of which is *abra* (or *habra*). Together, these terms embrace a variety of meanings: graceful one, handmaid, servant, favorite slave. Toni Craven has also suggested that she was no mere personal attendant but the woman in charge of Judith's household. Her status is underscored at the conclusion of the scriptural text where we learn that before her death, Judith "emancipated her trusted servant" (16:23). There is a certain appeal, then, both emotional and practical, to maintaining the familiar appellation, which I have sometimes done here, using quotation marks to remind the reader of its ambiguous status.

In the pioneering first monograph on Artemisia Gentileschi in 1989, Mary Garrard saw the figure of the maid as dominating the composition by virtue of her placement at its apex (310), an idea my observations further elaborate by stressing her head as the culmination of the painting's most visually interesting "field," the area bounded on the sides by her arms. The patterning of colors and textures in that region—lit and shaded crimson and white cloth, flesh, hair—seems to have a vivid life of its own. The strong light cuts under and over her right arm from the left, creating a vibrant color module along her flank: a piercing, attenuated triangle of bright red, with an almost flamelike upper extension, wedged between the black void of the tent interior and the dark shadow underneath the intersecting forearms. This is a device to which I will return.

Within the frame of arms, which are adroitly configured by the tactic of varying the lengths of the pushed-up red sleeves, an unsettling sense of three-dimensional space is constructed. Its spatial strangeness is partly a function of the disjunctive scale of the jabbing fist of Holofernes, and it is contrasted masterfully with the less elaborated area bordered by Judith's and Holofernes' arms on the right. The maid thus seems an oasis of aesthetic meditation in which the extroverted violence of the foreground is echoed but transmuted into subtler poetry by sophisticated formal means. The exhibition catalogue discusses "formal devices [that] are employed as narrative strategies" (84), and links them to contemporary baroque literature, but it does so vis-à-vis Orazio Gentileschi. I believe that the use of such formal devices is just as relevant to our understanding of the accomplishments of his daughter, especially at the early stage of her career represented by the Naples *Judith,* whose youthful *gaucheries* are often noted.

Among the contemporary seventeenth-century literary figures encountered in the literature is Federico Della Valle (1978), a playwright whose drama *Iudit* (Judith) has figured in recent scholarship ever since Garrard invoked it as a parallel to the Judith imagery of both Artemisia and Orazio.[7] First published in 1627 and now considered a masterpiece of baroque literature, Della Valle's play was even quoted in the Met's label for Orazio's *Judith and her Maid* in Hartford, to explain the motivation of the figures' poses (Christiansen and Mann 2001, 186–90). But thinking about the sophistication of Artemisia's maidservant brought to mind a line from Della Valle's *Iudit* that was not cited; indeed, I am not aware of its notation in any of the Gentileschi literature. I am referring to a dramatically ironic statement by Holofernes, whose ultimately fatal enchantment with Judith's beauty is central to the plotting of his destruction; gazing upon her, he observes: "*Gran macchina è bellezza*" (Della Valle 1978, 3.4.431).

In this definition of beauty (*bellezza*) as a great or impressive "*macchina*," Della Valle apparently intended the term to mean a "war machine" and by extension "machination"; modern dictionar-

ies provide a constellation of etymological and conceptual associa-
tions: "weapon," "engine," "instrument," "edifice," "body," "plot,"
"intrigue," "intelligence," "ingenuity." "*Gran macchina è bellezza*":
the more time I spent with Artemisia's *Judith* paintings, the more the
nuances of the phrase reverberated. Like the heroine they depict, the
paintings not only portray beauty as an engine of power, they themselves *are* such engines. It is to their power that we are drawn, and
that power is fundamentally aesthetic.

Artemisia's play with lighting and with spatial "modules"
bounded by arms and hands in the Naples *Judith,* her artful deployment of beauty, is interesting not only on its own terms, but
also in relation to earlier works in her stylistic orbit, both her own
and others. It immediately brings to mind her Pommersfelden
Susanna and the Elders of 1610 (see fig. 17), discussed in the previous chapter by Nanette Salomon, where the entire drama coa-
lesces in a similar segment of open space punctuated by gesticu-
lating limbs. There too there is some ambiguity, in both the
figural scale and the oddly projecting white collar of the elder on
the left, and there too there are delicious little optical touches, like
the shadow cast onto the wall by his sleeve. But the daylight scene
and the close proximity of the wall in the *Susanna* apparently did
not provide the same range of experimental possibilities offered
by the positioning and lighting of the maidservant in the nocturnal scenario of Holofernes' tent. When we look further afield to
the well-known prototypes of the Naples *Judith* by Caravaggio
(see fig. 23) and Rubens (fig. 25), keeping in mind the blinding
risks of reduction, generalization, and judgment inherent in the
comparative method (pointed out in the essay here by Mieke Bal),
we find that Artemisia is not "outclassed" by her elders in her
invention of savvy visual ploys. Caravaggio's seminal work may
have inspired the pose of Judith's parallel arms, but Artemisia en-
livens the area within them to a greater extent with her positioning of Holofernes and the resultant overlapping of limbs, itself
perhaps derived from Rubens's more agitated but less concentrated drama (c. 1600–10).

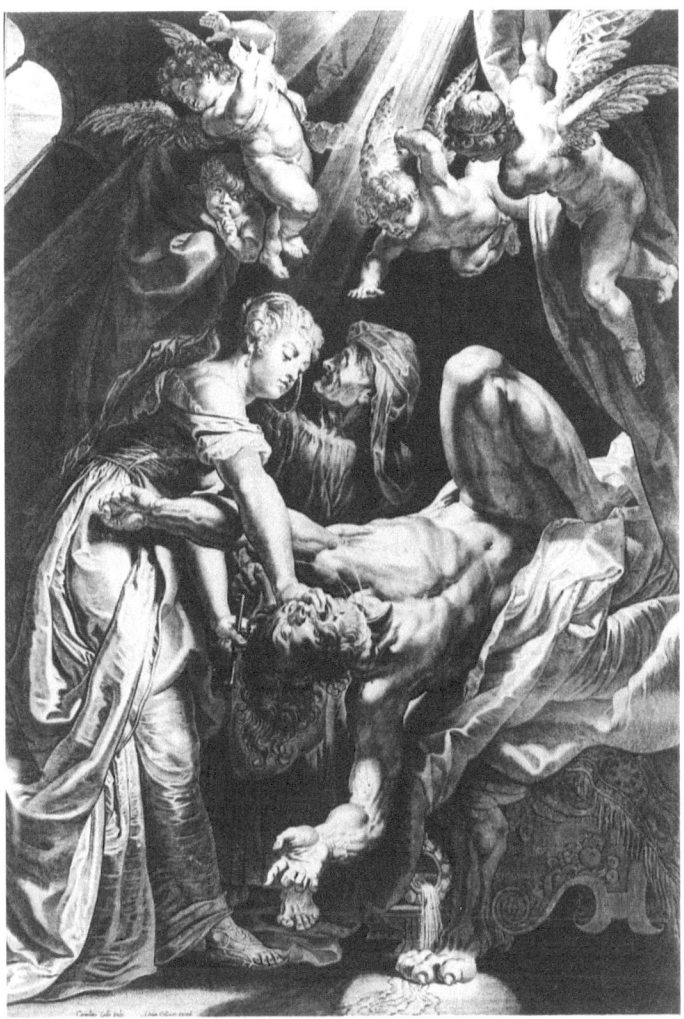

Figure 25. Print by C. Galle after Rubens, *Judith Slaying Holofernes,* ca. 1600–10. Engraving, 1610. New York, Metropolitan Museum. (Courtesy of Dr. Rembrandt Duits, Warburg Institute, Photographic Collection.)

All three painters exploit the tactic of extreme chiaroscural juxtapositions against unexpected slivers of illumination that produce
uncanny spatial and plastic moments. In Artemisia's painting, as we
have seen, the motif in question is the shard of light along the flank
of the maid. In Caravaggio's *Judith,* the chiaroscuro involves the
torso of Holofernes. On the left edge, the composition is closed by
the brilliantly calibrated geometry of Holofernes' shoulder and arm,
the climax of which is the sinuous curve of the band of cast shadow
under his armpit and around his chest, and it is given carnal force by
the two tiny perforations of bright light from behind. Indeed, there
is more lethal razor-sharpness in this configuration than in Judith's
actual blade working its way rather unconvincingly through
Holofernes' neck immediately to the right. Rubens too played with
the dialectic of ribbons of cast shadow and highlight, most notably
in the tense weave of the arms of Judith and Holofernes and in the
telling area between his right armpit and the sheet below. The latter
cuticle of light is a small but vehement indication of the galvanic
force which pulls Holofernes off the elaborate bed.

In all three images, passages marked with beautifully shaped
splinters of light are invested with a variety of tasks: they create
space, they enliven the design surface, and they simultaneously enhance the physical and psychic credibility of the gruesome beheading scene while providing the viewer with some relief from it. We
recognize such pictorial touches as small but important tools in the
early baroque arsenal of the "*gran macchina (di) bellezza.*" They remind us, in case we need the reminder, that, notwithstanding the
innumerable interpretive possibilities these paintings offer, they
are minutely calculated visual constructions to be appreciated for
their skill. Although the exact commission circumstances are not
entirely clear for the Gentileschi *Judith* paintings, we do know they
were intended not for churches but for private or princely collections, which is to say for patrons whose discernment was addressed
and flattered by the strategic deployment of aesthetic pleasure.

Of course, Artemisia was schooled by her father, a master of
chiaroscural and compositional sophistication, and two of his early

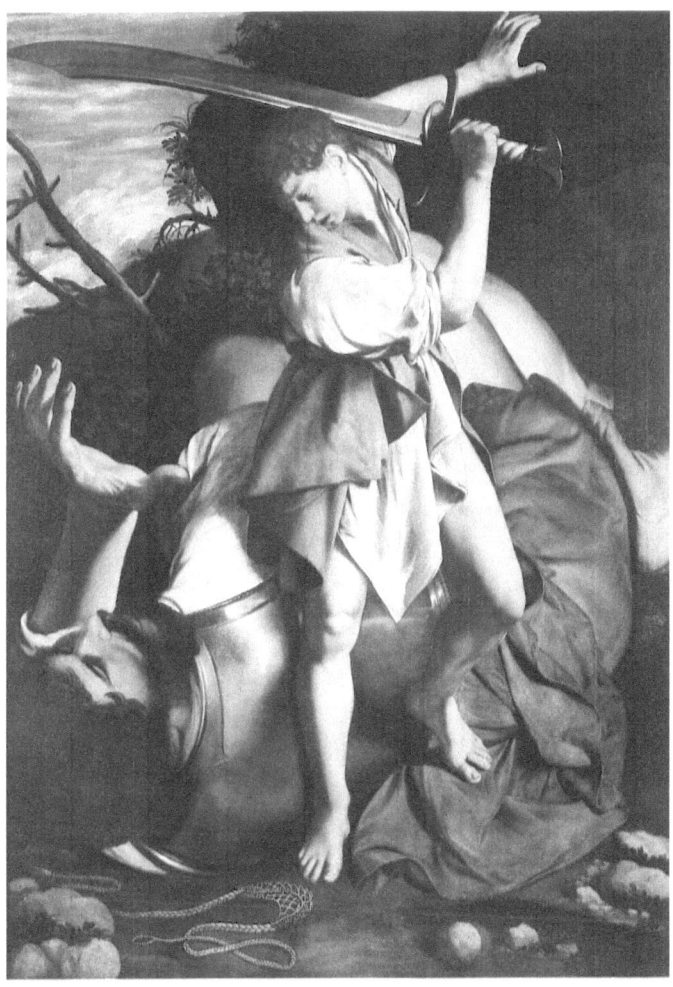

Figure 26. Orazio Gentileschi, *David Slaying Goliath*, ca. 1607–9. Oil on canvas, 73 1/4 × 53 1/8 in. (186 × 135 cm). Dublin, National Gallery of Ireland. (Photo credit: Alinari/Art Resource, New York.)

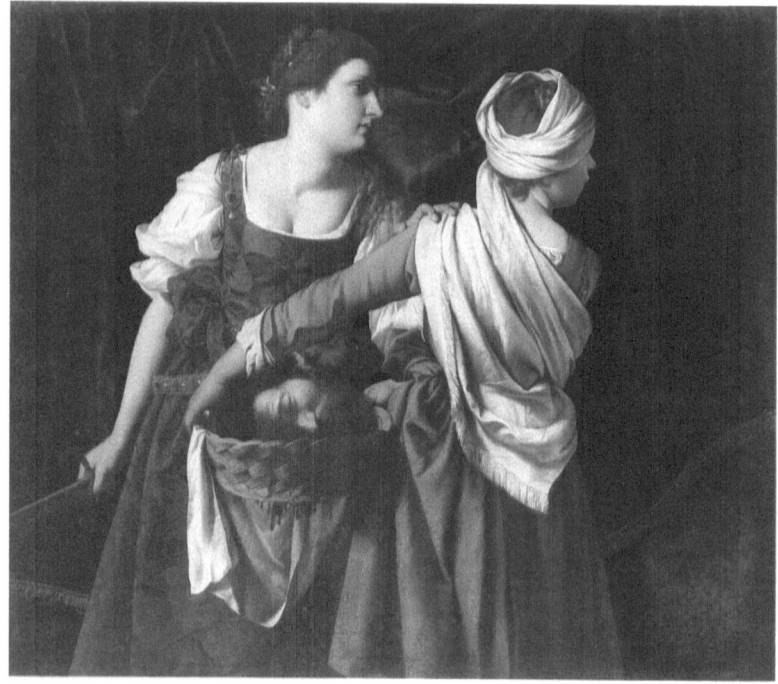

Figure 27. Orazio Gentileschi, *Judith and her Maidservant*, ca. 1608–9. Oil on canvas, 53 1/2 × 63 in. (136 × 160 cm). Oslo, Nasjonalgalleriet. (Photo credit: National Gallery, Norway.)

paintings on view at the Metropolitan are particularly relevant to her Naples *Judith* in this regard. One is his *David Slaying Goliath* in Dublin (fig. 26), dated by the exhibit's catalogue to ca. 1607–9, when Artemisia was certainly in his workshop; the pose of Goliath has been associated with that of the Naples Holofernes, and both drama and spatial complexity are again a function of the deft interplay of limbs. With Orazio's *Judith and her Maidservant* of perhaps ca. 1608–9 in Oslo (fig. 27), the links to Artemisia are even closer (Christiansen and Mann 2001, 82–86). Indeed, there is even a minority position in the scholarship which attributes this painting to her. We will return to its composition later, since it is so close to

Artemisia's second version of *Judith,* but here it suffices to point out the familiar light and space devices, even if they are more muted than those of Artemisia, Caravaggio or Rubens. The basket with the head of Holofernes, for instance, is again locked into a field composed of the servant's arm and flank, and her left hand provides an opportunity for a small but lively play of shadow and backlit brightness on the lovingly articulated white cloth draped on the basket. Orazio's style is celebrated for its decorative touches and for a more lyrical orientation than the more dramatic approach of his daughter, but she was well versed in his visual language and subsumed rather than rejected it in her own more vehement works. The visual complexity of the maidservant in Artemisia's Naples *Judith* is one indication of this.

Moreover, once the maid is allowed to exert her full visual force, even some well-known problems with this painting can shift. As the Met's label reminded us, Artemisia "clearly struggled with the composition. The scale of the figures is not consistent, and x-rays show that she made significant adjustments." No doubt. In the exhibition catalogue, Mann notes that the young painter was working out the logistical implications of the narrative, and Christiansen explains the inconsistencies with the hypothesis that her compositional method did not rely on "an action staged by three figures but a kind of patchwork of three models separately posed" (Christiansen and Mann 2001, 256, 12). But the scale disjunctions, intentional or otherwise, are expressively functional, especially where the massive fist of Holofernes collides with the foreshortened face of the maid: they create a sense of the inexplicable. If we cannot quite rationalize the sizes and the positions in space of the female protagonists, they therefore loom more persuasively as the enactors of an omnipotent cosmic force that transcends human parameters. We do not see them exactly as Holofernes would, but the composition flirts with a vertiginous *sotto in su,* or worm's-eye vantage point, which, together with the scale and position "problems," enhances the sense of the violation of the natural order inherent in the biblical story.

There is more than a little of the unspeakable here. The discursive disruptions, especially in the disquieting juxtapositions of foreground brightness with background void and of Holofernes's fist with the maid's head, also suggest the sensation of temporal abruptness, of a hallucinatory, freeze-frame tableau. Ultimately, the aura of Caravaggesque naturalism provided by individual details and the emphatic conviction of the overall chiaroscuro is thus undermined. It is irresistible to invoke here the contemporary American poet Charles Simic, who once said, "Beauty is about the improbable coming true suddenly."

Improbability also inhabits this painting at the narrative level, since the dispatching of Holofernes is here carried out by two women. Yet, the Book of Judith is explicit that Judith was alone in the tent with Holofernes, while her maid kept watch outside. The creation of such an overt physical role for "Abra" in the beheading itself is therefore an unbiblical innovation of Artemisia Gentileschi, one unique to her. Much has been made of this invention, psychologically and politically. It was first given a feminist reading in 1989 by Garrard, who argues for it as a statement of sisterhood, an idea that has aroused hostility on the grounds of interpretive excess and anachronistic implausibility.[8] But in the construction of the painting itself, the sense of sisterhood is not an intrusion. In the silence of the night, Judith and her servant work together, with no need for words. All the critics have observed that they are in sync physically and psychically, and the composition itself establishes this in its placement and posing of the figures.

Beyond this obvious device, there are subtler visual cues, such as the evocative twin highlights on the two women's eyelids and cheeks. This purposeful pairing, superb in purely optical terms in spite of the degraded surface of the canvas, reverberates throughout the upper half of the painting. The doubling highlight motif is carried onto the maid's neck and related to the adjacent twinned white stripes of her chemise, which in turn are echoed in her cuffs. A variation on this theme is provided for Judith, one result of which is the foregrounding of the naturalistic device of the women's pushed-up sleeves. Simultaneously mundane and psychologically astute, this device confers a matter-of-factness on the women's approach to their task and their solidarity in it. The cuffs, in their variety, placement, and coloristic contrasts with the sleeves, indicate another of those spirited pictorial decisions which attest to the painter's concern for artistry.

The eyelid and cheek highlights on Judith not only tie her to her partner but also contribute to the whole magnificent passage of her face, shoulders, and breasts, where deep shading is deployed in undulating, echoing arcs throughout. Although the face of Judith has suffered from deterioration and overpainting in the past, in its current condition it creates a complex and elusive psychology for the heroine. The frown and the soft, slightly pursed lips register a seriousness and total absorption that are neither seductive nor fierce, in spite of the calculated drama of the shading which conceals so much. In reproductions, this Judith usually appears deviously calculating, but in person, she seems rather to exude the confidence of someone secure in the virtue of her deed, and in this she is matched by her servant. This Judith's determined yet almost calm face, together with the much commented-upon physical plausibility of her entire figure, make her metaphorically and literally a figure of substance. She therefore inhabits an entirely different expressive universe from that created by Artemisia's predecessors in this iconography, one that is completely congruent with the spirit of the biblical text.

This painting thus forces us to redress the common misapprehension that inscribed in the story of Judith is her sexual seduction of Holofernes.[9] It must be stressed that such a possibility is explicitly denied in the biblical text. It is true that Judith is presented there as exploiting Holofernes' physical desire for her, verbally manipulating his expectations about her sexual availability with shrewd double entendre, but her behavior overtly subverts them. The language and the plot are replete with sexuality, but all versions of the text are emphatic regarding the heroine's avoidance of "defilement." Even her town's name, Bethulia, refers to (her) sexual abstinence: it is etymologically close to the Hebrew word for virginity, *bethula.* Indeed, like Jael and other biblical heroines, as Babette

Bohn has discussed elsewhere in this book, Judith was long paired
typologically with the Virgin Mary by the Catholic Church.

Once I looked at the Naples *Judith* with Della Valle's "*gran
macchina (di) bellezza*" in mind, the deep correspondences between the painting and its source came into sharper focus, since
both share an eeriness submerged in overt rhetorical bombast. The
biblical tale, for all its exotic opulence, is verbally laconic about the
climactic scene in Holofernes' tent, thus ensuring a mysterious aura
of both directness and elusive introspection. Artemisia's painting
does exactly the same thing. There is no denying the overt force of
the central action, and yet even the notorious blood seeps into the
sheets almost stealthily, in telling contrast to both Caravaggio's
and Artemisia's own subsequent versions of this scene. One might
say that although the dramatic temperature is high in the Naples
Judith, its aural volume is very low. Like its implacable protagonists,
this is an excruciatingly silent picture.

The Uffizi *Judith*

One cannot say the same for the version of this scene which
Artemisia painted approximately eight years later, the renowned
Judith Beheading Holofernes of ca. 1620 in the Uffizi in Florence
(see fig. 24).[10] Almost certainly commissioned in Florence for the
Medici grand ducal collections, this large (almost 78 by 64 inches)
and impressive canvas befits a courtly provenance. The canvas reg-
isters in every way as a mature and expansive restatement of the earlier composition in Naples, one is tempted to say an inflation of it,
with far more attention to monumental formality and luxurious
effects. The result is a painting that is supremely accomplished and
extroverted, a painting whose visual expertise is so assured as to
need no defense. Its status as a Della Vallean "*gran macchina*" has
been abundantly confirmed in the literature, wherein eloquent
paeans to its stylistic sophistication abound. Nonetheless, in New
York, I couldn't help but agree with the minority position that there
is a price paid for Artemisia's proficiency here: the mystery of the

Naples prototype is gone, as is its tense *pianissimo*. The Uffizi *Judith* is operatic, and its decibel level is stentorian.

As Nanette Salomon has pointed out in the preceding chapter, it is Artemisia's "best-selling" image, the one most associated with her, the pillar on which her popular reputation rests. So grandiose in its scale and its effects, and so relentlessly scrutinized from every possible angle, the painting is daunting to contemplate. Coupled with, but overshadowing, the version in Naples, it has inspired a dizzying number of competing interpretations.[11] It has been variously seen, and this is an incomplete list, as an image of sadism, sacred ritual, irreligious profanity, self-portraiture (both psychic and physical), heroic feminism, misogyny, murder, sexual intercourse, castration and penis envy, childbirth, and even science, whereby the arc of Holofernes' spurting blood either illustrates the unpublished discovery of the parabolic law of projectiles by Gentileschi's friend Galileo or visually anticipates the effects of the circulatory mechanisms discovered later by Harvey.

The tally goes on: together with the Naples *Judith*, it has been said to recall impassive slaughter by both a rural butcher's wife and a cut-throat prostitute, to invoke the Virgin Mary, to arouse aesthetic disgust, and to reveal a diverse range of contending traits, such as the painter's wanton lasciviousness, her unresolved conflicts with men, her "womanly" tendency to profuse ornament, her "masculine" tendency to fierceness, and her anxiety of influence vis-à-vis Orazio and their shared inspiration, Caravaggio.

At the Metropolitan it was at least finally given a worthy presentation, something of a historic novelty for this work. In Florence, it has until recently been relatively inaccessible in the Corridoio Vasariano of the Uffizi, to which it had been relegated from Palazzo Pitti, where a disapproving grand duchess had apparently consigned it to a dark corner in the eighteenth century. Damaged in the terrorist bombing of 1993, it was subsequently restored and replaced in a visually maladroit corner in the Uffizi itself, rather hard to find and harder to see. The condition of the canvas was seriously compromised across the centuries, even before 1993, sustaining what Mann in the exhibition catalogue describes as "considerable losses and repaintings throughout" (Christiansen and Mann 2001, 350). But unlike the even greater deterioration of the *Judith* in Naples, the damage was not especially disconcerting to the naked eye at the Met. Some of it was visible, but not enough to cancel the general impression of glowing surfaces. The painting was hung in a dominating position on a wide, burgundy wall, its visual grandeur given every opportunity to exert itself. Not surprisingly, it drew a great deal of attention.

It may seem redundant, perverse even, to insist on a pictorial exploration of such a widely acclaimed masterwork, but at the exhibition I felt a certain urgency in the task. More than any other painting by Artemisia, this is the one which has been looked to, one might say *through,* for evidence about its maker's psychobiography and her multifaceted connections to her society and culture, as well as her relevance to our own. I do not wish to suggest that there is a paucity of stylistic considerations of this painting in the art historical literature; on the contrary, discerning accounts of it exist, generally within larger arguments about such important matters as chronology, provenance, sources, relationship to Orazio, historical significance, and more. The exhibition gave me the chance to indulge a more narrowly defined pictorial focus.

It is impossible to think about the visual achievements of the Uffizi *Judith Beheading Holofernes* alone, without reference to its predecessor in Naples. The much discussed nature of their interrelationships is too complex to be plumbed to its depths here, but some comparative factors cannot be avoided. Issues of size and scale are central to any such discussion, with the larger size and broader focus of the Uffizi version often adduced as evidence for the original dimensions of the truncated painting in Naples. There is no question that the Uffizi canvas's greater space across the top and the much fuller articulation of the trunk and lower limbs of Holofernes on the left mitigate the claustrophobic expressivity of the earlier work. And they contribute in no small measure to the sense of greater spatial consistency and therefore mastery.

The Uffizi figures are virtually identical in their positioning to those in the Naples canvas, yet they seem to have a more convincing envelope of air around and between them, and the more central placement of the focal point of the composition, the head of Holofernes, creates a newly calibrated sense of equilibrium. The presence this time of his legs, and the careful angle of their placement, furnish a strong balance on the left to the arms of Judith on the right, thus broadening both the geometry and the fluidity of the compositional sweep. The more legible logic of space and scale alone in the Uffizi image guarantees the erasure of the sensation of the uncanny at the heart of the Naples scene. But we are not sure of the original parameters of that earlier work, a point not always given adequate weight in the interpretive literature, and so we must admit the possibility that accidents of history account for some of the major differences now seen between the two paintings.

But certainly not all of them. Indeed, whatever we cannot say about Artemisia's original intentions for the space, we can say much about her use of color. Both the warm tonality overall and the individual color designations of the Uffizi *Judith* are worlds apart from her earlier choices. Judith's electric blue dress, which almost disrupts the composition in Naples, is transmuted into gold now. (Incidentally, these are the garments that inspired the quip by Longhi about "the house of Gentileschi" as the finest purveyor of silk in seventeenth century Europe, after Van Dyck [1916, 258].) To be fair, it must be recognized that the maidservant's dress in the Uffizi painting would have maintained a blue accent, but its effect is impossible to assess now, since the color has deteriorated and darkened over time. Fully integrated into the burnished chromatic design, the honey-toned dress of Judith and the drapery over Holofernes, now deep red and trimmed with gold, strike us immediately as vigorous changes vis-à-vis the earlier version, and they signal the move towards visual opulence, which is universally recognized as pervasive in this work.

Textures are more varied here, and folds are more convoluted, along with a greater degree of elaboration in the details of the cos-

tumes. For instance, while it's true that Artemisia has now aban-
doned the Naples painting's gold and black ribbon trim on Judith's
dress, she more than compensates by clothing the heroine in gold
damask, whose patterning makes a more insistent note; moreover,
Holofernes' new crimson drapery is clearly velvet. Equally revealing are the contrasting red linings introduced into the pushed-up
cuffs of both Judith and her assistant, a simple change with a variety of consequences. The decorative ante is instantly "upped," while
the already noted compositional balance is underscored, since the
cuffs' tones not only echo the velvet cover over Holofernes (Judith's
match it exactly; the maid's are a paler variant), but they overtly
contribute to the pyramidal geometry established by the poses. In
addition, the cuffs announce in a declarative voice the bond between Judith and "Abra" more quietly invoked in the earlier version
in Naples.

The new prominence of red accents in the Uffizi canvas is of
course most salient in the notorious treatment of Holofernes'
blood, which now spurts out in energetic arcs and even spatters the
women's bodies and clothing. This is a staggering device, horrifying in its anatomically realistic suggestion of the pressured eruption
from the severed carotid artery and, one hates to admit it, visually
elegant in its sinuous linearity. In both regards this is Artemisia's
correction of Caravaggio and of her own Naples version, and perhaps a variation on Rubens. The jets of blood in the Uffizi *Judith*
call attention to themselves not only by their exuberant design but
by their frontal placement and their contrast with the lighter skin
and sheets behind them. Formally, they reiterate the shapes of the
folds in Judith's dress and Holofernes' bedclothes, and they slyly
echo the composition's celebrated organization around the radiating spokes of limbs. Additionally, they draw attention to Judith's
bracelet, a prominent embellishment not indulged in the painting
in Naples. Thinking about Holofernes' blood, as Artemisia certainly intended her viewers to do, we cannot help but admire her
audacity and her skill in exploiting simultaneously both the lurid
and the exquisite possibilities of this violent story.

One cannot attend to the blood without considering the sword, which is longer and more vertically placed than in the Naples *Judith;* the blade is now framed by the blood, and together they achieve a more calculated integration of the painting's lower stratum with the rest of the design. The blood continues the downward trajectory of the sword, insinuating itself into the mattresses in a more plausible and yet more refined cursive route into the white passages of the bed linens. "Butchery . . . on a sheet . . . worthy of Vermeer," Longhi famously put it (1916, 258). While this is no doubt hyperbole, one is grateful for the extensive respite from the brutality of the scene offered by those soft and mellifluous white folds.

The fringed fabric draped over the edge of the bed in the lower right is familiar from the Naples version, but its better state of conservation in the Uffizi canvas allows us to appreciate its sensuous yet subtle handling, especially of the fringe itself, with its frothy arabesques and tactile variety. Perhaps a garment (a shirt?) rather than bed linens, this drapery straddles the corner of the bed, thereby anchoring the composition in two directions and concluding in the lower right corner the progression of radiating intervals set in motion on the far left by Holofernes' thigh. It is thus essential to the design of the painting. Moreover, it is here on the exposed corner of the bed that we find the artist's signature: EGO ARTEMITIA / LOMI FEC[IT], Lomi being a familial Tuscan surname, which she naturally stressed in her Florentine commissions.[12]

Artemisia further uses the white zone of the bedding as the base on which to develop more fully another reinforcement of the figural pyramid above, namely, the equilateral peaking rhythm of vivid whitish accents in the three protagonists' garments. The pinnacle of this configuration is the head of the maid, whose light head scarf has been expanded to enframe her face more fully than in the painting in Naples. Although the precarious condition of the blue pigment on her sleeves makes the artist's intent about the exposure of the white blouse underneath hard to discern with any certainty, it is clear that the light accents are generally doubled, as in the two women's two cuffs, and sometimes they form white bands framing

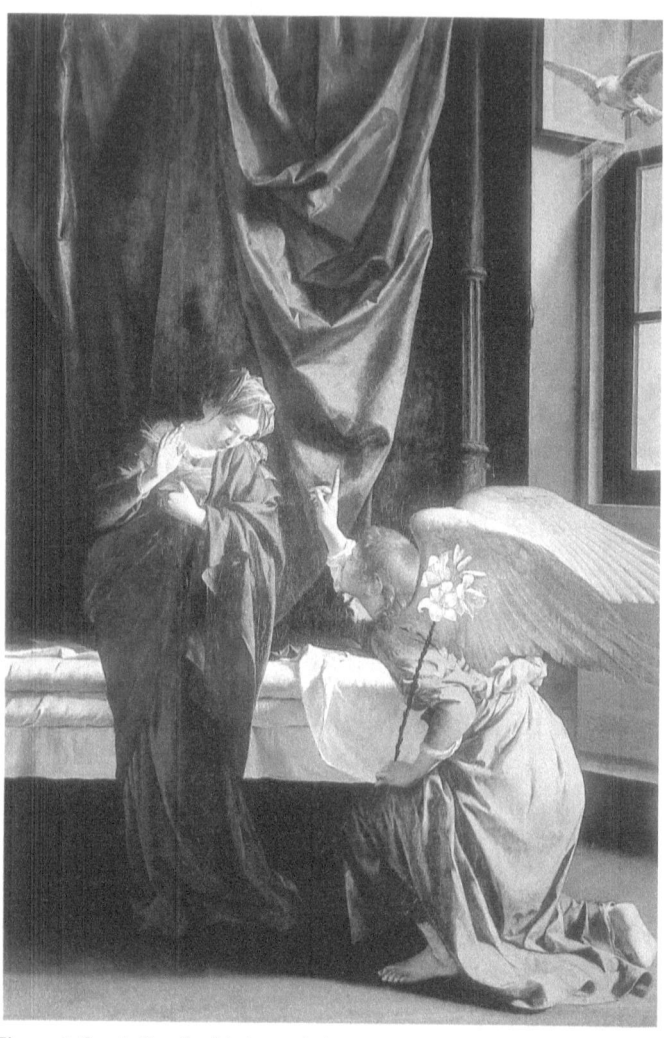

Figure 28. Orazio Gentileschi, *Annunciation,* 1623. Oil on canvas, 112 5/8 × 77 1/8 in. (286 × 196 cm). Turin, Galleria Sabauda. (Photo credit: Scala/Art Resource, New York.)

a darker intervening tone passage, as in the sheets around Holofernes's red cover or the cloth around the servant's face. They thus form a subtle, curvilinear counterpart to Artemisia's inventive compositional strategy of the terse pairs of accented and expressive limbs.

As I walked through the exhibition at the Met, I couldn't help but be struck by how often, in painting after painting, both Artemisia and her father deployed white highlights, usually provided by blouses and underclothing, to organize and animate their compositions in this way (e.g., see Christiansen and Mann 2001, 39, 51). Frequently, we find their canvases given over to interlocking color fields punctuated with a pattern of white cloth units that coalesce or articulate the overall design. On the related subject of sheets, Orazio was clearly also a master, especially in his Genoese period from 1621–24. In his two versions of *Danae* and his *Annunciation* (fig. 28), for instance, we encounter splendid beds with sophisticated textural and draping effects. Tremendous care is given to distinguishing their specific textures, but most seem to use more refined fabric, with more threads per inch, one might say, than Artemisia employed in her Uffizi *Judith*. Attention to such details was obviously prized in both Gentileschi's studios, and a high degree of the conviction exerted by their paintings depends on it.

If the spatial, coloristic, and surface mastery of the Uffizi *Judith* bespeak a new level of visual elaboration for Artemisia, other stylistic components underscore the point. It occurred to me in New York that these are some of the causal factors in the dilution of the minor key *frisson* of the Naples version. For instance, Judith's patterned gold gown provides the opportunity for brighter illumination effects than its blue precedent in the swatch of skirt behind Holofernes's arm, thus filling in with decorative allure what was virtually a mysterious black void in the earlier painting. In the process, the later canvas detaches the heroine more emphatically from the dark background, increasing her three-dimensional credibility but concomitantly defusing her otherworldly air. The gold dress in the Uffizi canvas is also used to make Judith's knee more visible behind Holofernes's torso, thus underscoring the physical logic of her strained position astride the bed. The greater brightness in this area is further exploited as the field against which the wider *quillon* of the sword hilt and the newly emphatic blood are marked. In the earlier work in Naples, the right armpit of Holofernes, replete with soft hair, is exposed, a poignant human touch which accentuates the superhuman scale of the force which vanquishes him. In the Uffizi painting, this telling little anatomical detail is hidden behind the far less subtle thrust of the sword handle and the aggressive spurt of blood.

One final example will suffice. In the Uffizi *Judith*, Artemisia transfers the already discussed sharp highlight along the flank of "Abra" to Judith, with important shifts in the balance of visual emphasis between them. One of the most evocative aspects of the Naples *Judith*, as we have seen, is the unbiblical prominence given to the maidservant. While she is almost identically configured in the later canvas, the greater brightness and attendant richness of Judith subverts the visual preeminence of the maid and therefore much of the compelling strangeness of Artemisia's earlier vision. In this sense, then, the Uffizi *Judith* conveys a somewhat more orthodox religious spirit, although the scene is scarcely normative or conventional, even by the operative standards of Caravaggism. The head of Judith in this version reinforces the point: she is more coiffed or bewigged and therefore more formal a presence than she is in the Naples work, not to mention older and more explicit in the frowning set of her features. She presides with authority over the ambitious and grandiloquent baroque spectacle, at one with it in every way.

The Pitti *Judith*

To turn now to our third painting, Artemisia's *Judith and her Maid-servant* from Palazzo Pitti in Florence, is to deviate from the declamatory mode, in both content and form (fig. 29; Christiansen and Mann 2001, 330–33). Usually dated to somewhere in the period between 1612 and 1618, this work is therefore chronologically situ-

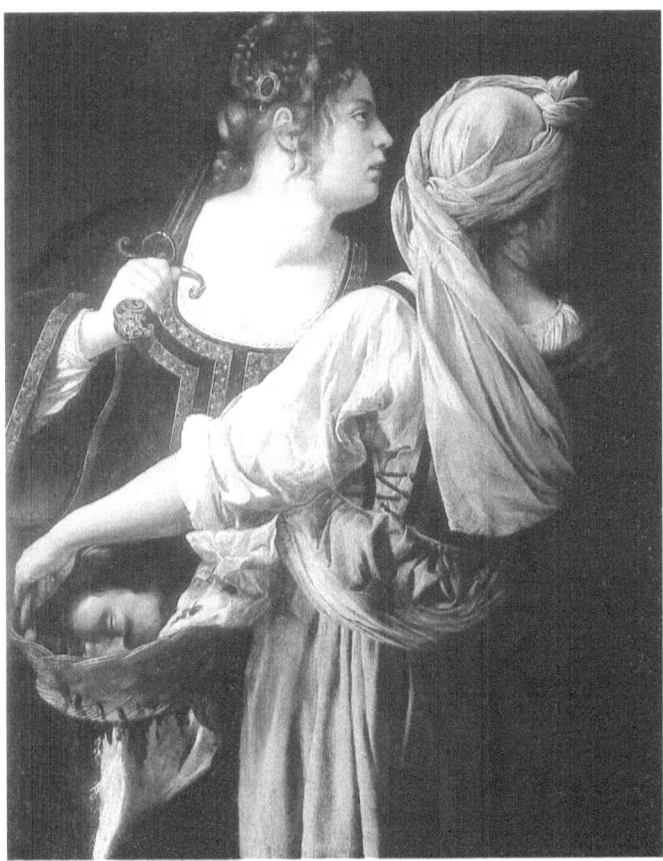

Figure 29. Artemisia Gentileschi, *Judith and her Maidservant,* ca. 1612–18. Oil on canvas, 44 7/8 × 36 3/4 in. (114 × 93.5 cm). Florence, Galleria Palatina, Palazzo Pitti. (Photo credit: Scala/Art Resource, New York.)

ated between the two images of the beheading of Holofernes already discussed. The narrative moment chosen is inherently less harrowing than in those, which affects its style as well. The painting treats the decapitation as a *fait accompli,* with Judith and her servant frozen in their tracks, as it were, no doubt in response to a startling sound outside the tent. Their senses are on high alert; a sound could mean their undoing as they undertake their dangerous escape from the Assyrian camp with their incriminating booty. There is, of course, graphic suspense here, but the grisly moment is past, and so the bold dissonance of the Naples *Judith* is replaced with a narrower range of colors, less intense chiaroscuro, and more constrained forms, and the operatic opulence of the Uffizi version is still in the future. In many ways the tone here is the closest of any of the *Judiths* to the slightly later *Jael and Sisera* analyzed in this volume by Babette Bohn.

Painted in Florence and documented in the Medici grand ducal collections by 1637, the Pitti canvas is the smallest of Artemisia's *Judiths*, about 45 by 37 inches. Like the others, it too has suffered considerable damage in the past, and it almost certainly was cut down at the top and left. I did not find the compromised surfaces to be as visible to the naked eye as in the canvas from Naples, however, and in New York the Pitti painting was comfortably hung, a nice change from its home setting in Florence, where the splendid décor of its room in Palazzo Pitti with its tiers of closely packed paintings provides almost overpoweringly rich visual competition. At the Metropolitan, it had space to breathe, and it looked magnificent. The face of Judith appeared unexpectedly rosy and fresh, which cast an appealing aura across the entire work. This is an altogether more subtle and consistent painting than its predecessor in Naples, and it is more accessible than its successor in the Uffizi; it is commonly referred to in the scholarship as a "masterpiece." Without the heroic scale of a "*gran macchina (di) bellezza*," it is nonetheless just that.

I'd like to examine the Pitti *Judith* as an inventive amalgam of strength and tenderness. The former is hardly news, given the subject and what we have seen of Artemisia's talents so far. As in the decapitation paintings, the anatomical configuration of the heroine alone bespeaks an imposing forcefulness, but in this case there is a more compressed and tightly interlocking composition to reinforce this effect. At first glance, the heavy, accurately portrayed sword with its shrieking pommel merely underscores the theme,

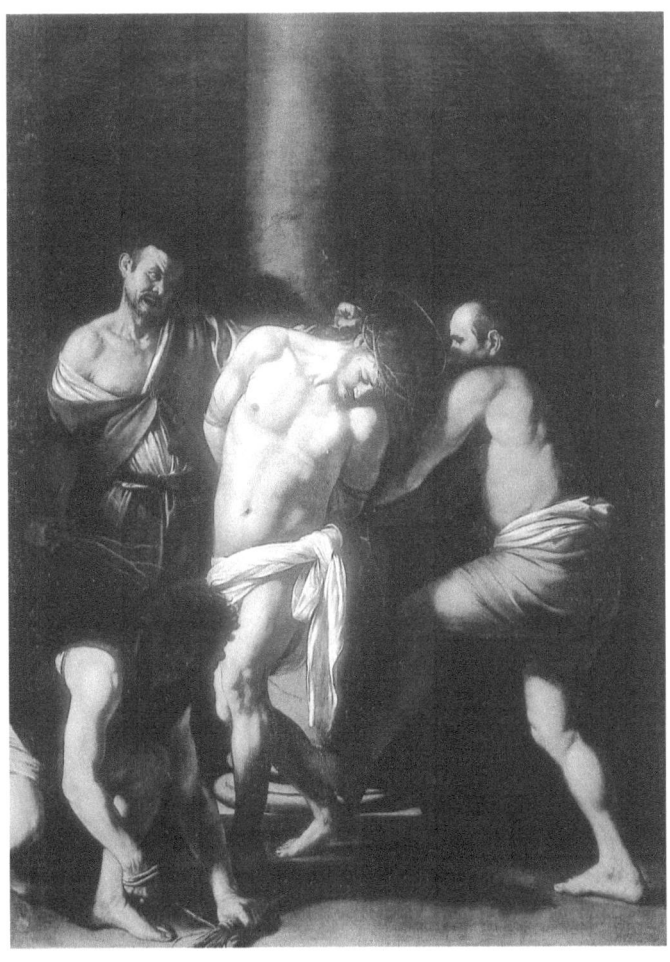

Figure 30. Caravaggio, *Flagellation of Christ,* ca. 1607. Oil on canvas, 112 3/5 × 83 4/5 in. (286 × 213 cm). Naples, Museo di Capodimonte. (Photo credit: Scala/Art Resource, New York.)

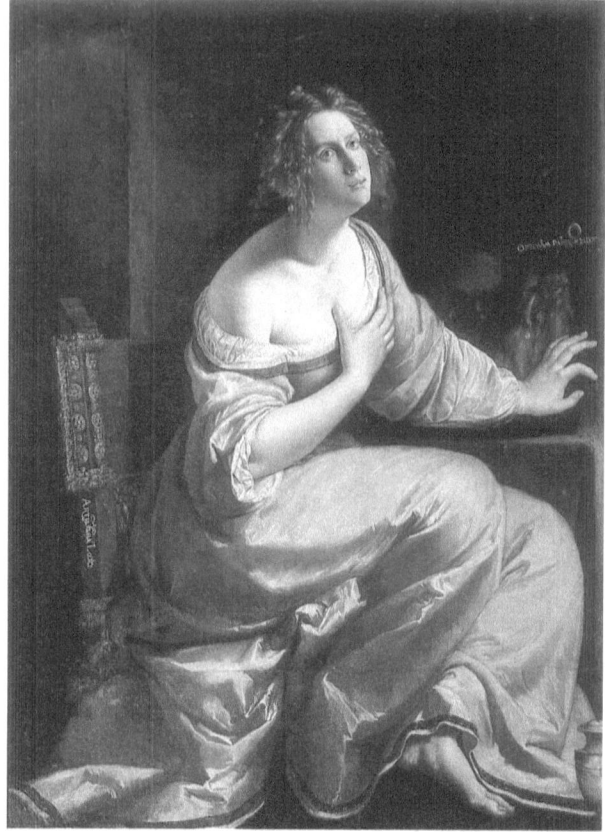

Figure 31. Artemisia Gentileschi, *The Penitent Magdalen,* ca. 1615–16. Oil on canvas, 57 5/8 × 42 1/2 in. (146.5 × 108 cm). Florence, Galleria Palatina, Palazzo Pitti. (Photo credit: Scala/Art Resource, New York.)

until we consider its unexpected placement. The sword may refer symbolically to Judith's historic personification as Justice, but within the Caravaggesque parameters of naturalism, it is rather improbably hefted onto Judith's exposed upper shoulder, threateningly close to the vulnerable flesh of her insistently featured neck. In classical literary fashion, this inevitably refers us both backwards in the narrative to the decapitation of Holofernes and forward to the danger of Judith and her maid while they are still surrounded by the camp of Assyrian soldiers. It also recalls the motif of the naked shoulder and neck so poignantly explored by Caravaggio throughout his career.

From his earliest secular work, such as the *Boy with Fruit Basket* (ca. 1594), to his final dark utterances, like the celebrated *David with the Head of Goliath* (ca. 1606–10), both in the Galleria Borghese in Rome, Caravaggio probed and extolled the plangent expressive possibilities of the bared shoulder and neck. Whatever constellation of elusive meanings accrues to this motif in his hands, vulnerability and/or its opposite are signaled, often in scenes associated with violence. A single illustrative example, the magisterial *Flagellation of Christ* (ca. 1607), combines both thematic valences in the contrasted shoulders of Christ and his assailants (fig. 30). The dichotomy there between vulnerability and aggression is in a sense fused in the heroine of Artemisia's Pitti *Judith,* the executioner who exposes her own neck to the blade. As with Caravaggio, we meet variations of the exposed shoulder motif across Artemisia's oeuvre, perhaps most memorably in her paintings of the Magdalen (fig. 31).

Another way Judith's sword in the Pitti image participates in an aesthetic of tenderness is that it ushers us visually into passages of great softness and delicacy: upward to Judith's wispy hair and downward to her smooth, fine-grained hand. Our eye is then inexorably drawn by the gold trim on her sleeve to another sensitive exposure, the inner wrist of the maid, and thence to the gentlest moment of all, the poetically agonized head of Holofernes nestled softly in the straw basket. Eyes closed as if in sleep, dark hued, and very subtly lit, the beautifully molded head seems almost tranquil, in spite of the devastating open mouth and the thick trickles of blood oozing from the maid's basket.

The entire area from Judith's hand to the basket is a masterful achievement of design and tonality. We note, first, that the irregular oval shape of her gold-rimmed sleeve opening, with its pro-

truding arm, is related to the rim formed by the basket and the arm
of the servant, and then, secondarily, that the basket's back edge (or
is it, even better, the ear of Holofernes?) picks up the concavity of
Judith's sleeve above it. The startling scarlet of the sleeve lining am-
plifies the conceptually important but otherwise modest amount of
blood; indeed, it is the major red accent in a scene which could have
been awash in crimson. Again, one cannot escape the recollection
of Caravaggio's *Judith,* where the prominent red drapery behind
Holofernes comments like a visual analogue of a Greek chorus on
the foreground action. The extroversion of Caravaggio's device is
inverted by Artemisia; the beautiful red sleeve is a quiet but
nonetheless artful substitute for the missing telltale bloodstains on
the women's clothes.

In the tracing of tenderness in this modest "*macchina,*" we can't
help but be moved by the gentle touch of Judith on her maid's
shoulder. More than any other detail, this light grasp has been recognized by scholars as underscoring the intimate partnership of the
two women, a theme we have already located in both the Naples and
the Uffizi *Judiths.* But the matter is more complex here, because it
involves Orazio as much as Artemisia. There is no doubt that the
composition of the Pitti *Judith* bears a very close relation to Orazio's
painting of the same subject in Oslo, noted earlier (see fig. 27). Indeed the literature on these two works is largely given over to the un-
raveling of their interrelationships, a tangle which also includes the
other *Judith* canvases by Orazio. None of the works in question has
clear documentary support for dating, and so the issue of chronological and therefore conceptual precedence is a minefield. If we assume, with Christiansen and Bissell, that Orazio's Oslo painting
was painted before Artemisia's Pitti canvas, her version can be said
to both derive from and develop beyond her father's concept. Although Orazio's Judith does not prop the sword on her shoulder, the
poses are otherwise extremely close, explained perhaps by Christiansen's insightful hypothesis that both artists employed tracings of
favorite compositional designs throughout their careers. Judith rests
a hand on the shoulder of her servant in both.

Even a cursory comparison reveals Artemisia's format, for all of its similarities to Orazio's, to be more taut and concentrated than his. To be fair, this may be at least to some extent accidental, since the original canvas apparently provided perhaps as much as five more inches along the upper and the left borders, which would have lessened the spatial confinement of the figures that contributes so much to the tension we read now. But the other compression device was unquestionably intentional: the positioning of the two women closer together, an effect encapsulated in the transference of Judith's hand from her servant's left to her right shoulder. The result is the increased sense of intimacy and solidarity noted above.

It is interesting that by collapsing the separation between the figures, Artemisia denied herself the zone of space- and light-play between the arm and flank of the maid, which Orazio's Oslo painting exploits and which figures so strongly in her Naples *Judith*. Indeed, in his painting Orazio built his entire composition around a central spatial void—bound by the maid's blue sleeve, the gathered folds of her rust-toned dress, and the head of Holofernes—which is a tour de force of visual effects. Its sinuous contour is a window opening past Holofernes' partially revealed ear onto the masterfully illuminated vista of Judith's red and white costume beyond it. When Artemisia closed that recessional unit by moving "Abra" closer to Judith, she filled in the remaining space with the white basket cloth, the ambiguous configuration of which blurs the three-dimensional give-and-take in which Orazio reveled. At the same time, she made other compensations, some involving the kind of design-enhancing manipulation of white fabric we noted in the Uffizi *Judith*.

For instance, she reconfigured the light cloth which wraps around the maid's head and drapes across her shoulders and down her back, with substantial formal and expressive results. In Orazio's Oslo painting, this splendid cloth becomes a shawl whose rhythm of folds and fringe provided him with an irresistible field for the kind of textural elaboration in which he specialized. He even doubled the possibilities by creating a visual pendant for it in the remarkable white fabric suspended from the basket; as a pair, they are major structural components of the composition. In the Pitti *Judith,* Artemisia expanded the maid's wrap to cover more of her head, but she abbreviates its extent over the shoulders and back, in the process revealing more of the bodice and blouse beneath.

Eschewing the blue oversleeve so central to Orazio's design, she emphasizes the white blouse, whose generously cut sleeves both invest her "Abra" with far more physical heft and provide the opportunity for energetic passages of billows and folds. The blouse then meanders downward behind the echoing zig-zag lacing of the bodice into the gathers of the skirt just below the waistband. This area is bound at the lower edge by a new motif not found in Orazio's maid, a loop or impromptu belt of light cloth that might be a tightly tied continuation of the head cloth, wrapped around her torso and waist.

This new arc or crescent is one of Artemisia's devices in the all-important task of intensifying the visual links between the two protagonists established in Orazio's Oslo composition. It picks up both the curve of white lace peeking above Judith's neckline and the parallel rim of the maid's blouse visible above her bodice, a pairing not possible in Orazio's version, where the shawl conceals so much. Similarly, in Artemisia's painting, both the maid's and Judith's bodices repeat the arc motif in their trim: gold on black for Judith and reversed to black on gold for the servant—again, an option not exercised by Orazio. Artemisia also uses these shapes to call our attention to the wider network of crescent design forms reverberating downward along the painting's diagonal axis from the servant's headwrap to the basket with Holofernes's head.

In Orazio's Oslo *Judith,* we see the echoing arcs, but they are largely limited to the upper section, again in the head scarf of the maid and the neckline of Judith, and this time picked up in the folds of the green background curtain instead. There is also the slanting axis, anchored by the related pendants of the white basket cloth and the "Abra's" shawl noted earlier. I am not arguing here for the superiority of one painting over the other; this is not a contest. But I am, with Bissell, making a case for the sophisticated visual techniques of Artemisia's painting in an effort to insert more nuance into the unavoidable comparison between father and daughter. Artemisia's style is generally held to be the more dramatic and Orazio's the more elegant. But this dichotomy, correct as far as it goes, doesn't do either of these two paintings quite enough justice.

Take, for instance, their color schemes. At first glance it would seem that the conventional wisdom obtains, since Orazio employs a palette with a far wider range and more sheerly beautiful tonalities than his daughter. We have already seen that she avoided in this Pitti *Judith* the kind of striking color accent he emphasized with the foregrounded soft blue sleeve of the maid. And while Orazio gave Judith a magnificent brocade dress of gleaming scarlet, Artemisia clothed her heroine this time not in the electric blue sheen of her earlier Naples *Judith* nor in the strong gold damask of the later Uffizi version but in velvet of muted deep burgundy, which today appears almost black. Her Pitti *Judith* is replete with tonal play nonetheless, primarily around a fascinating variety of related shades: whites, creams, beiges, and ochres.

The subtle contrast between the maid's headdress and her blouse is the crux of this, but the coloration throughout the canvas participates, offering another unifying tactic. It is as if Artemisia has decided to experiment with a chromatic scale of closer intervals than Orazio's. The lower key of the interrelated tonalities contributes to the hush that is, after all, the subject of the painting. So while it is certainly true that the daughter eschewed the dazzling color contrasts and textural differentiations of the father, she did not sacrifice artistic niceties to her more sober vision. Indeed, hers is a painting of extraordinary subtlety, coloristically and compositionally. Bissell has written of Artemisia's "sensitivity" to Orazio's "gift for understatement" in the Pitti *Judith*, a position I heartily endorse (1991, 12).

In addition, an overinsistence on Orazio as the more decorative of the two painters can distract us from realizing that his Oslo *Judith*

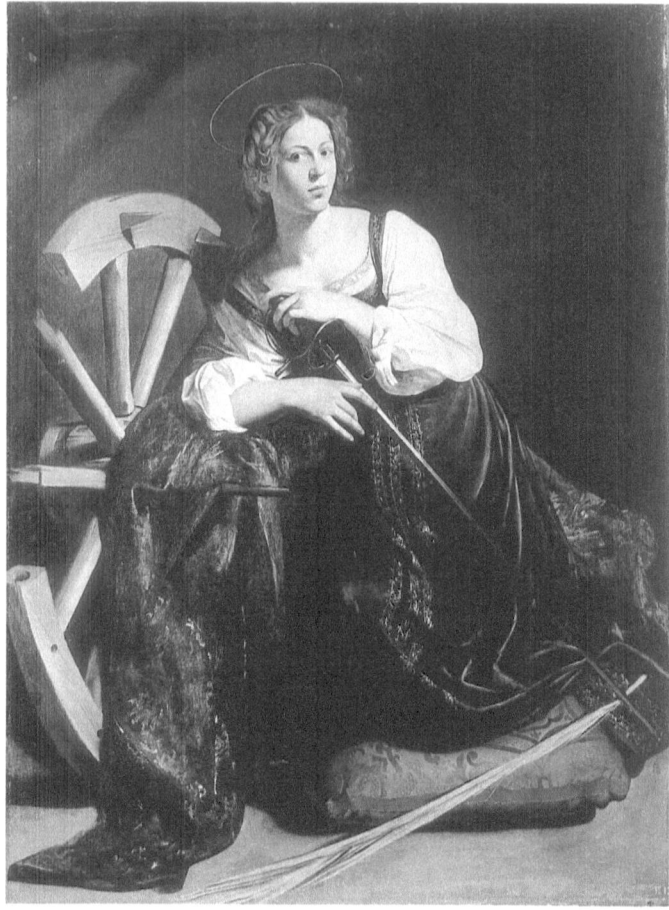

Figure 32. Caravaggio, *St. Catherine of Alexandria,* ca. 1598. Oil on canvas, 68 × 52 1/3 in. (173× 133 cm). Madrid, Fundacion Coleccion Thyssen-Bornemisza. (Photo credit: Scala/Art Resource, New York.)

has a significant dose of dramatic impetus. Ironically, it is partly provided by the tonal contrasts in which the painting's beauty resides. But it is also elaborated in a variety of ploys that one might have expected more from Artemisia: the heightened chiaroscuro overall, for instance, with the consequently more brightly lit and more gruesome head of Holofernes and the sharper shadow cast by the basket onto the servant's skirt. Even more to the point, perhaps, is the tiny hint of a smudge of blood on his Judith's sword, an idea which sends us yet again to Caravaggio, whose *St. Catherine of Alexandria* (ca. 1598) establishes a suggestive psychological bond between heroine and crimson-tinged rapier (fig. 32). Of course, both Gentileschis learned valuable lessons from Caravaggio, but they were not always the same ones. Indeed, the operative relationship between the Oslo and the Pitti *Judiths* of Orazio and Artemisia may be not so much a contrast between what the Met's labels called his "elegant sense of formal composition" and her "action-packed moment" as a kind of slant rhyme—two different and related varieties of both ingredients.

The Detroit *Judith*

With the last of our four paintings, Artemisia's *Judith with her Maidservant* (ca. 1625–27) in the Detroit Institute of Arts (see fig. 5), whatever disparity might be thought inherent between drama and formal elegance is resolved decisively (Christiansen and Mann 2001, 368–70). The two qualities not only coexist, they are both in-dividually raised to a high magnitude and made to fuse. A large canvas, 72 by 56 inches, it is not only often considered the "most ac-complished" of Artemisia's *Judiths* (Met label) but the "finest work" of her entire career (Christiansen and Mann 2001, 368). Less ag-gressive than the disquieting beheading scenes in Naples and the Uffizi, and more glamorous than the Pitti painting, whose narra-tive moment it shares, the Detroit *Judith* seems to please all tastes.

The firmly controlled complexity of its composition, palette, and lighting is invariably held as evidence of the artistic maturity of its creator, her fullest mastery of her pictorial tools. If the assigned dating is correct, Artemisia would have been in her early thirties when she painted it. Neither the commission circumstances nor the pre-nineteenth-century history of the canvas is known, but a plau-sible case has been made for its Neapolitan provenance. Its condi-tion is comparatively good and it was well presented at the Met. It had been twenty five years since I had last seen the painting, in the epochal Women Artists, 1550–1950 exhibition at the Brooklyn Museum of Art, where it was a revelation. I remember only that I found it thrilling and completely satisfying. At the Metropolitan, it took a while for the anticipated magic to do its work, no doubt because of an initial fear that it was perhaps too superficially beautiful and, like the Uffizi *Judith,* too self-consciously a "*gran macchina.*" However, with sustained and patient scrutiny, the sheer visual pleasure deepened to something even more substantial.

In terms of pictorial flash, of which there is no shortage in the Detroit *Judith,* the lit candle on the left has pride of place. Derived perhaps from Northern European examples known to Artemisia in Rome, such as Elsheimer's tiny *Judith Beheading Holophernes* (ca. 1601–3), it reminds us of the mysterious hypothesized candles in the Naples and Uffizi *Judiths* and the grievousness of their presumed loss. The powerful sense of suspense, even more graphic here than in Artemisia's related Pitti version (fig. 29) and Orazio's intense paintings in Hartford and Oslo (fig. 27), is largely a function of the candlelight, which immobilizes the figures in its grip. It is, in Spear's phrase, "the primary bearer of (the) drama" (1971, 61). Although problematic because it does not account for the illumination on the figures with complete accuracy and may even have been a late addition to the design, the candle nonetheless accentuates the diagonal dialogue of postures and gestures that constitutes the composition. It justifies the sharpness of the collision of light and shade throughout and the hallucinatory clarity of individual highlit elements, like the sheen of Judith's dress and the hilt of her sword, and perhaps even the rather jarring white headwrap of the maid. Indeed, it is hard to imagine the painting without it.

There is no question that Artemisia reveled in the pictorial possibilities of the candlelight in the Detroit *Judith,* as we see from the sparkle on the curls, earring, and diadem of Judith, not to mention the entire magnificent passage of her profile. The play of the mediated shadow that articulates the fleshy cheek and the bone structure of forehead and eye, with its silhouette of lid and lash, struck

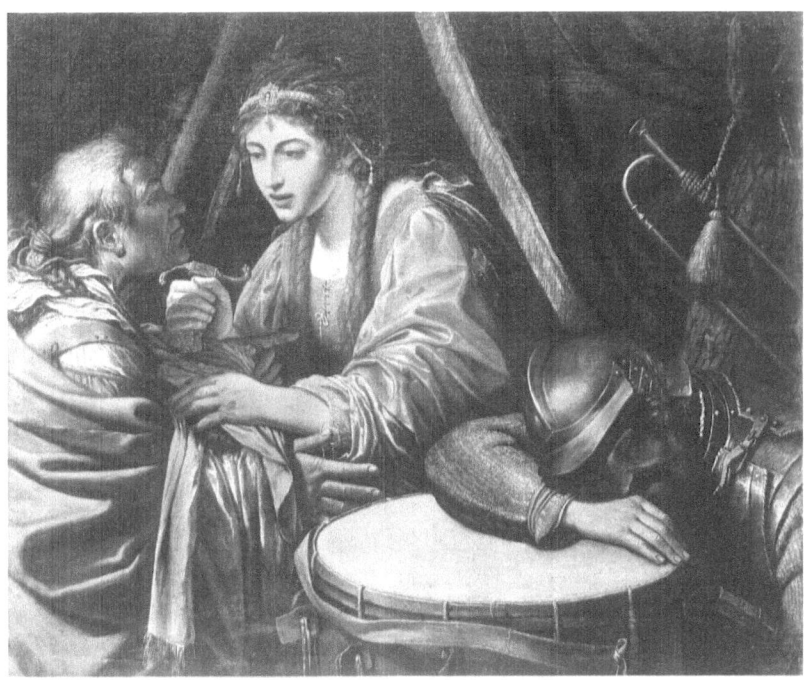

Figure 33. Lionello Spada, *Judith and her Maidservant,* ca. 1610–20. Oil on canvas, 43 1/3 × 53 1/2 in. (110 × 136 cm). Bologna, Pinacoteca Nazionale. (Photo credit: Alinari/Art Resource, New York.)

me in New York as one of the supreme passages in baroque painting. The candlelight is also indulged along the edge of the red curtain, in the border of jaunty little gold fringe. This dramatic curtain, surely the canopy over Holofernes's bed, cannot fail to remind us of the similar device in Caravaggio's *Judith,* and it is identical in color and texture to the bed cover over Holofernes in Artemisia's Uffizi canvas, even down to the exact fringe. It is the most assertive of the backdrop curtains in either Artemisia's or Orazio's *Judiths,* the only one to at least imply the significant role of this prop in the biblical tale itself. There we are told that the canopy was torn down by Judith and her servant after the death of Holofernes and carried back in triumph to Bethulia, along with the head; a war trophy, it adds another note of humiliation to the Assyrian defeat, like Judith's gender and her use of Holofernes's own sword to kill him. I have often wondered why more explicit use has not been made of it in paintings of this subject.

Perhaps the canopy in the Detroit *Judith* is a transmutation of the sanguinary excess of the Uffizi painting: it is certainly the most powerful red accent in the scene. Blood has not been completely banished here, however, as we see from the dark, dripping beads along the sword blade and the even more disconcerting besmirched hands of the maid in the foreground shadows. Mary Garrard shows in her contribution to this volume how significant hands are in Artemisia's work, and in the biblical text Judith herself repeatedly emphasizes that Holofernes was vanquished "by the hand of a woman" (13:19). But the bloody hands in this painting are not Judith's, and, perhaps more surprisingly, they are unique in the entire Gentileschi *Judith* canon; in fact, they are rare even in the larger history of Judith imagery. The closest parallels of which I am aware are contemporaneous paintings by Lionello Spada (1576–1622), the Bolognese artist known at the time as "Caravaggio's ape" ("*scimmia del Caravaggio*"), especially for his *Judith* in the Pinacoteca Nazionale in Bologna (fig. 33).[13] In this work, the bloody hands do belong to Judith, and they are prominently illuminated and placed, as she consigns the grisly bundle to an elderly "Abra" in the immediate presence of a sleeping Assyrian soldier. Spada thus not only makes conspicuous what is more understated in Artemisia's scene but renders visible the menace of detection which is lurking beyond the frame in both the Detroit and the Pitti *Judiths* of Artemisia, as well as those in Oslo and Hartford by Orazio.

This latter work by Artemisia's father, dated in the exhibition catalogue to ca. 1621–24, that is, close to the date of her painting in Detroit, can be paired with it further on several levels. Considered the best of the *Judith* images of their respective painters, they depict a similar moment in the narrative, after the beheading but before the escape, which ties them closely to the Oslo and the Pitti paintings, and they go to great lengths to create a sense of dramatic tension, within the framework of their diverse stylistic inclinations. Both depend on the most splendid textural and tonal displays of which their creators were capable, subtler in Orazio's and more intense in Artemisia's. Again, the predictable expectation of greater nuance for Orazio and drama for Artemisia is both realized and insufficient, since Orazio achieves a high sense of theatrical suspense in the facial expressions, and Artemisia deploys a palette of unusual subtlety. The figure of Artemisia's maidservant is a particularly successful component in this regard, since her cool blue and lilac tones are made unexpectedly congruent with the predominant warm golds and reds and the olive green table cloth on the left. Orazio's Hartford *Judith* makes use of a similar but more muted range of these colors; for Artemisia, the canvas in Detroit demonstrates expanding chromatic ambitions that go well beyond the more limited ranges of her earlier *Judiths*.

One of the key coloristic tactics in the Detroit *Judith* does not leap out at first view, namely, the head of Holofernes. It is shrouded in shadow in the middle of the lower edge, unlike the brighter and more immediately prominent face at the core of Orazio's composition in Hartford. Given the narrative moment depicted in the Detroit *Judith*, when the success of Judith's enterprise, not to mention the safety of the two women, hinges on the maid's hiding of the head, Artemisia's subdued treatment is an ingenious stroke. The head of Holofernes is flanked by the related accents of Judith's heavy shoe and the horny toes of the servant, which together create a tonal unit of umber and beige. This dusky note is subtly allied to the gold skirt of Judith and the green tablecloth nearby, and to the sword hilt, the candle, and the shading of Judith's sleeves and hair ornaments above. At the same time, the severed head, the goal of the biblical narrative, is located at the lower terminus of the central zig-zag vector that begins with Judith's head and organizes the entire composition. The shadowed head thus functions as a unifying pictorial and thematic device on multiple levels. Form and content are one.

If the issue of theatricality adheres to all of Artemisia's *Judiths,* as it does also to Orazio's, nowhere is it quite as literal as in the Detroit canvas. This is the one that most appears as an onstage scene, with plausible stage lighting, props, and posed actors behind an implied proscenium. Even the scale of the scene contributes here, since we see the figures fully, as they would appear to a theater audience, unlike the three-quarter lengths of all the other Gentileschian *Judiths.* As for the focal point of the protagonists beyond the frame on the left, Garrard has reminded us, apropos of Artemisia's Pitti *Judith,* that stage noises in baroque theatres were produced in the wings (1989, 316). And as in so much baroque and classical drama, the violence also occurred off stage.

We are again in the world of Federico Della Valle, whose own *Iudit* play was praised in 1929 by Benedetto Croce for its gravity and its Clytemnestra-like heroine, a characterization not inconsistent with either the overall tone or the rather fierce physiognomy of Artemisia's Detroit *Judith.* Finally, I think we *hear* the suspense of this scene, as we would in the theater: and what we hear is not only silence, as the two protagonists are riveted by an offstage threat, but a sudden, ominous, larger-than-life cessation of sound. In my discussions of Artemisia's Naples and Pitti *Judiths,* I argued for a silent aural dimension, which I associated with eeriness and subtlety in the respective paintings' pictorial qualities. The very different scale, palette, lighting, and composition make the Detroit *Judith* silent in a different way: grandly silent. *Fortissimo pianissimo.*

Conclusion

As I noted at the outset of this essay, I went to the Metropolitan's Gentileschi show while in the midst of research focused not on the formal construction of *bellezza* but on iconography. Nonetheless, in the back of my mind, I think I was hoping that the chance provided by the exhibition to embed my scholarly enterprise in face-to-face contact with its subject would offer me the means to confront an issue I had found increasingly vexing, namely the gap between the discourses of artists and art historians. As an art historian who has been teaching for over twenty-five years in a college department composed of both art historians and studio artists, I live daily with the vast gap between the ways the two groups talk about the same thing. It seems a conundrum. It is a divide I find more troubling than the familiar rifts within art history itself, although I expect they are related phenomena.

I take it as axiomatic that historians of art have much to learn from artists; it seems so obvious a point as to be unworthy of utterance. And yet my experience has been that art historians' academic practices, both scholarly and pedagogical, including my own, do not often proceed from such a premise. Conversations with artist colleagues have helped me to think about what it could mean to redress this imbalance, to teach and write an art history which they would recognize as congruent with their concerns, rather than merely ancillary or parallel to them.

It is harder than it sounds. It is not about turning back to "mere" formal analysis, as if that were possible or desirable. It would be idiotic, not to mention irresponsible, to fail to profit from the immense expansion in recent decades of art history's methodologies and foci of inquiry. I understood that my iconography project, any iconography project, by definition would not offer the opportunity to address even tentatively the discursive chasm between artists and their historians. But it seemed to me that one essential tenet of any such venture would be the kind of informed devotion to the visuality of works of art themselves that animates their makers.

Not surprisingly, in spite of my desire to really see the paintings, I initially had difficulty sidestepping the phantom haunting virtually all art historians: the obstacle of our own preparation. In direct encounters with our beloved objects and monuments, we often have to find ways to battle through the wall of data and theory we've erected between ourselves and them. I did my best to focus my thoughts on the paintings' visual strategies by the unsophisticated tactic of writing detailed descriptions as I stood before them at the Met. Were I an artist, I'd have made careful sketches.

Neither a review of the Gentileschi literature nor an intervention in the current theoretical, historical, or iconographic debates, this essay has nonetheless been affected and enriched by them. I trust that informed readers will recognize where my observations intersect and diverge from the published record and where implications may be drawn. From the start, I have framed this project within my desire to look at the Judith paintings of Artemisia Gentileschi as artful constructions, naive as that may sound, yet recognizing full well that this approach is as individually variable as any other and that paintings are also documents susceptible to many other methodologies.

The stakes are very high in Artemisia's case, especially for feminists, because we have invested in her so much of our quest for justice for women, historically and currently, intellectually and politically. Having reemerged as a figure of consequence after centuries of critical neglect, Artemisia has become a star, but as we all know, fame can become a defining and limiting trait of its own. The Gentileschi exhibitions gave us the chance to test the ascendant art-historical reputation of the painter against the visual realities of her paintings themselves. In my encounter with the pictorial strategies of her *Judiths,* I recognized and hope to have affirmed in these pages the pertinence, the justice of Artemisia Gentileschi's modern renown.

Acknowledgments

I owe many debts of gratitude: to Mieke Bal for her initiative and her support; to the staff of the Clark Art Institute, especially its Director of Research and Academic Programs Michael Ann Holly, for providing the ideal environment for research; to Janet Braun-Reinitz, Nanette Salomon, Keith Christiansen, and Christian Minnick for illuminating conversations in front of the paintings; to Toni Craven for help with Greek biblical terminology; and to my colleagues at Hobart and William Smith Colleges, especially Claudette Columbus and Susan Henking for their critical reading of this manuscript, Nick Ruth for raising some central questions for me, and above all Jim Crenner for his generous collaboration in every stage of this project. I wish to further acknowledge a special debt to Mary Garrard, for the inspiring example of her work, her integrity, and her love for Artemisia Gentileschi.

DEATH, DISPASSION, AND THE FEMALE HERO
Artemisia Gentileschi's *Jael and Sisera*

Babette Bohn

Artemisia Gentileschi's *Jael and Sisera*

Although Artemisia Gentileschi has achieved near cult status with modern audiences as a feminist heroine, her painting of *Jael and Sisera* (fig. 34) has received curiously little attention or acclamation. Despite its representation of a woman's triumph over a man, ostensibly a quintessentially Gentileschian subject, no one loves this picture, and it is rarely cited to exemplify Artemisia's heroic women. Although it is included in several recent studies of Gentileschi, the work is either discussed in neutral terms or denigrated as a disappointing picture that somehow never achieved the *frisson* of her contemporary *Judith Beheading Holofernes*. For Judith Mann, the painting is characterized by restraint and contemplation rather than drama (Christensen and Mann 2001, 344). Ward Bissell dismissed the *Jael and Sisera* as "passionless, stilted, and derivative," a work of minimal importance that betrays Artemisia's own lack of interest in the subject (1999, 212). Artemisia's quiet Jael, in contrast to her dynamic Judiths, demonstrates no athletic prowess, has no need to struggle with her sleeping victim, and conveys no evident fury in her act of violence. Is such quietude appropriate to a scene of assassination? The painting, to be sure, is in problematic condi-

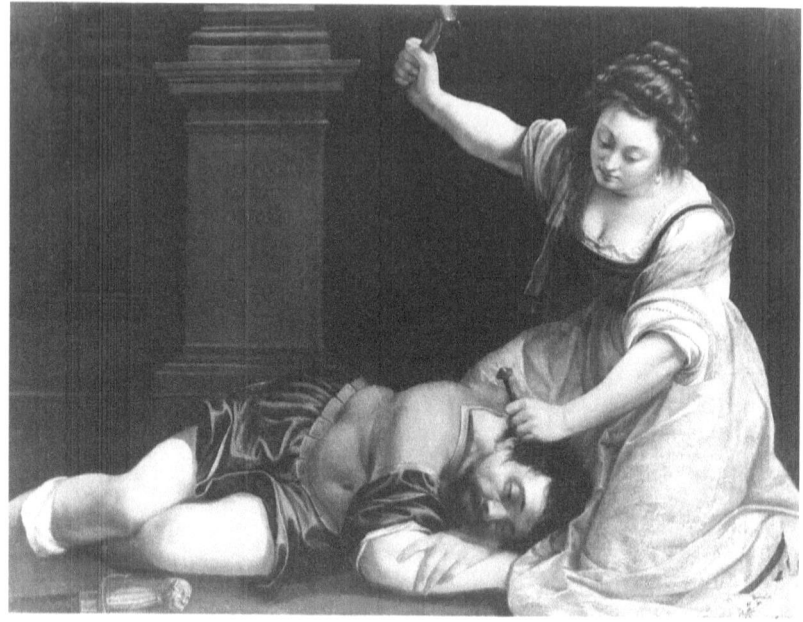

Figure 34. Artemisia Gentileschi, *Jael and Sisera*, 1620. Oil on canvas, 86 × 125 cm. Budapest, Szépmüvészeti Múzeum. (Photo credit: Szépmüvészeti Múzeum.)

tion, but this hardly seems to account for its lukewarm critical reception since its rediscovery in 1974, when it was acquired by the Szépmüvészeti Múzeum in Budapest.

The Old Testament subject of Jael and Sisera has also met with a mixed reception (Bal 1988, 24–27; Bos 1988, 37–40). Although the story of a woman killing a man may be intrinsically problematic in a patriarchal culture, in which this represents a reversal of the "natural" order, Jael's mixed reception history contrasts markedly with that of the similar but more popular subject of Judith and Holofernes, a text that is thematically related to the older Jael and Sisera story. Why did Jael kill Sisera? Is she a temptress and criminal, or are her actions divinely sanctioned? Her motivation and character are less clear and more morally complex than Judith's in killing Holofernes, as I will explain in this essay.

In contrast to the theological and artistic traditions, which often portrayed Jael as a morally compromised seductress and murderess, Gentileschi paints a picture at odds with this tradition. In her painting, the two figures are effectively contrasted in terms of pose, color, and physical appearance, suggesting a moral discrepancy to match their visual differences. Gentileschi's Jael acts with quiet deliberation rather than uncontrolled passion, reinforcing the notion of her moral superiority and divine support. Her downcast eyes, kneeling pose, restrained gesture, and fine but not excessively decorated clothing portray a figure of virtue and refinement who differs markedly from the sexual temptress type favored by most of her contemporaries. This characterization reflects Artemisia's innovativeness as a painter and may also reflect the influence of her unknown patron, social attitudes towards female murderers during the period, and the context of Counter-Reformation theology, which constructed Jael as a prefiguration of the Virgin Mary. To appreciate how unusual Gentileschi's positive portrayal of Jael was in 1620, we must examine the very different characterizations that typified the theological and artistic traditions in early modern Europe. Moreover, we need to consider how, during the seventeenth century, the subject of Jael and Sisera was often shaped by contemporary religious, political, and social considerations.

I wish to argue that Artemisia was sensitive to the ambiguity of Jael's motivation, tempering her presentation of Jael in the painting with characteristic originality. An impassioned Jael whose righteous fury matched Judith's divinely driven ferocity would not have been appropriate to the text.

The Old Testament Subject of Jael and Sisera

The Old Testament subject of Gentileschi's painting is related in the Book of Judges. The Israelites were at war with the Canaanites, whose formidable general was Sisera. Deborah, a prophet, summoned the Israelite leader Barak and predicted his triumph over the Canaanites. As she had prophesied, the Canaanite army was annihilated, and Sisera fled to the tent of Jael, wife of Heber the Kenite. Jael invited Sisera into her tent, reassuring her frightened visitor and giving him milk to drink. When Sisera fell asleep, Jael took a tent peg and hammer and "drove the peg into his temple, until it went down into the ground—he was lying fast asleep from weariness—and he died" (Judges 4:21). Deborah had predicted rightly that God would "sell Sisera into the hand of a woman" (Judges 4:9), and she and Barak celebrate the Israelite victory and the triumph of Jael, "most blessed of women" (Judges 5: 24). Their victory song provides a somewhat different account of Jael's actions from that given in chapter 4; there is no mention of Sisera being asleep, and he is described as falling (from a standing position?) at Jael's feet after the blow.

As Mieke Bal has noted, such triumphs of women over men in the book of Judges, which also includes the story of Delilah and Samson, disprove the traditional notion that women play a minor role in history (1988, 14). Jael's killing of Sisera was pivotal in helping to establish the Israelites in Canaan.

But was Jael's act morally justified? This question has been hotly debated in the history of Judaism and Christianity alike. Although Sisera was the enemy of the Israelites, several issues complicate the assessment of Jael's morality. Her actions violated the traditional laws of hospitality that mandated protection of one's guest (Matthews 1991, 13–21). She also transgressed the alliance of her husband and his family with the Canaanites (Bos 1988, 53). No doubt Sisera trusted Jael for both these reasons. Nevertheless, many writers have endorsed the morality of Jael's actions, on the basis of both her support of Israelite interests and Sisera's character. Rabbinic tradition often portrayed Sisera as an evil giant reminiscent of Goliath and a blasphemer of God (Gunn 2005). For Martin Luther, Sisera personified the ungodly man and the sin of pride (Luther 1976, 2:129–31). Such views suggest that Sisera's death was morally justified, given his evil nature and enmity toward God's chosen people.

If Sisera was characterized as unequivocally transgressive, however, Jael is a more complex figure. Although the biblical text says nothing about her appearance, rabbinic tradition characterized

Jael as formidable in her powers of seduction, effective in inspiring lust and seducing her guest (Gunn 2005), an erotic reading of the text that many modern writers have endorsed (Good 1988, 119; Niditch 1989, 41–53). In the Middle Ages, Jael was understood as a prefiguration of the Virgin Mary, and her killing of Sisera was seen as prefiguring Mary's triumph over the Devil (Réau 1956, 2:327–28).

But despite her association with the best of all women, Jael's negative profile persisted. Chaucer transposed Jael into an evil wife who drove a nail into her husband's brain while he was sleeping (*The Wife of Bath*). Luther was ambivalent about Jael, arguing that her tent peg signified the Word of God, but the hammer by which she drove the nail in symbolized the coming judgment (Luther 1976, 2:129–31). This ambivalence continued during the seventeenth century, when the Reverend John Gibbon argued, "When sin, like Jael, invites thee into her tent, with the lure and decoy of a lordly treatment, think of the nail and hammer which fastened Sisera dead to the ground" (Nichols 1981, 1:98). In this view, Jael is a sinner and temptress, not God's instrument whose actions are justified by her connection to the divine.

Although popularly represented in book illustrations and prints, particularly in series devoted to the wiles of women or to women from the Old Testament, Jael's story was far less popular in monumental painting than the story of Judith, whose history resembles Jael's in that both women killed formidable Israelite enemies. But if Judith's motivation, as a devout and patriotic Israelite, is clear, Jael's motivation is decidedly murky. Why did Jael kill Sisera?

Although some writers hypothesized that Jael was an Israelite or at least a Yahwist sympathizer, Fewell and Gunn observed that no such allegiance is specified by the text. In this view, since her husband's alliance with the Canaanites placed him on the losing side, Jael pragmatically killed Sisera to align herself with the victors, acting from motives of self-preservation rather than from more spiritually elevated reasons (1990, 394–96). Such a motivation would make Jael less admirable than Judith, who acted for her God and her people.

Jael is more morally complex than Judith, and not only because of the ambiguity of her motivation for killing Sisera. The sexual elements seen in the story by many modern writers also rob Jael of Judith's purity. Although Judith pretended to invite Holofernes's sexual interest as a ploy for gaining the opportunity to kill him, she affirmed her chastity after Holofernes's death: "I swear that it was my face that seduced him to his destruction, and that he committed no sin with me, to defile and shame me." (Judith 13:16). After killing Sisera, Jael spoke only once, to announce Sisera's death to the Israelite leader Barak, and she never explained her actions. Like Esther, Jael employed deceit to achieve her ends, but unlike Esther, who risked her own life to save her people, Jael's motives are ambiguous. Although the church understood Jael, Judith, and Esther as Old Testament prefigurations of the Virgin Mary, their moral definitions were not equivalent. Nevertheless, this connection to Mary was crucial in sanitizing actions that, in all three cases, resulted in the violent deaths of powerful men who had opposed God's chosen people.

The Artistic Tradition

Jael's moral complexity is illustrated by her representation in art. During the Middle Ages, Jael appeared occasionally in cathedral sculptures and more often in moralized Bibles and Psalters (Réau 1956, 2:328), where, like Judith, she prefigured the Virgin Mary's triumph over the devil. In the *Speculum humanae salvationis* of ca. 1360 (Darmstadt, Hessische Landes- und Hochschulbibliothek), a depiction of the Virgin Mary standing over the devil is grouped with illustrations of Jael, Judith, and Queen Tomyris (Wolfthal 1999, 123). The association between Jael and Mary is also expressed in sixteenth-century northern European prints. Maarten van Heemskerck's series of eight engravings from around 1560 included depictions of Mary, Jael, Judith, Esther, and Susanna. In other print series from the period, Jael appears, without direct reference to Mary, as an exemplar of a virtuous woman from the Old Testament. Thus Hans Burgkmair the Elder's engraving of "three good Jewish women" featured Esther, Judith, and

Jael (Russell and Barnes 1990, 1), and Pierre Le Moyne's famous "Galerie des Femmes Fortes" of 1647 included Jael (Garrard 1989, fig. 150).

However, in late fifteenth-century and sixteenth-century Northern European art, Judith, Jael, and Tomyris were sometimes transformed from virtuous heroines into evil temptresses, to illustrate how women's wiles led to men's destruction (Wolfthal 1999, 122–23). This revised conception of Jael may be found in the prints of Lucas van Leyden, who included Jael in a series of woodcuts from 1516–19 conventionally entitled the *Power of Women* (Jacobowitz and Stepanek 1983, 172–75). Susan Smith has discussed the development of the Power of Women, a topos dating back to the thirteenth century. The specific religious and secular subjects included in this series varied, but all illustrated the reversal of the natural order when women employed their sexual wiles to overcome heroic or accomplished men like Hercules, Aristotle, or Samson. Lucas van Leyden's print portrayed three events: Jael gives Sisera milk to drink in the background; dressed in clinging garments that reveal the form of her body, she greets the Israelites in the middle-ground; and Jael kills the sleeping Sisera in the foreground. In a later state of the print, a quotation deriving from Ecclesiasticus didactically condemns Jael's actions: "Nothing exceeds the malice of a woman" (Ecclesiasticus, 25). This comment repudiates any notion of Jael's virtue or divine sanction.

In Italy, the subject of Jael and Sisera rarely appeared in monumental painting until after the Council of Trent (1545–63), when the renewed emphasis on the Virgin Mary by the Catholic Church led to a revival of interest in portraying her Old Testament prefigurations in art. Mary Garrard has shown that Jael was one of a number of virtuous women whose images became more popular around 1630, a popularity influenced in part by the art patronage of Queen Marie de' Medici (1573–1642) and Anne of Austria (Garrard 1989, 157–65). Although Jael was sometimes depicted as an isolated figure with mallet and tent peg, in prints and occasionally in paintings (as in an example by Antiveduto Grammatica in the Palazzo Pallavicini, Rome), she was more often portrayed in a narrative context.

Two different approaches to depicting the narrative of Jael

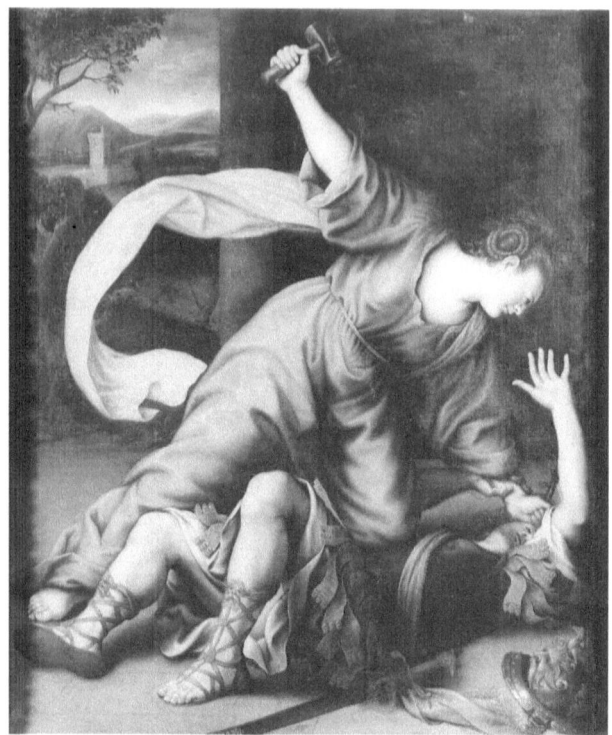

Figure 35. Camillo Procaccini or Girolamo Siciolante, *Jael and Sisera,* late 1500s. Oil on canvas, 190 × 160 cm. Bologna, Museo Davia Bargellini.

killing Sisera emerged in late sixteenth-century Italian painting. The first type portrays a scene of manifest violence, with a dynamic Jael forcefully wielding her mallet to subdue a struggling Sisera, perhaps reflecting the version of the story given by Deborah in Judges 5. This violent depiction contrasts sharply with the second type, which features a quieter and less dramatic interpretation of the narrative, with a sleeping Sisera, consistent with the narrative in Judges 4.

The earliest example I know of the first type (fig. 35) was painted in Bologna during the last quarter of the sixteenth century by an artist variously identified as Camillo Procaccini or

Girolamo Siciolante (Grandi and Medica et al. 1987, 89). In this work, Jael's large body, diagonal pose, extended right arm, and billowing draperies fill the picture. Sisera is awake and struggling, rather than asleep and helpless, but he is completely overcome by a woman who is both larger and stronger than he is. The artist's conception derives from traditional depictions of Virtue triumphing over Vice, as exemplified by Giambattista Zelotti's painting of this subject in the same collection (Grandi and Medica et al. 1987, 88). In both works, a huge woman stands astride a male adversary, filling the pictorial space and forcefully asserting her moral and physical superiority. This type of depiction unambiguously portrays both the virtue and the imminent victory of the female protagonist. Although Sisera's position between Jael's legs may allude to sexuality, her body is not suggestively revealed beneath its covering draperies.

This dynamic and morally unambiguous Jael type is unusual in Italian art, but it reappears in a few seventeenth-century Emilian examples. Luca Ferrari's triumphant Jael looks up toward Barak and God as she raises her mallet above a struggling but defeated Sisera. Ferrari painted this fresco during the 1640s for the Basilica of the Madonna della Ghiara in Reggio Emilia, where it was included due to Jael's significance as a prefiguration of the Virgin Mary (Benassi et al. 1983, 66). Guercino also painted a picture of Jael and Sisera (ca. 1619–20). Although this painting is lost, it is recorded in a series of preparatory drawings, a photograph of the lost painting, and a reproductive woodcut by Giovanni Battista Coriolano (Mahon 1969, figs. 49–52; Turner and Plazzotta 1991, 54–56). These demonstrate that the artist began with a depiction of Jael showing Sisera's body to Barak. Guercino then decided to depict the murder itself, and his next preparatory drawing portrays a violent struggle between Jael and an awake and struggling Sisera (London, Mahon collection). A later drawing rejects this dynamic interpretation in favor of a quieter depiction, with a sleeping Sisera (Paris, Institut Néerlandais, Lugt collection). This quieter depiction with a sleeping victim, as described in Judges 4, seems to have been much more popular during the early modern period in Italy than the more active version.

The second type of Jael and Sisera narrative, based on Judges 4, may also have originated in late sixteenth-century Bologna, although it was popularized in Florence. A drawing of ca. 1588 by the Bolognese artist Ludovico Carracci (Milan, Biblioteca Ambrosiana), probably the design for a chapel's ceiling painting, depicts an unemotional Jael calmly hammering the tent peg into the temple of a sleeping Sisera (Bohn 2004, fig. 44). Although it is unclear whether this lost work was influential, Carracci's drawing, conceived during the same quarter-century as Siciolante/Procaccini's painting, marked the inception of a quieter and morally more ambiguous depiction of the story, in contrast to the more violent and morally less ambiguous portrayal of Siciolante/Procaccini.

Cigoli's *Jael and Sisera*

Cigoli's painting of *Jael and Sisera* (fig. 36), painted in Florence between 1596 and 1603 for a private collection, was evidently the best-known example of this second, quieter type of depiction. In Cigoli's picture, a beautiful and richly dressed Jael kneels gracefully over a sleeping and hence unresistant Sisera. The general is dramatically foreshortened and splendidly attired, in ornate armor and a golden cape that clearly attest to his high status, to which the gesture of his right hand, resting on his discarded helmet, also testifies. This Jael is noticeably smaller than her male adversary, but she neither struggles nor grimaces at her exertions. Instead, she looks down at Sisera in quiet concentration, with the light that signifies God's favor falling upon her and leaving most of Sisera's doomed body in shadow. In the distant landscape at the left is a soldier, probably Barak, the Israelite leader to whom Jael later revealed her deed.

Jael's rich feminine attire and beautiful face imply her use of sexual temptation against Sisera, although her quiet demeanor and the

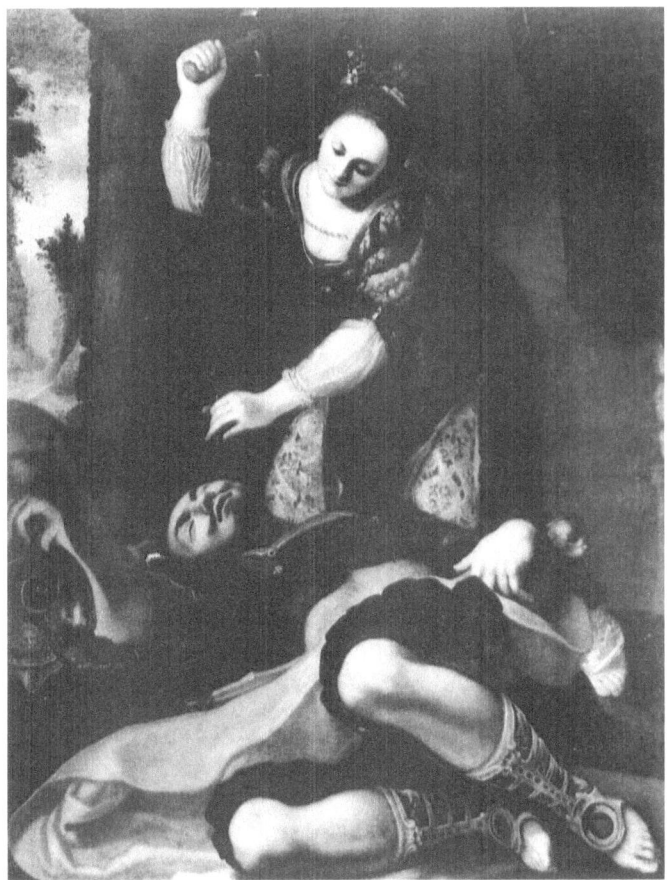

Figure 36. Ludovico Cigoli, *Jael and Sisera,* ca. 1596–1603. Oil on canvas, 162.5 × 132.5 cm. Turin, private collection. (Courtesy of Gianni Pavesi.)

divine light that shines upon her testify to the moral rectitude of her act. Cigoli's compact and carefully constructed composition was devised in several preparatory drawings (Cecchi 1992, 88–89), and his two figures are harmoniously united in an eloquently curvilinear construction. These graceful, unemotional, and beautifully attired figures seem far removed from the gory violence that is imminent, permanently frozen in a state of implicit rather than explicit action that projects a very different sensibility from Siciolante/Procaccini's violent picture.

Cigoli's interpretation of Jael and Sisera was extremely influential in Florence. It is known in at least three early painted copies and influenced paintings by Felice Ficherelli, Orazio Fidani, Ottavio Vannini, and Jacopo Vignali (Cecchi 1992, 91). Elsewhere in Italy during the seventeenth century, some artists followed Cigoli's lead. Others, like Luca Giordano (Naples, Santa Maria Donnaromita and Chambéry, Musée des Beaux-Arts) and Alessandro Tiarini (Reggio Emilia, Pinacoteca Fontanesi), shifted the narrative even farther away from violence to depict Jael and Sisera after the latter's death. Whereas Tiarini's Jael is characterized as a sexual temptress, as her bodice slips down revealingly, both of Giordano's Jaels evoke a clear sense of virtue by assuming reverent poses as they look upwards toward God. Some other artists went farther than Cigoli in eroticizing the figure of Jael and thus rendering her more of a sinner and less of a divine instrument. The Milanese artist Cerano, for example, provocatively positioned a bare-breasted and brilliantly illuminated Jael in the central foreground of his painting (Milan, Fabbrica del Duomo; Arslan plate 31), assaulting the viewer with Jael's qualifications as erotic temptress.

Cigoli's subtler interpretation of Jael's sexual attractiveness, however, remained a more popular model for most artists and typifies the subtle but unmistakable misogyny that most male Italian artists during the period brought to this subject. This type of portrayal emphasizes Jael's beauty and sexual attractiveness in lieu of her connection to the divine. This artistic interpretation did not derive from the biblical text, which does not discuss Jael's appearance, but had its roots in a rabbinic tradition that remained current for many early modern theologians. Jael was depicted less as God's instrument than as a female sinner, a wily temptress whose skills destroyed a powerful man. In such scenes as Cigoli's, female virtue is subsumed into the sexual dynamics of male versus female, and male strength is subverted by female sexual attractiveness in a titillating reversal of the natural order.

Gentileschi in Florence

Scholars agree that Artemisia Gentileschi's *Jael and Sisera* was painted either just before or just after her departure from Florence for Rome in 1620. Artemisia worked in Florence from about 1613–20, and her painting of *Jael and Sisera* is signed and dated 1620. This date, the form of her name employed on the signature (Lomi, reflecting the Florentine antecedents of her family), and the style of the picture have all been cited as support for dating this work either during or just after her stay in Florence. In addition, many scholars agree that the work was painted for a Florentine patron. In short, the picture was painted either during or just after Artemisia's stay in Florence, where she might well have known Cigoli's influential picture (Contini and Papi 1991, fig. 17; Bissell 1999, fig. 11; Christiansen and Mann 2001, fig. 61).

Artemisia's Florentine sojourn was the first period of her life when she was separated from her father Orazio, her teacher and mentor, and has been described by Roberto Contini as a turning point for Artemisia in achieving a new sense of rich color and a new level of literacy and education (Christiansen and Mann 2001, 313–14). Although in 1612, Gentileschi declared that she was unable to write and could read only a little, she had learned to write by at least 1619, the date of her earliest extant letter. During her Florentine years, Artemisia was friends with the great scientist Galileo, became the first female member of the Florentine Accademia del Disegno, and developed a professional relationship with Michelangelo Buonarroti the Younger, the erudite nephew of the great Florentine sculptor. All three of these connections brought the artist into contact with intellectual circles. It was in this context that Artemisia began to produce some of her most original interpretations of subjects, a course that presumably required the reading and rethinking of texts.

Gentileschi's *Jael and Sisera* and Cigoli

Gentileschi's *Jael and Sisera* is a modestly sized painting in oil on canvas, measuring 86 by 125 cm., with two slightly under life-sized figures. Jael and Sisera are positioned in the foreground of the painting, a placement that augments the strong visual emphasis on the two figures. Attired in brightly colored clothing and strongly illuminated by a light from the right, both figures emerge powerfully from the dark and largely unarticulated background. Sisera is portrayed as a dark, bearded man with unidealized facial features who lies on the ground, sleeping. Jael, a handsome woman with downcast eyes and an elaborate, upswept coiffure that gleams with light, lifts a mallet in her right hand and holds a nail against Sisera's head in her left. Although some writers have questioned the viability of Jael's grip on her hammer (Bissell 1999, 212; Christiansen and Mann 2001, 344), both of her hands grip their instruments in firm, strong fists, consistent with Artemisia's characteristic portrayal of women's hands, as discussed by Garrard in this volume. The feet of both figures are cut off by the picture frame, which also truncates Sisera's sleeping, lion-headed sword, a feature that, as Judith Mann astutely observed, provides an analogy to Sisera himself (Christiansen and Mann 2001, 344). The darkened background provides only a minimal setting, featuring the base of a column or pilaster that is inscribed with the artist's signature and date: ARTEMITIA. LOMI / FACIBAT / M. D.CXX.

Gentileschi's picture has often been seen as reflecting the impact of Cigoli's painting of the same subject (Contini and Papi 1991, 145; Bissell 1999, 212; Christiansen and Mann 2001, 346). Is this a fair characterization? Certainly Gentileschi's Jael, like Cigoli's, looks down quietly at her sleeping victim, as she raises the mallet in her right hand and holds the tent peg against Sisera's temple with her left. However, the two conceptions are otherwise very different. Whereas Cigoli's Jael rises up above the foreshortened Sisera, in a uniformly vertical composition that emphasizes the cohesion between the two figures, Gentileschi's heroine is distinctly separated from her male adversary. She is positioned vertically, her body parallel to the right boundary of the picture; and Sisera's body is placed at a 90-degree angle to hers, along the lower axis of the painting. Gentileschi's composition thus emphasizes the separation—both physical and spiritual—between the two figures, who form a more homogeneous unit in Cigoli's conception.

Artemisia emphasizes difference and distinction between her two figures in other ways as well. Her Jael is clothed in paler colors, white and yellow, in contrast to Sisera's red and blue. Jael's hair is light auburn, whereas Sisera's is black. Her arms are outspread in action, but his arms are motionlessly folded together, to cushion his head. Thus Artemisia's Jael is distinguished by pose, position, coloration, and gender from Sisera. Whereas Cigoli's Sisera is visually emphasized by being closer to the viewer and by wearing a golden cloak that provides the strongest color accent in the painting, Gentileschi's Jael is closer and more brilliantly colored than her companion. Although the light that traditionally signifies God's presence falls on both of Gentileschi's figures, setting them off from the dark background, there is no question as to which of her two figures is more virtuous. Jael's proximity, verticality, and distinctive visual differences from Sisera clearly express her virtue and her imminent victory. Although Cigoli's painting also conveys Jael's impending victory, her moral superiority is left decidedly less clear.

In Gentileschi's painting, Jael's clothing and setting may also be understood as signifiers of her virtue. Her golden dress and white blouse match the costumes Artemisia employed for other biblical heroines during her Florentine period and for more than a decade afterwards, including Judith, Mary Magdalen, and Esther. Although her dress is brilliantly colored, Gentileschi's Jael wears much simpler clothing than Cigoli's figure, who wears a rich brocade dress over a silk blouse trimmed in gold lace that emphasizes her role as worldly temptress. The stark setting, primarily articulated by the vertical accent of the column base upon which Artemisia signed her name and the date, avoids all suggestion of lush sensuality or opulence. This is a Jael whose violent actions are undertaken on God's behalf, and she is less sullied by the implications of secularity and eroticism that shaped Cigoli's conception. Gentileschi's Jael is a protagonist worthy of Deborah's song of celebration, which concludes triumphantly: "So perish all your enemies, O Lord!" (Judges 5:31).

Thus Gentileschi's Jael is only superficially indebted to Cigoli's example. Unlike the depictions of her male contemporaries during the seventeenth century, her Jael is distinguished as virtuous, divinely inspired, and above all different in every way from her male adversary. Artemisia did not adopt the violent interpretation with an awake Sisera utilized by Siciolante/Procaccini. Instead, she followed the text of Judges 4 and most of her fellow artists in depicting a sleeping Sisera. However, like Siciolante/Procaccini's, her Jael is unambiguously portrayed as a virtuous person in the service of God. Since such an interpretation of Jael was unusual in Italian art of the period, it seems possible that it was influenced by Artemisia's patron for the picture.

Patronage

Although Gentileschi's patron for the *Jael and Sisera* is unknown, most scholars agree that it was painted for a Florentine (Contini and Papi 1991, 143–45; Bissell 1999, 212; Christiansen and Mann 2001, 344–45). Most of Artemisia's Florentine pictures—seven of her ten known works from this period, according to Bissell—were painted for the Medici, who were also probably influential in supporting Gentileschi's admission to the Florentine Accademia del Disegno (Bissell 1999, 21–25). These circumstances raise the interesting question of whether this work too might have been produced for the Florentine grand ducal family.

Bissell has suggested that Gentileschi's Jael may have been intended as a positive allusion to the Grand Duchess Maria Maddalena, a hypothesis that, if true, might help to account for Artemisia's unusually positive interpretation of the biblical heroine (1999, 24–25). Maria Maddalena of Austria, wife of Cosimo II de' Medici, grand duke of Tuscany from 1609 to 1621, was one of Artemisia's most important Florentine patrons. Gentileschi's two paintings of *Mary Magdalen* from these years were probably produced for the duchess or her husband, to honor the name saint of the deeply religious duchess. The grand duchess also commissioned paintings featuring virtuous women from other artists, including four canvases depicting Lucretia, Artemisia, Semiramis, and Sophonisba, painted between 1623 and 1625 for a room in the Medici Villa del Poggio Imperiale (Bissell 1999, 24–25).

Although Gentileschi's interpretation of Jael and Sisera may thus be linked to her patron's religious concerns, other paintings of Jael and Sisera during the period were made for patrons whose political circumstances explain their interest in the subject. Cigoli's *Jael and Sisera* was commissioned in ca. 1595 by Ascanio Pucci, whose father and brother had both been executed for allegedly conspiring against the Medici. Alessandro Cecchi has argued that this family history inspired Pucci's commission from Cigoli. Cecchi suggested that Pucci, who moved to Rome from Florence after the executions of his father in 1560 and his brother in 1575, chose this subject in lieu of the more popular Judith and Holofernes to recall the two family members who had sacrificed their lives in attempting to overthrow the ruling tyrants in Florence (Bissell 1991, 90–91).

The Bolognese painter Barbara Sirani (1641–92), sister of Elisabetta Sirani, was the only woman besides Artemisia Gentileschi to depict the subject of Jael and Sisera in seventeenth-century Italy. Barbara painted her now-lost picture of *Jael and Sisera* for Count Ercole Bentivoglio (Malvasia 1841, 2:411; Crespi 1769, 75). The Bolognese Bentivoglio family was notorious for its history of conflict with the established political order. In 1506, the Bentivoglio had fled Bologna when Pope Julius II restored the city to papal rule; and in 1507, following the Bentivoglio's failed attempt to reenter Bologna, papal authorities punitively destroyed the Bentivoglio family palace. The Jael and Sisera subject was unusual for Sirani, her only Old Testament subject among some twenty known works, and probably reflects a sense of political reminiscence by her patron, Count Ercole Bentivoglio. Like Cigoli's *Jael and Sisera,* Sirani's painting was probably intended to provide a biblical parallel to recent attempts by the patron's family to overturn the established political order.

The examples of Cigoli and Sirani suggest that contemporary political issues often figured in commissions for paintings of *Jael and Sisera.* But if Gentileschi's picture was painted for the Medici rulers of Florence, rather than for patrons whose families had been overthrown by the established order, it did not reflect political concerns. Instead, the artist's interpretation seems to have been primarily religious. In this context, it is understandable that Jael's significance would have shifted from that of a rebel against an established power to that of a paragon of female virtue who prefigures the Virgin Mary. But how plausible was the construction of a female assassin as virtuous in seventeenth-century Florence?

Murder in Early Modern Italy

Women in early modern Italy, like women throughout the history of Western civilization, were far more likely to be the victims of violent crimes than the perpetrators. Despite a literary tradition from Euripides to Kipling that viewed the female of the species as more deadly than the male, all modern scientific studies of violent crime have arrived at the same conclusion: women rarely kill. Coramae Richey Mann provides convincing statistical evidence that "there is no known human society in which the level of lethal violence among women even begins to approach that among men" (Mann 1996, 1). Studies of violent crime in various parts of early modern Europe confirm this hypothesis. Ulinka Rublack's study of Germany between 1500 and 1700 found that murder was a crime almost invariably committed by men (1999, 81, 167). Malcolm Greenshields's study of violent crime in France between 1557 and 1664 found that women comprised less than 2 percent of the suspects tried for assault or homicide (Greenshields 1994, 240). Samuel Cohn's study of female crime in Renaissance Florence showed that between 1455 and 1466, only four women were prosecuted for murder, compared to twenty-three male defendants (Cohn 1996, 26–27). These studies all suggest that the story of Jael and Sisera provided seventeenth-century Italians with an unusual social phenomenon: a woman's violent murder of a man.

Female murderers were not entirely unknown in early modern Italy, however. It is likely that Gentileschi was acquainted with the circumstances of a famous murder trial in Rome of 1599, a case suggesting that female murderers of men were likely to receive severe punishments, particularly if those women owed a family allegiance to the victim. The notorious case of the Roman noblewoman Beatrice Cenci, who arranged her abusive father's murder in 1599, was well known throughout Italy. Although her father had beaten her, virtually imprisoned her, and prevented her from leading any sort of normal life, a Roman court condemned the twenty-two-year old Cenci to death. She and her collaborators were all decapitated in Rome in 1599, despite considerable public sympathy for the young woman that produced a series of romantic depictions in painting and literature (Bevilacqua and Mori 1999). Cenci's tragic history provides a chilling example of how female murderers of powerful men might expect to be treated in early modern Italy. If Gentileschi intended to evoke an association between Jael and the virtuous Maria Maddalena of Austria, or between Jael and the Virgin Mary, it was prudent to de-emphasize the violence of the crime.

Gentileschi's Quiet Women

Although in the absence of documented information about Gentileschi's patron for her *Jael and Sisera,* we can only speculate about the Medici's possible influence on this work, we can see how the picture fits with Artemisia's other depictions of strong biblical heroines. Although Gentileschi is deservedly famous for her dramatic and sometimes violent depictions of Judith and Susanna, her works also include a number of quieter depictions of biblical women and saints. Artemisia painted several representations of

Mary Magdalen as an introspective, thoughtful penitent. Mary Garrard has discussed how Gentileschi's melancholic and meditative portrayal entitled *The Penitent Magdalen* in Seville, painted during the early to mid-1620s, provides a quiet and dignified alternative to the erotic Magdalens painted by many of her male contemporaries (2001, 35–48).

Gentileschi's painting of *Esther before Ahasuerus* in the Metropolitan Museum of Art in New York (ca. 1630), which has been thoroughly analyzed by Judith Mann, depicts another Old Testament heroine who saved the Jews through her courage and determination (Christiansen and Mann 2001, 373–77). Gentileschi followed the apocryphal additions to the biblical text in showing Esther fainting as she appears before her husband, King Ahasuerus. Esther had fasted for three days before risking her life to approach the king, so here her quiet portrayal as a fainting figure expresses her devoutness as well as her fear in risking her life. Other examples by Gentileschi of quiet and often introspective female religious figures include St. Catherine of Alexandria, St. Cecilia, and further depictions of Mary Magdalen. Although these pictures do not conform to sensationalist notions of an Artemisia Gentileschi whose pictorial conceptions were shaped by her sexuality and anger towards men, they do represent an important part of the artist's achievement.

Conclusion

Artemisia's Jael is one of several quiet and contemplative women portrayed by the artist whose strength, courage, and virtue are expressed through subtler means than those used in her better known and more forceful depictions of Judith and Susanna. These quiet women do not conform to popular, melodramatic notions of Artemisia's furious feelings towards men. Instead, they show the artist rethinking traditional subjects with characteristic originality. In the case of her *Jael and Sisera*, this originality involves a careful consideration of the biblical text and a rejection of those aspects of the artistic tradition that did not conform to it. In addition, Artemisia's unconventional conception of a quietly virtuous Jael whose actions, sanctioned by God, prefigure the Virgin Mary's triumph over Satan, may have been influenced or inspired by the virtuous Grand Duchess Maria Maddalena.

Whoever commissioned Artemisia's picture, however, the artist herself was clearly sensitive to Jael's problematically ambiguous morality and motivation in the Old Testament story. By avoiding explicit eroticism and violence, she sanitized her heroine, emphasizing her role as God's instrument and a prefiguration of the Virgin Mary in lieu of her traditional characterization as a temptress whose character and motivations are ambiguous. This type of original iconography, involving a fresh look at the biblical text, a critical rethinking of pictorial traditions, and a sympathetic and positive characterization of the female protagonist, constitutes a characteristic feature of Artemisia Gentileschi's remarkable creative ingenuity.

Griselda Pollock has argued, cogently and convincingly, that Artemisia's current fame is "more a matter of notoriety and sensationalism than of any real interest in or comprehension of 'Gentileschi' as a set of artistically created meanings" (1999, 97). If we can eliminate our sensationalist preconceptions about Artemisia Gentileschi to examine her *Jael and Sisera,* the painting can be understood, not as a rather unsatisfactory mirror of her personal life, but as a serious and original interpretation of the biblical story, seen through the lens of contemporary religious and political realities.

Acknowledgments

I am deeply grateful to David Gunn, for sharing with me the relevant portions of his soon-to-be published reception-history commentary on the Book of Judges (Blackwell Bible Commentary Series).

GROUNDS OF COMPARISON

———

Mieke Bal

Comparison, Judgment, and Antivisualism

Compare and contrast—as Nanette Salomon has argued in her contribution to this volume, this is the basis of judgment in the field of art. Comparison reigns supreme, and "versus" is the implied logic that underlies it. Not only in art history, where the parallel slide projection has been the pedagogical tool for decades now, but also in society at large, where artworks are consumed as if they had the same format, texture, and dimensions. Perhaps in the wake of art history—but it might just as well be the other way around—comparison there, too, has become the privileged basis for judgments of taste. We compare the artworks in front of us with others—by the same artist, by artists of the same movement, or by predecessors. There is a certain lack of self-confidence involved in this compulsion to compare. Most people are not so sure about their taste, and comparison helps to give a work meaning, a relative place.

Consequently, comparison has two drawbacks. It quickly becomes a ground for (relative) judgment and establishing hierarchies, and it distracts from looking. Indeed, art thus seems to be an area where judgment is compulsory. Instead of "just looking," the ordinary as well as the expert viewer feels compelled to judge. The concept of art itself is grounded in judgment: What is, and what is not art? Is it art or kitsch? Great art or secondary art? Museums exhibit their treasures in architecturally construed itineraries that lead up to the most important masterpieces. Temporary exhibitions thrive on the juxtaposition of works, one of which is judged superior to the other.

There are, however, other forms of comparison, not built on a logic of oppositional judgment. Comparison can be a tool for analysis as long as one of its terms is not established as normative. It can help careful and sustained looking by focusing it. Moreover, comparison can help us to make distinctions. In addition, comparison serves a particular kind of art history, namely, that of connoisseurship—the decision to attribute a work to a particular artist and thus to compose that artist's oeuvre. Hence, there is no point in rejecting something so central in our dealings with art.

But in spite of the traditional usefulness generally attributed to comparison, there are other aspects to art of the past that matter, and for which comparison might well end up being a curse. As soon as comparison promotes judgment and one term is instituted as the norm, there will always be the lesser work, and we are discouraged from taking a good look at it because we already "know" it is less valuable, less pleasurable, less intelligent—in short, less masterly. In this sense, comparison not only serves a cultural compulsion to pronounce judgments of taste; it tends to lead away from a personal confrontation with the artwork itself. For this reason, comparison when grounded in or serving judgment is antivisual. Moreover, since the judgment of taste is by definition anchored in the present, comparison does not help a historical understanding of a visual culture from the past. This essay is based on the conviction that Artemisia Gentileschi's paintings have fallen prey to all of the negative, and rarely any of the positive, aspects of comparison. The authors included in this volume are exceptions to this tendency, along with an increasing number of others. I will make a case for this view of the reception of Artemisia's work through a discussion of recent exhibitions of it.

I examine here three exhibitions as cases of comparison, in order to exorcise its negative—antivisualist and judgmental—aspects and

to enhance its positive potential as a method of analysis, understanding, and—simply?—looking at art. And since, as I mentioned earlier,
I believe the boundary between "art history" and "popular taste" is
permeable, exhibitions offer a relevant and seldom-studied middle
ground between academic and general conceptions of art. In all three
exhibitions, comparison steers the visitors' engagement with the art.
The first, The Genius of Rome, 1592–1623, curated by Beverly Louise
Brown, was held at the Royal Academy in London (20 Jan.–16 Apr.
2001), and later at the Palazzo Venezia in Rome (May–Aug. 2001).
The ground of comparison here is the master-student relationship:
Caravaggio is the master, Artemisia the student. Judgment is based
on chronology and cast as influence, conceived as emulation.

The second, Orazio and Artemisia Gentileschi: Father and
Daughter Painters in Baroque Italy, was held at the Museo del Palazzo di Venezia in Rome (15 Oct. 2001–6 Jan. 2002) and subsequently
at the Metropolitan Museum of Art in New York (14 Feb.–12 May
2002) and the St. Louis Art Museum (15 June–12 Sept. 2002).
Its theme, as the title overtly suggests, is the father-daughter
relationship, and the ground of comparison is age and authority,
again cast as influence. This time, influence is conceived of as imitation, and the primary issue in the relationship appears to be the attribution of works to either artist.

The third case is Kathleen Gilje's exhibition titled *Susanna and
the Elders (Restored)*, staged around a single artwork, which was
held at the Gallery Braven, Post, and Lee in New York in 1998, and
later at the National Museum of Women in the Arts in Washington,
DC (18 Oct. 2001–21 Jan. 2002) and the Contemporary Art Museum
in St. Louis, Missouri (23 Aug.–12 Oct. 2002). The ground of comparison here is the question of rape, and the comparison takes the
form of quotation, commentary, and reframing in the present.

Judith, Inc.

Other contributions to this volume reconsider in great detail
Artemisia's versions of the mythical story of *Judith Beheading*

Holofernes, particularly Ciletti's, and her versions of *Susanna and the Elders*, particularly Salomon's. My first case concerns the former painting, and my third the latter, of these two signature themes. To avoid repetition, I will limit my remarks on the issue of comparison to what the other authors do not elaborate.

The comparison in the London exhibition, The Genius of Rome, which is avoided in its Rome counterpart, is the most frequently alleged one involving Artemisia's oeuvre: her depictions of Judith slaying Holofernes are compared with Caravaggio's treatment of the same theme. Having these pictures together in one exhibition offered a wonderful opportunity to take a closer look at this case, made famous long ago by Mary Garrard (1989).

The comparison is both obscured and framed by the exhibition's title. This title, The Genius of Rome, is wildly ambiguous, and at first sight, does not induce the compulsion to compare for judgment. That it ends up doing just that, in manners characteristic of such blockbuster shows, is a reason to take a closer look at it. After all, titles do sum up a program and as such, are a tool to attract and predispose the public. Its curatorial meaning is this: In Rome, at a specific moment in time, the genius of the baroque was born; the simultaneous presence of painters, patrons, and other power brokers during two and a half decades made "the birth of the baroque" possible. Naturally, the actual organization of the show, in practice limited to painting, could not convey the diversity of the birth of a cultural concept that took hold of architecture, sculpture, music, philosophy, science, literature, politics, and city planning, as well as of painting. Nor could it be expected to. Instead, the exhibition was an attempt to convey the temporal and spatial convergence implied by the title—through a *thematic* distribution. This is a rather frequently deployed strategy in contemporary exhibition practice.

Superimposing themes onto genres or other art-historical categories—still lifes, "painted music," landscapes, nocturnal scenes characterized by chiaroscuro (an art-historical category), saints "between sacred and profane" (a theological, specifically Catholic set of expectations)—is a way of powerfully laying out the notion that, in Rome, artists of genius converged. Rome, as a city, "had," or housed, people of genius, whose joint work can retrospectively be recognized as "baroque." A historical geography of painting thus leads to a thematically constructed exhibition.

A second meaning of the title facilitates a view of the works as embedded in a historical, visual culture. Subliminally, one can also take the title to refer to Rome not simply as a location, as a site where things happened to happen, but as a social, institutional, and political unit with causal powers. Rome, then, not only houses people of genius; it has genius itself. Given the power of the Catholic Church and its Counter-Reformation ideology, such an interpretation certainly makes sense. On the one hand, it helps us to understand that art does not emerge out of the blue, that artists, like other people, are subject to political pressures, and that the horizon of their imagination is limited by what is thinkable, to what the powers-that-be allow the brainwashed mind to foster. This view turns artists into artisans without a vision of their own—a historicist notion that usefully struggles against Romantic notions of the "artist as lone genius." On the other hand, it also contributes to the naturalization of such power over creativity. This second meaning, I submit, encourages a dubiously uncritical view of political subordination, a repetition, even an unwitting endorsement, of the determinist ideology that those powers have a vested interest in promoting.

This attempt to historicize the phenomenon of the artist as well as to frame historical aesthetics, while necessary, is also risky. To be sure, artists, then as now, depend on the sale of their work. To please patrons, they cannot avoid adhering to the stipulations of the commission, the taste of the day, and the politics that reign as a frame within which to work. But while all the old artists did that, only a handful of them still interest us enough today to be included in this exhibition. The question of aesthetic criteria begs that of power. Simply explaining pictures historically through their commissions may be useful as an account of what happened in the art market, which is why such an endeavor approaches "cultural history" but fails to explain how these pictures end up in an exhibition of this nature *today*. The "versus" implied in choices is neither made explicit, nor justified. To be truly historical, in the sense of cultural history, the tedious, the failed, the imitative, and the rejected works would need to be included, along with one or two "great" works. But we do not want that. This is "us"—the contemporary public and the art historian working for us—acting as unwitting judges. Judgments of taste resulting from "versus" comparisons underlie the selection.

The second interpretation of the show's title suggests a historical explanation but fails to give one. Instead, it takes our "taste" for granted, while accepting the political powers of patrons as a given and as implicitly positive—they yielded great painting!—and ignoring, even obliterating, what characterizes the paintings as what we nevertheless assume them to be: works of art. As a result of the repression of our own intervention in the historical material, the view underlying the second interpretation of the title easily becomes a condescending "othering" of historical phenomena. It suggests more tyranny, more constrictive dependency than we can even conceive of, let alone explain, for today's artists, who, post-Romantically, are considered free.

A third connotation equally subliminally active in this exhibition is the individualizing, narrativizing one. This is where the topos of Caravaggio's and Artemisia's *Judith*s comes in. The genius of Rome, like the Hunchback of Notre Dame, the Phantom of the Opera, or the Murderer of Amsterdam, is a man of as yet unknown identity who roams about Rome—and is a genius. The story of the show leads to the discovery of his identity. It is clear who that guy is—not Artemisia, but Caravaggio, of course—yet it remains interesting to see what this narrativizing structure of meaning does to the comparison.

As it happened, in the Roman venue the name Caravaggio was the main title of the exhibition, while the London title became the subtitle. In both locations Caravaggio was not alone: his fifteen-odd works were surrounded by paintings by others, among whom were well-known, "great" old masters such as Rubens, Annibale Carracci, Adam Elsheimer, and Artemisia, together with many "minor" artists. But most of the sections and essays in the exhibition catalogue present Caravaggio as the measuring stick. He is portrayed as both recal-

citrant and "great," so that he becomes interesting as an artist by being interesting as a man. His paintings hung in central places and,
with the help of juxtapositions and captions as well as their own im-
manent qualities, outshone the others. This connotation, I contend,
reinstates the anachronistic conception of genius against which the
exhibition, as suggested in the "official" meaning of its title, argues.
Instead of cultural history, it becomes a display of connoisseurship.

I will consider the anachronistic conception of genius with regard
to the implications of, especially, the first and third interpretations of
the exhibition's title for the practice of art history as it plays itself out
in the comparison in which Artemisia is so inevitably entangled. The
catalogue essay "Between the Sacred and the Profane" attempts to
clarify the historical issue of the ambivalent reception of primarily
Caravaggio's ambiguous saints in Counter-Reformation Rome. Es-
pousing chronological treatment, art history's primary dogma, curator Beverly Louise Brown first discusses Caravaggio's *Judith*. She
writes two things about it, which I contend to be in contradiction
with each other. First she writes, "Not yet dead he [Holofernes]
screams in violent protest, while Judith with complete composure
and icy self-determination merely frowns" (Brown 2001, 292). Visually this rings true enough. Garrard based her critical assessment that
Caravaggio wasn't interested enough in women on this composure.

Brown's remark suggests a different interpretation: Judith's pro-
fessionalism as a heroine in the service of her nation motivates the
depiction of her as "icy." But Brown's next sentence shows how her
discourse contradicts itself, unwittingly endorsing another dogma,
that of misogyny: "Her erect nipples indicate a state of sexual
arousal that often occurs at the moment of hysterical violence"
(Brown 2001, 292). If such referential details matter at all, let me say
that women know, as some men perhaps do not, that nipples
harden under stress owing to adrenaline as much as to sexual
arousal. There is little reason to favor the latter explanation over the
former. But more significant seems to be the selection of this tiny
bodily detail in an analysis of barely a paragraph, half of which
speculates on what Caravaggio may have seen in the streets of

Rome. What I am most interested in here, though, is the contradiction between the two sentences: complete composure and icy self-
determination seem to be at odds with sexual arousal and hysterical violence. For the latter remark, a source is cited in a footnote. By
repeating uncritically what predecessors have claimed, Brown reiterates the sexist collocation of hysteria and women, thus reducing
Caravaggio's "graphic realism" to a near-pornographic cliché.

More disturbing still for those interested in these images as works
of art is the comparison that fatally turns Gentileschi's painting from
a few years later into a mere imitation. Not that imitation is a negative
project, certainly not in seventeenth-century Italy. But if the comparison is couched in terms that establish one artist as the master and the
norm, the other as derivative, then imitation, even in a culture where
emulation was more appreciated than today, is a negative notion. That
her two paintings of Judith slaying Holofernes have scared critics out
of their wits in ways that Caravaggio's has not has been obvious for a
long time (see Bal 1996, 225–311; Ciletti 1988). But what is the implica-
tion of this comparison whose chronology translates into influence?
The differences are articulated on the basis of the earlier work, and the
similarities are foregrounded: "Much of his grisly realism and sexual
innuendo is *repeated,* but Abra is now a young co-conspirator and the
action is more compact and intensified. Both pictures stress the brutality of Judith's actions rather than the more traditional heroic aspects of her courageous deed" (Brown 2001, 292; emphasis added).
Here, we see the particular ground of comparison as emulation at
work. There is a standard (Caravaggio), relative to which similarities
and differences are meted out. Embedded within two similarities that
justify the comparison on the basis of the standard, the differences are
relative to that standard, and they are not interpreted qualitatively but
quantitatively. What remains unaddressed is the feature that characterizes Gentileschi's painting most profoundly and that bears no resemblance whatsoever to Caravaggio, even though it defines the
painting's very baroqueness: its composition.

Since Germaine Greer (1979) first wrote her early feminist intervention in art history, many have written on the unusual composition

of Gentileschi's *Judith* (fig. 22), in which the scene is so crammed that it is readable only with the greatest difficulty.[1] In the present volume, Elena Ciletti's analysis in particular elaborates on this. This dark, steamy scene, centered around the head that emerges from shoulders that look like thighs, conflates birth, sex, and death as the three key moments of confrontation between men and women. Three moments, that is, where women can wield power over men. In fact, no other *Judith* from the immense corpus on this theme in Italy—and specifically Rome—or elsewhere is remotely comparable with Gentileschi's dramatically staged scene. More than a hysterical exercise in violence, it is primarily an inquiry into the baroque-inflected confrontation of bodies that can no longer be disentangled.[2]

If comparison is so compulsive, then perhaps it is more helpful to establish a different standard. The culture of baroque thought about representation and life, about the body and the person, suggests that we displace the focus from a master-student chronology to a comparison of two different interventions in a historical, visual culture. There is no need for the normative status of one term of the comparison; no need for "versus." Where Caravaggio challenges two-dimensional representation in the left-hand corner of the scene where the blood spurts forward, but otherwise keeps to the format of the scroll, Gentileschi's work offers a much more radical exploration of three-dimensionality within painting, on the basis of an irresolvable movement between pushing forward and receding backward, characteristic of the most profound philosophical thrust of baroque thought.[3] With the two paintings installed for comparison, and with Caravaggio's earlier date and higher status dictating the direction of the dual assessment, Gentileschi's unique representation is flattened out into a lesser imitation that allegedly shares the misogyny (wrongly) imputed to the great master, and thus loses its innovative work entirely. Without imposing a romantic myth of originality, denying Artemisia her innovations is an objectionable form of censorship.

What I have attempted to show with these remarks is how thematic organization puts an exhibition at risk of triply reiterating art history at its most mechanical—in its use of normative, Oedipal comparison. In the first place by conflating themes with art-historical categories of genre, the reiterative nature of thematics is, so to speak, naturalized: since we know the categories already, they appear to be the only ones possible. The repetitive nature of thematics encourages us to look at the paintings from the knowledge we already have, or think we have, of the story in the Bible. Second, the method of comparison is put in place as, again, already naturalized, so that the standard is self-evidently the earlier master, and seeing similarities, not differences, becomes the most ordinary mode of looking. Third, combined with connoisseurial evaluation and chronological reasoning, the comparison reiterates the hierarchies among Old Masters as well as the clichés of interpretation. As a result of these three drawbacks, Artemisia's *Judith*—and hence, Artemisia as an intelligent, searching baroque artist—is incorporated, cannibalized, into a canonical hierarchy that keeps the visual specifics of her work at bay.

Facing the Face

In order to counter such tendencies, I suggest we move away from the emblematic, canonical masterpieces too easily linked to the kind of biographist sensationalism on which Pollock writes in this volume. In accordance with Bohn's decision to dwell on a noncanonical, quieter picture, I now move to a comparison of an altogether different nature. Many comparisons occurred on the basis of biographical assumptions in the Orazio and Artemisia Gentileschi exhibition, even regarding the less sensational paintings. One such comparison rests on the represented face. As it happens, and as has often been remarked, Artemisia's paintings frequently depict a generic, Artemisia-like face, a tendency critiqued in this volume by Mary Garrard. Here, the faces are implicitly compared to the face that, but for an incidental etching, we only know through paintings. The comparison is circular, and, like the comparison with Caravaggio, it obscures the paintings in that it makes us search for the woman "behind" the paintings. To call these recognizable faces hidden self-portraits goes a long way to sustain the biographical frenzy that so frequently overrules the visual evidence of the paintings—especially in the case of Artemisia.

The generic faces are all the more striking because, while Artemisia's face as we have first construed it can be recognized in many history paintings, even her most generic self-portraits "other" her self. They do this mostly by means of allegorization: *Female Martyr, Self-Portrait as an Allegory of Painting,* and *Lute Player* (see figs. 1, 37, and 8). Mary Garrard discusses some of these images in her contribution to the present volume. This allegorization is paradoxical in that these allegories, or discourses of otherness, play the personal (self) off against the other, who is not even the commensurable other of the "second person" but the incommensurable other of abstract theory.[4]

Instead of qualifying these faces as hidden self-portraits, I therefore propose to give them a name according to their play between "self" and "other." The composite term "allo-portrait" recalls self-portrait but infuses that genre with the otherness of allegory. The most famous of these—*Self-Portrait as an Allegory of Painting* from 1630 (fig. 37)—folds this othering back onto the self. Here the glance as trace of the mirror has been completely omitted or obliterated. Instead, the hand holding the palette almost cuts into the space of the viewer, thus standing at the cutting edge between the self and her "second person."[5]

But rather than remaining in the realm of allegorical abstraction, this image brings the face to life, not as the face of the artist in the biographical sense, but through the insinuation of narrative into an ostensibly static pose. The image, indeed, comes to life, not only in the generic act of painting, for which more muscle is mustered than abstraction requires, but also in the chain that hangs obliquely, sliding off her breast because of the figure's frenzied activity. The small pendant of the mask, traditionally read as a sign of mimesis, stubbornly remains the mask as a sign of theatricality, abstraction's counterpart.

In view of this late work's staging of the complexities of allo-portraiture, I take it as a key to the many earlier works (history paintings) in which the artist appears to have used her own face. The relevance of the standard interpretation that the artist is her

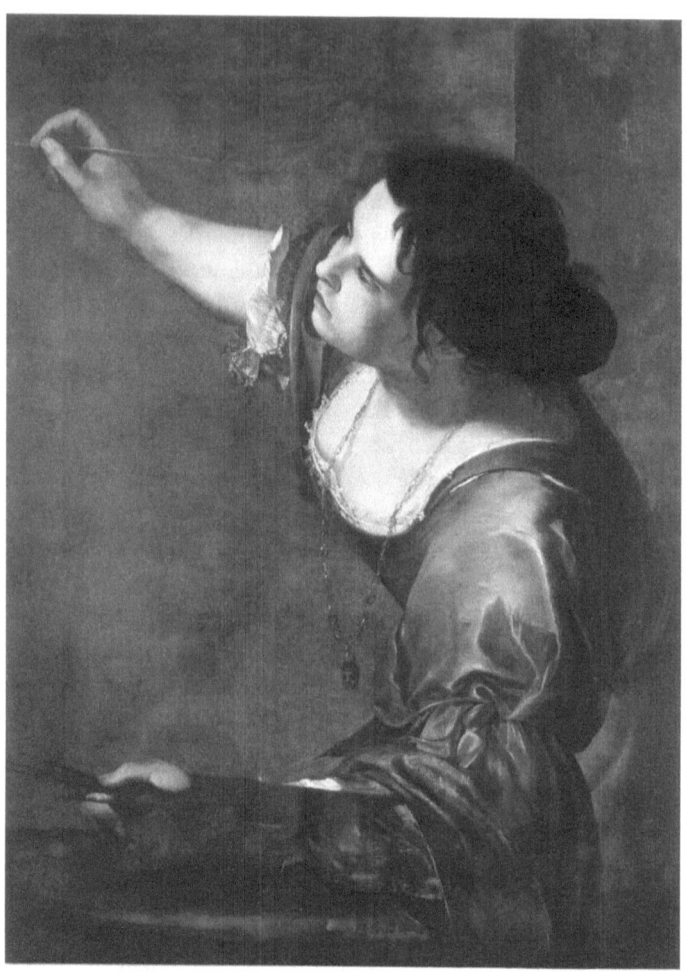

Figure 37. Artemisia Gentileschi, *Self-Portrait as an Allegory of Painting*, 1630.
London, Her Majesty Queen Elizabeth II, Royal Collection, public domain.

own cheapest model is quickly exhausted. Instead, I consider the extreme frequency with which Artemisia's face seems to appear in her paintings as a statement on self/other relations. Going beyond humanistic sentiment, a theatrical representation of well-known and well-worn scenes from the catalogue of ideologies made concrete and naturalized in myths raises questions that I find more important to attend to as questions than to answer too hastily.

Artemisia's face has been recognized in—or projected onto—two of the most famous and overquoted paintings: the harrowing representation of Susanna when she is being threatened by two overbearing elders (1610; see fig. 17), and the equally harrowing representation of Judith slaying Holofernes (1612–13; see fig. 22), central here in the contributions by Salomon and Ciletti respectively. Instead of reading these two works as continuous with each other, as rape and revenge in relation to a widely abused story of real rape, I propose to heed the insistence of the *Self-Portrait as an Allegory of Painting* that each are different instances of alloportraits. As such, they mirror each other. Each positions the self-as-other in an intense relationship with social others at moments of equally intense threats to the self. Being raped, as the subject in the *Susanna* is threatened to be, is just as self-estranging (depriving the self of its reassuringly stable subjectivity) as killing. No more, no less.

The use of the face of the artist is not to be totally ignored, however. It is infused with meaning when we realize that the two paintings thematize both the loneliness of one against the collaboration of two, and the trace of the mirror that characterizes the self-portrait. In both, the mirror's trace resides in the face's closeness to the picture plane. In the *Susanna,* the cropped foot and the water that spills over into the viewer's space signify this. Moreover, water as a reflecting surface recalls the mirror. In the *Judith,* this function of pushing the face forward is fulfilled by the spurts of blood. These are two liquid ways of implicating the viewer as "you," as second person. The I/you interaction is foregrounded in the drops of blood that stain Judith/Artemisia's dress and breast. This is how killing is self-alienating; resonating with allo-portraiture, it contaminates the self with the other who is being discarded.

All this is quite poignant, and certainly contributes to the emotional charge of the paintings. Clearly we don't need a naturalized humanistic individualism to convey emotion. On the contrary, here the emotion comes with the threat to or destruction of the self as autonomous individual. Perhaps this emotional charge is best seen as a case of what Deleuze called the "affect-image." This type of image stands between the perception-image, which offers insight into what, from the perceptible universe, is most useful for the viewer's own life, and the action-image, which offers suggestions for acting upon that insight. In between, the affect-image moves us but suspends action. There is a special relationship between affect in this sense and the human face. Deleuze identifies the affect-image he spotted in the close-ups of classical cinema not only *with* but *as* the face. Deleuze wrote, "There is no close-up of the face. The close-up is the face, but the face precisely in so far as it has destroyed its triple function [individuation, socialization, communication] . . . the close-up turns the face into a phantom . . . the face is the vampire" (1986, 99). In this light, I would like to raise the question that the recurring face poses: How does recognizing or projecting the artist's face help?

Sharing Garrard's doubts, I am not sure it helps at all, certainly not *in general*. Instead, I propose to use this recognizable, generic face, this recurring allo-portrait, as a critical tool. Here I wish to use it to drive a wedge into the father-daughter topos and its "versus" ground of comparison. For the question of the meaning of this face becomes ironical—most emphatically in the case of an artist whose audience is relentlessly in search of the biopic within art—when we realize that this use of the face also occurs at one more remove: in the other painter's images.

Artemisia's father, Orazio, as those of us who saw the exhibition in the Metropolitan Museum had the opportunity to realize, used the face we think of as Artemisia's as frequently as she did herself. This fact brings me to the outer limit of the idea of the allo-portrait. If we consider the oeuvres of Artemisia and Orazio separately, the two uses of Artemisia's face would be completely distinct. Orazio's masks of Artemisia would have no meaning beyond the ones imported by the actress playing the roles and the roles themselves. There would be no connection, then, between Orazio's two depictions of the story of *Lot and His Daughters* (in which an increasingly drunken, sleeping father disavows complicity with the incestuous event imported from the biblical pre-text) and Artemisia's choice to give her face to the victim (in the thrice-depicted story of Susanna under threat of rape) in her oeuvre.

If, on the other hand, we consider the two oeuvres as one *corpus,* as is implied in both this joint exhibition and art-historical discourse in general, a disturbing suggestion is implied. In choosing his daughter as model for a story of father-daughter incest, Orazio gives her own self-depiction as "other" an authenticating gloss. We can't have our cake and eat it too: either we sever the ties between life and representation in both cases, or we sever them in neither. Treated as part of two independent oeuvres, Artemisia's *Susanna* can be considered independently from her life myth. In continuity with Artemisia's allo-portraits, in contrast, Orazio's painting overrules the male figure's innocent sleep.

This suggestion, which I make deliberately transgressive of art-historical decorum, serves various purposes. First, on a rather mundane level, the irresolvable contradiction is meant to contribute to curing us, "homeopathically" as Derrida would say, from the obsession with artists' lives and intentions as a ground for comparison. Second, it offers the outer limit of allo-portraits as undermining the humanistic certainties of self-portraiture.[6] Third, it establishes a conceptual continuity between depiction of self and identification. The latter is a projection of self—of the artist as well as the viewer—onto the image of another (*allo-*). As a means of identifying subject or sitter, emotion or mood, ideology or obsession, such projections can be terribly problematic. As a mode or code for reading that grants the projective nature of its results, it can constitute the outer limit of allo-portraiture as a ground for a comparison of a different kind, one not predicated on chronology and authority.

Let me try this out on two paintings, one by each Gentileschi, both on the same utterly conventional subject. Figure 38 represents Orazio's stunning *Madonna and Child;* figure 39 shows Artemisia's depiction of the same. Displayed together, with only one larger painting between them, this was one of several opportunities for analytical comparison between Orazio and Artemisia that existed in the Metropolitan exhibition. Predictably, the exhibition abused that opportunity by reconfirming Orazio's superiority as a painter, thus entirely missing the opportunity to compare on a basis other than judgment.

I would like to read the exhibiting of these two paintings, their wall captions as well as their hanging, as a sample of museum practice in its incapacity to deal with allo-portraiture because of an obsession with the artist's life. To be sure, exhibition captions may appear to be too easy a mark for critical analysis. But if I take them as seriously as I do here, it is because of their mediating status between academic and popular art history. Precisely because they represent the ideas of scholars to the public at large, captions and wall texts are keys to understanding how a culture as a whole, not just its intellectual specialists, deals with art.

The captions that accompanied these two works are radiant examples of the kind of antivisualism that inheres in the compulsion to judge on the ground of "versus": that is to say, polarization and hierarchization. In order to understand the collusion of contemporary museum practice with this compulsion and the conflation of art and life that subtends it, I quote the captions in full next to the figures. (See figs. 38 and 39.) The standard captions for figures in this volume also appear. The exhibition captions are reproduced in a different typeface, just as they appeared with the exhibited works.

Remarkably, the quotation from a historical source constitutes the bulk of the caption text for figure 38. Some of this seems luxuriantly redundant in a text constrained by a standard maximum number of words ("the child nude except for a little swaddling band . . . "). Why quote so extensively? As a taste of historicity, it supports the historical reliability of the exhibition, like an "effect of the real" (Barthes 1991). It thus draws its justification, precisely, from the unreflective commitment to "period thinking." I use the phrase "period thinking" to estrange my account from the self-evident value attached to "historical thinking." Period thinking is unanalytical and paraphrastic, and works by means of the dogmatic value attached to "authenticity." When taken seriously for what it has to say, the quotation supports a single, albeit complex, idea: it supports the positive judgment on naturalism through the humanistic judgment on positive affectivity ("they look at each other with great affection"). This conflation of social and aesthetic judgment has the effect of closure. It is so satisfying that no more questions need be asked. This closure is the hallmark of humanistic ideology and is the reason I probe below, in a discussion of Richard Brilliant's study on portraiture, the kind of humanistic discourse in which it is steeped.

The first element that is hardly an incentive to take a closer look at the painting is the part of the caption for which the curator from the twenty-first century alone is responsible, which characterizes the painting first of all as an "influence" on Artemisia. The second element that acts as a disincentive to look at each work independently is the negative formulation: the naturalism that the quotation infuses with affectivity is now a case of the anxiety of influence, a "rejection" of earlier and rivaling styles. Neither element encourages a visual engagement with the painting at hand.[7]

With the caption accompanying Artemisia's *Madonna and Child* (fig. 39), the viewer eager to be guided into the image fares no better. Again the viewer is referred to the other painting. The effect of the comparison is judgment. Orazio's is good, Artemisia's less so, and the condescending tone attributes the alleged lesser quality to her young age ("understandably"). It thus contributes to the painter's status as the eternal daughter of her superior father.

But what is the standard? The phrase "conveys the use of a model less effectively" suggests that we compare the two works in terms of naturalism. The remark that there is "a mood of domestic intimacy that is very engaging," is again premised on the conflation of art and life and the humanistic sentimentality that sustains it. It also alludes to a conventional sense of femininity. The remark is vague

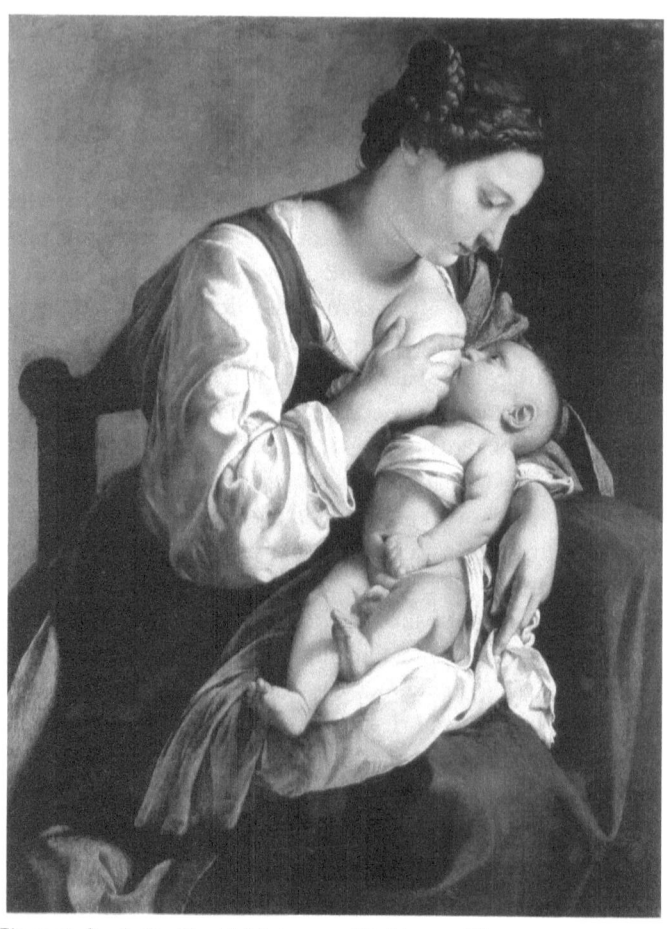

Figure 38. Orazio Gentileschi, *Madonna and Child*, 1609. Oil on canvas, 38 3/4 ×
29 1/2 in. Bucharest, Muzeul Naţional de Artă al României.

Orazio Gentileschi
Madonna and Child
1609
Oil on canvas
Signed and dated: (lower left, reverse)
Horatius Gentileschi facibat 1609

A version similar to this picture was painted for the
Duke of Mantua, whose agent visited Orazio's studio
in 1609 and described it as "a seated Madonna, with
the child in her arms, the child nude except for a little
swaddling band. . . . And they look at each other with
great affection, for all that the child is no more than
one month old. . . . In sum, [the picture] demonstrates
that naturalism is a very good thing."

The models for this picture would seem to be ordinary
people, and we know that the wife of Orazio's tailor
let him use her children as models. Orazio's picture
inspired one of Artemisia's earliest paintings and is
a vigorous rejection of high-style Mannerism and
classical idealism.

11 Naţional de Artá al României, Bucharest

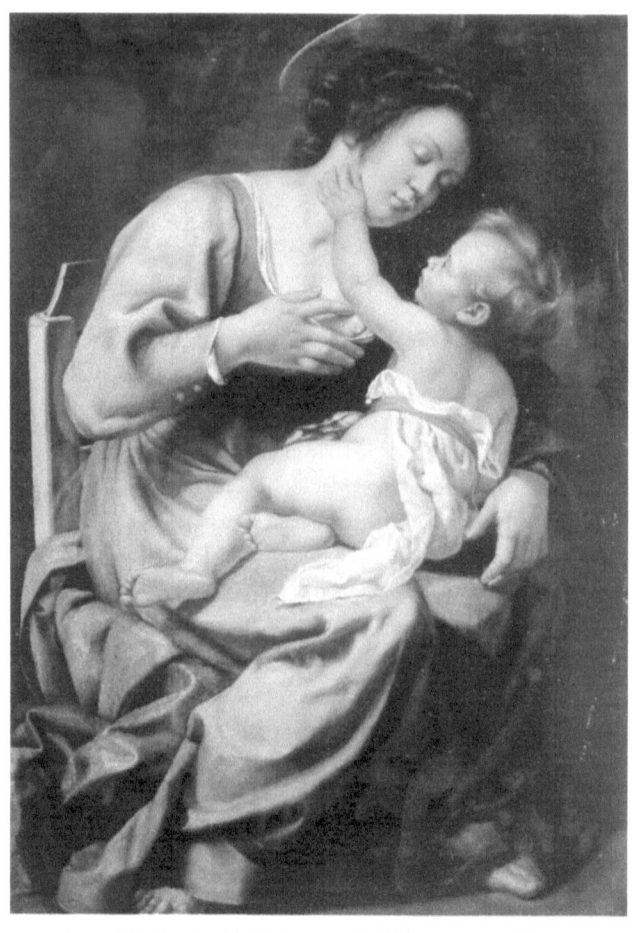

Figure 39. Artemisia Gentileschi, *Madonna and Child*, 1610–1611. Oil on canvas, 45 7/8 × 34 in. Rome, Galleria Spada.

Artemisia Gentileschi
Madonna and Child
1610–1611
Oil on canvas

The pose and general composition are closely related
to Orazio's depiction of the same theme (cat. no.15).
Given its early date, Artemisia's picture is understandably
not as accomplished and conveys the use of a model
less effectively. At the same time, there is a mood of
domestic intimacy that is very engaging.
The picture was owned by Alessandro Biffi, who
also owned "David Contemplating the Head of Goliath"
(cat. no.18) by Orazio. An inventory of 1637 describes
the painting as a work by Artemisia. Another version
(Galleria Palatina, Florence) has also been ascribed to
Artemisia but is more likely by another artist.

Galleria Spada, Rome

enough, however, to also leave room for a different kind of comparison, one based not on judgment but on difference—on an interpretation of the face. Intimacy, as Catherine Lord has suggested in a different context, is, indeed, the key (1999).

The face is often a primary trigger for identification. But since this term is felicitously ambiguous—identification *with* and *as*—we can use each of the two meanings as a ploy to complicate the other. Hence if identification *as* (the face of the painter) is continuous with identification *with* (either figure depicted), the naturalism of Orazio's painting can be given a different meaning. The naturalism is impressive indeed. Let me take it as a tool for analysis, not as a self-evident standard, and not for comparison between ("versus") but for comparison *within.* For its foregrounding is not equally distributed across the image. In the mother, it translates into a certain plainness. The phrase most clearly entangled with the humanistic value assigned to realism—"they look at each other with great affection"—distracts from a significant unevenness that harks back to the classical study on portraiture in the humanistic tradition that I mentioned above. In this study, the author, Richard Brilliant (1991), makes an anthropological generalization. I allege his study and its definitions here as a backdrop for the kind of comparison I propose to substitute for the more common kind, which I consider a curse for art.[8]

Brilliant defines portraits as "art works, intentionally made of living or once living people by artists, in a variety of media, and for an audience" (1991, 8). This definition is generously vague. It posits the circular argument of intentionality as what defines the object. Brilliant's provisional definition is vague in that it does not stipulate, for example, that the portrait requires depiction of the face. Not because this is not a criterion but, on the contrary, because it goes without saying. This primacy of the face appears to be a given in all the publications on the subject that I have consulted. For the face, as the saying goes, is the mirror of the soul, the visibility of interiority. A bit later, Brilliant clearly endorses the naturalness of the centrality of the face, when he explains the genre with reference to babies: "The dynamic nature of portraits and the 'occasionality' that anchors their imagery in life seem ultimately to depend on the primary experience of the infant in arms. The child, gazing up at its mother, imprints her vitally important image so firmly on its mind that soon enough she can be recognized almost instantaneously and without conscious thought" (1991, 9).

We all know that entire new disciplines can be grounded in speculations about what babies see, do, and desire. But although psychoanalysis can and must be challenged for its generalizations, a theory of the psyche can get away with assuming that a human feature is a feature of all humans, while a theory of a historically and culturally specific genre cannot.

What interests me here is the anthropological, functionalist argument that seeks to explain the appeal of portraiture in the culture of Western individualism through an appeal to human universals. This reasoning is fundamentally humanistic: it exalts human nature through an artistic tradition that exalts human nature. It is also anthropomorphic, in that it shifts thought about a cultural genre— here, of painting—from the object of thought to the human being doing the thinking. It collapses the subject and object of analysis. This collapse is common in considerations of art, academic or not. It is overdetermined in the case of Artemisia.

The shift operates through the self-evident importance attributed to documentary realism, a second unquestioned value in Western humanist culture. The point of the portrait is a belief in the real existence of the person depicted, the "vital relationship between the portrait and its object of representation" (1991, 8). A third assumption of Brilliant's argument concerns the nature of identity as a basis for communication. This again is based on the baby, so that the ontogenetic perspective is constantly mapped on the phylogenetic one, in which development is the matrix, and old equals primitive.

A little later on the same page, Brilliant writes the statement that made me allege his text here in the first place: "Here [in the mother-infant visual interaction] are the essential constituents of a person's identity: a recognized or recognizable appearance; a given name that refers to no one else; a social, interactive function that can be

defined; in context, a pertinent characterization; and a consciousness of the distinction between one's own person and another's,
and of the possible relationship between them" (1991, 8).

The "given name that refers to no one else" is particularly striking here since the only example of this in the description on which
this generalization is based is "Mama," an eminently social role.
This identity emerges not only out of appearance and naming, but
also out of distinction. Moreover, the recognition of appearance
triggers interaction and expression. The two are practically the
same: "Visual *communication* between mother and child is effected
face-to-face and, when those faces are smiling, everybody is happy,
or appears to be. For most of us, the human face is not only the
most important key to *identification* based on appearance, it is also
the primary field of expressive action" (1991, 10; emphasis added).

The link, or lack of it, between these two sentences posits the
equality of communication with identification. This equation is
grounded in the double sense of identification—*as* and *with*—that
I contend underlies the problem of self-portraiture in general and
of the two Gentileschis' use of the face in these two paintings of the
Madonna in particular.

Orazio's Madonna does not have the generic Artemisiesque face.
Although both figures are depicted in the naturalistic mode or
code, the focus of attention is the baby. Not only is it placed closer
to the picture plane, with its flexed feet almost available to our
touch, but its detailed genitals that assert its sex and the clenched
little fist also make it remarkably real. The dimples in the arm and
the slightly translucent ear are both touching and almost photo-
realistic. The mouth clamped onto the nipple emphasizes the
mouth's tininess, and the breast's closeness to the little nose recalls,
to those who have experienced breastfeeding, that a baby would almost rather suffocate than miss the treat of mother's milk.[9]

The absolute focus of this picture is the baby's gaze. Its eyes seem
riveted on its mother. It must be on the basis of a picture like this
that Brilliant saw this gaze as the origin of portraiture. The obsessive quality of this gaze, its urgency, is what makes this baby neither

divine nor the emblem of humanism that the patron's agent tried to make it. It is psychological, a necessity, a condition for physical and psychic survival. Across the centuries, this gaze for us, as—who knows?—for contemporary viewers, turns this baby into an object of identification. I thus propose this baby as an instance of the kind of disguised self-portraiture that exists at the outer edge of the field of allo-portraiture. It belongs to the same category as Caravaggio's Goliath and Holofernes. The baby "is" Orazio.

Although this assessment is no more without judgment than any other description (of the success of the picture's naturalism), it is primarily an attempt to interpret and understand what is going on here. In other words, I attempt to use comparison here as an analytical tool. The issue here is the interactive quality of this painting, not its relative quality compared to the other one. Comparison can thus help to understand how this interactivity works. On this basis— hence only *after* the work has been contemplated for its own sake— an analytical comparison with Artemisia's *Madonna and Child* becomes possible. The comparison no longer needs to be based on naturalism and its anchoring in aesthetic-humanistic judgment, those twin standards. Nor does it need to be considered in terms of influence, whether as emulation or as learning—the "Inc." of my first case. After all, only the composition in its barest outline is identical, as is the case for hundreds of Madonna paintings. Instead, the comparison can be shifted to the common term between the two paintings: identification. This term helps an assessment of the two paintings on the basis of the idea of allo-portraiture.

Let me bend over backward and start first with comparison on quantitative grounds of more or less. In Artemisia's work, the scene is more dynamic. Second, comparison in terms of the presence or absence of a feature stipulates a difference on the terms of the Orazio. In the Artemisia, the child is not cramped in the effort of feeding, nor is its gaze fixated on the source of satisfaction. With these two comparisons out of the way, we can move to a third kind of comparison, as analysis of relative difference. In Artemisia's painting, the relationship between the two figures is not primarily based on the combined

senses of taste and sight. Instead, it is entirely played out through the
sense of touch. Here, too, there are feet that come close to us, but the
closest are the mother's. The child does look at his mother, but not in
an exchange of looks. For, significantly, the mother closes her eyes.
The baby is actively touching his mother.

This leads to an assessment of how comparison can make visible
a difference that is not automatically bound up with judgment. This
touch, equivalent yet very different from Orazio's baby's tense activity, is the trigger of difference in this painting. The face, vaguely reminiscent of the almost generic face of the artist as it permeates both
artists' oeuvres, is primarily striking as a representation of bliss.
Moreover, the baby—older here—is actively exercising his capacity
to touch as a means of communication, beyond the anthropological
universality of the gaze on which Brilliant rests his case for the meaning of portraiture. On his own initiative, Artemisia's baby is establishing a relationship of physical love, perhaps seducing his mother.
But, whereas Orazio's painting is concentrated on the baby's fixating
gaze on his mother, here the focus of affect is the mother's quiet response. The resulting difference in mood is so striking that, for me, it
characterizes the two paintings in relation to each other, the one a
sharp expression of desire (Orazio), the other an equally intense expression of bliss. Two affect-images, painted in totally different
modes, yielding totally different effects and equally strongly affective.
The Madonna in Artemisia's painting savors the pleasure bestowed
on her. In terms of affect, then, this difference can be put even more
clearly in theoretical terms: in Artemisia's painting, the object of
identification *as* (the artist) is also the object of identification *with*.
This is how her painting is most convincingly an affect-image.

Many details contribute to this effect. First, the attractive flesh of
the baby—defined not in terms of its tender age but of the desire to
caress that it elicits—"explains" why being touched by this creature
is such a strong source of happiness. Second, the naturalism may be
less consistent than in Orazio's painting, but for that very reason it
contributes to the overall identificatory effect. For, in terms of naturalistic depiction, the most elaborated element is the right hand,

an excellent case for Garrard's argument in this volume. This hand holds the life-giving breast that has just satiated the child. But it is the same hand that paints in the *Self-Portrait as an Allegory of Painting*, that kills in the *Judith*, and that wards off the assailants in the early *Susanna*. In the latter painting, too, there is a gap between the forefinger and the middle finger.

It goes too far to project into this image a desire to assert the position of the artist as who she is; to identify her in the sense of ascribing an essential identity to her: that of a woman-artist, two aspects of her self that are bound, not separated, by a hyphen—a hyphen as "not-versus." This would be my own desire speaking. But the possibility of performing such a projection, on which Pollock has much to say in her contribution to this volume, is no less given by the painting than by all those other projections that subordinate this artist to that artist, daughter to father. If the baby's hand recalls simultaneously the feeding that allegedly just took place, the pleasure of the touch (the breast as erotic), the act of painting, and the act of self-defense, it sustains the function of the face. And that function is to solicit the bond between identification-*as* and identification-*with* that defines the allo-portrait.

Referring to a visual representation of the self as other, the concept of the allo-portrait raises more questions than it answers. Its virtue is that it reorients our questions. I find it important to heed that proposal for reorientation. For it is only if we do this that art from the past will come to life and inspire new ideas. The face we know, but only from already having seen it, solicits identification-*with* in the present of viewing. Hence the face becomes a critical tool to establish that primary relationship that makes art matter— the one between artwork and viewer. It can thus be put in the service of what I have called elsewhere a "preposterous history" (1999).

Catastrophe and Aesthetics

This last aspect—the primacy of the present of viewing in our intercourse with art—is the subject of my third and final case. Here, I wish to shift moods and take up an aspect of art that seems far removed from the pleasurable experience of seeing all those wonderful paintings that such momentous exhibitions as I have discussed so far invariably provide: social catastrophe. Indeed, that pleasure all but makes us forget that art can also offer a philosophically relevant analysis of important issues in the world. One such issue is violence. I broach this issue through a debate that is acutely present in contemporary thought on art, especially in the context of the Holocaust and of Adorno's alleged indictment of poetry "after Auschwitz" as "barbaric" (2003, 162). In its various formulations, Adorno's objection remains as paradoxical as it is valid. He argued that turning horror into beauty, far from being a civilized thing, is, indeed, barbaric (362–63).

Allegedly, art would destroy the civilized world, or at least be in collusion with that destruction, because it makes violence palatable, even risks making it pleasurable. The effect is the total obliteration of the violence. For there is no more radical way of erasing violence than to make something appealing out of it, thus mitigating it, giving it beauty, and, whether intentionally or unwittingly, redeeming it. It is important for this volume's attempt to connect art-historical with larger social-cultural concerns to realize that Adorno's original statement appears in the context of a rather savagely critical examination of what was later to become cultural studies: the progressive, critical study of culture—which is the context within which we propose this volume. And although some of Adorno's statements in this essay, "Cultural Criticism and Society," suggest that self-reflection is urgently necessary, he equally relentlessly points out the limitations of that activity: "Even the most radical reflection of the mind on its own failure is limited by the fact that it is only reflection, without altering the existence to which *its failure bears witness*" (160; emphasis added).

Within this last phrase resides the continuing relevance of Adorno's thoughts on post-Holocaust art for cultural reflection. Is it possible to deploy art not as reflection only, but as a form of witnessing that does alter the existence of what it witnesses?

It is at the end of this in-depth commentary on radical cultural critique that the famous indictment of poetry after Auschwitz first appears. In a later essay, devoted to what he calls "committed art," and in which he again primarily discusses literature, the issue is not *sense*, as in entry into acceptance or even redemption, but, plainly and disturbingly, *pleasure:* "The so-called artistic rendering of the naked physical pain of those who were beaten down with rifle butts contains, however distantly, the possibility that pleasure can be squeezed out from it" (252). The danger here, to put it bluntly, is akin to the effect of pornography. An effect that, one might think, is almost inevitably at stake in the representation of subjects that are themselves "about" the pornographic, or at least voyeuristic, effect.[10]

This context compels me to return briefly to the story of Susanna and the Elders and to Artemisia's most famous painting on that subject. For the presence of at least a hint of the pornographic effect is visible in the biblical story, where seeing the bathing Susanna entices the two men to decide to enforce intercourse on her. In relation to the theme of voyeurism, power-inequality and the social status of men and woman respectively are woven into the story in ways that affect the representations of it in painting—by definition, an act of making public. An important element of the story is the high social status of the two elders, public functionaries, in sharp contrast to Susanna, who is taking a bath in her private domain.[11]

The opposition between private and public is notoriously problematic. Nothing has made this more painfully clear than the abuse and rape of children by a family member. Perpetrators got away with this criminal practice for so long because the domain of privacy protected them instead of the children it should protect. Contemporary artists work to undermine this false and dangerous opposition. One such artist is the Colombian Doris Salcedo, who painstakingly preserves and integrates in her sculptures the traces of people who were victims of the civil war that rages in her country, but whose disappearance erased even their memories because they fell into the black hole of anonymity. There is no reason to deny that artists from the past also had an interest in the social consequences of the private-public boundary.

Like Salcedo's work, the story of Susanna sharpens the dilemma of whether a provisional endorsement of the distinction (not opposition) between private and public might not help rather than hinder the endeavor of making an aesthetic that addresses catastrophe work for today's culture. For art helps to break the wall between the private and public that protects the perpetrators of violence while erasing its victims. Aesthetics as a cultural attitude is inseparable from the notion of canon and canonicity. As has been argued by many, most prominently by Nanette Salomon and Griselda Pollock, the canon is less a mechanism for the selection of aesthetic excellence than it is a tool for exclusion. For the focus of this third case of comparison, it is primarily important to assess Artemisia's place in a preposterous history of art for the purpose of understanding some of her works as a paradigm for an aesthetics of catastrophe. This may well be the reason why both her *Judith*s and her *Susanna*s benefit today from so much critical attention.[12]

In view of the specific recasting of it in the work that constitutes my third case, I need to recall here the story of Susanna and the Elders that has been told by other authors in this volume. As she takes a bath in her private garden, two elders, each lusting after her, put their heads together. Indeed, as Salomon demonstrates in her contribution, Artemisia "saw" these heads as together. For only together, in collaboration, are they "able"—that is, culturally strong enough—to put the screws on her. They threaten to tarnish Susanna's public reputation for chastity if she does not yield. Astonishingly, she resists the attempted rape, and her life, which these two public officials threaten to stone out of her, is saved by the young Daniel. He exposes their lie by interrogating them separately. Break the cultural collaboration between men, and their strength melts away. No rape, no suicide. A pretty uplifting story.

As we know, Western art's first great heroine, Artemisia, was not so lucky. Her rape by the teacher appointed by her father, led to her torture in court. In 1998, two art works were produced and exhibited that tried to update this double myth: of Susanna and of

Artemisia; of threatened and exposed rape and of real but denied rape. Two catastrophes challenging the dividing line between private and public that made the crimes possible, thinkable, in the first place. One of these two contemporary works (the first a film, the second an exhibition) offers a solution to the double dilemma of comparing life and work, and of aestheticizing catastrophe.

As I see it, the first one, Agnès Merlet's feature film *Artemisia,* romanticizes the rape out of the story. Griselda Pollock discusses this film from a perspective quite different from mine. In my view, instead of representing the catastrophe of rape—and reassuringly for a culture that flaunts itself as "postfeminist"—Artemisia is technicolored in as a liberated young woman who acts on her own sexual impulses, a role model for today's middle-class girls who don't need one. Rape is edited out, in the spirit of the troublesome "postfeminist" parody of feminism fashionable today, which is fun-oriented and tired of complaining.[13]

Gentileschi's most direct and disturbing painting of the threat of sexual violence is, predictably, not used in the rape episode of the film. But, anachronistically from that perspective, her rapist is recast as a prefeminist teacher, in a scene that Germaine Greer might have staged in her 1979 book *The Obstacle Race.* Catastrophe is so firmly aestheticized that it disappears altogether from sight. In the face of the historical moment we are currently living, I contend that this "solution" must be firmly rejected. It puts history at risk of losing its cultural visibility, and puts aesthetics at risk of losing its affective, binding function.[14]

A "preposterous," willfully anachronistic comparison that can retrieve this aesthetic function may help to exorcise the demon of the kind of comparison that has turned this mode of argumentation into the curse of art. An instance of such a preposterous comparison is the third Artemisia exhibition I wanted to discuss in this chapter. In her work, New York artist Kathleen Gilje chooses to confront the dilemma of aesthetics and catastrophe head-on. Over a long period of more than a year, she copied Artemisia's harrowing *Susanna and the Elders* (fig. 40). Carefully paying homage—aes-

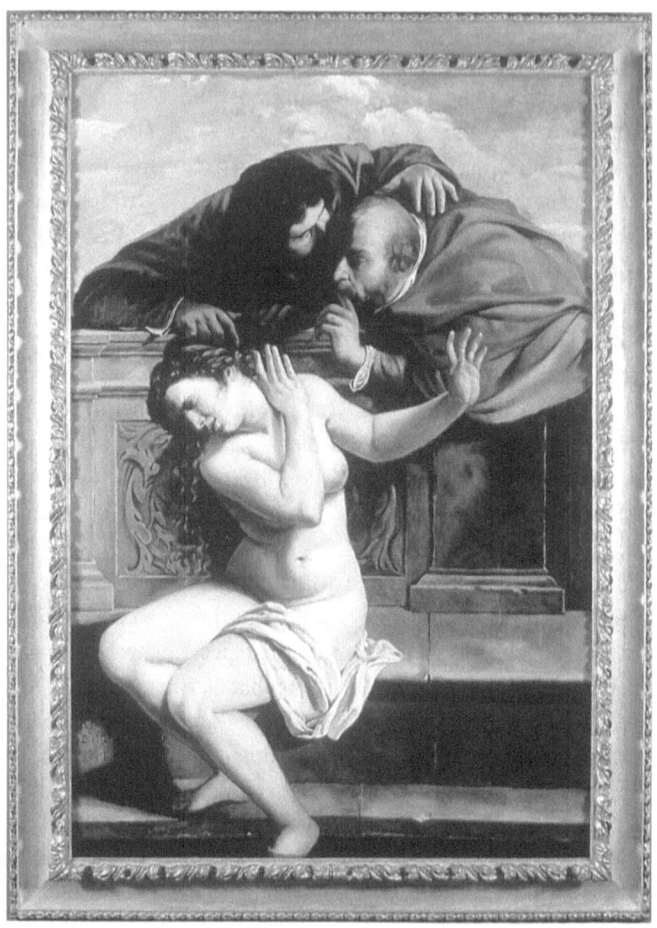

Figure 40. Kathleen Gilje, *Susanna and the Elders, Restored*, 1998. Oil on linen, 78 ×
58 in. (framed). New York, Gorney Bravin + Lee. (Courtesy of Kathleen Gilje.)

thetically—and attention—semiotically—to the aspects of this
work that make it successful as an aesthetic representation of catastrophe within the limits of public acceptability, Gilje, in her
work, performs two comparisons. First, by literally copying the
painting, she "quotes" it. Second, she "X-rays" it.[15]

Quotation is an important device that is frequently deployed in contemporary art to pay homage, revise, reinterpret, or critically engage art from the past. Gilje has quoted the entire painting. She thus re-emphasizes Artemisia's shallow depth, which confines Susanna's private space to a narrow band between water and stone. She quotes the overbearing closeness of the two threatening men looming over Susanna, signifying that Susanna's private space is only private as a limiting—not a protecting—space. The one slight change Gilje makes is to darken the white fragment of the younger elder's shirt—to bind the two men together even more, like a concrete wall that no one can break (fig. 41). Gilje thus appears to support Salomon's interpretation of this painting as abstract.

She also quotes the age difference between the elders, interpreted by many as an indication of what Artemisia was trying to depict with these two mythical figures. Artemisia's painting focuses on the collaborating men who engineered Susanna's vulnerability to rape—Artemisia's father and the somewhat younger Tassi. Hence the hand of the younger man pressing the older man into acceptance of the sacrifice required to keep the cultural order going. Unlike Merlet, whose update of Artemisia's and Susanna's story superficially aestheticizes the catastrophe out of it altogether, Gilje pays homage to Artemisia, who, in 1610, broached the issue of the predicament inscribed in the private/public divide. She creates aesthetically effective objects that violate the social order, so that the "uninterest" is chased out of disinterested contemplation.[16]

But simply to copy the older work would not be enough to make it work for today's culture. For, in keeping with the limits of public taste of her day, Artemisia was only able to go so far. She made the most of the cultural limitation put on an aesthetics of catastrophe in her own day, by "foreshortening" time. Foreshortening, as it is commonly understood, is a technique that can be used in the service of producing an illusion of three-dimensionality on a flat surface. It partakes of the perspectival rendering of space. Elsewhere, I have attempted to translate this term—the technique and its effects—into its temporal equivalent (forthcoming). In what Sa-

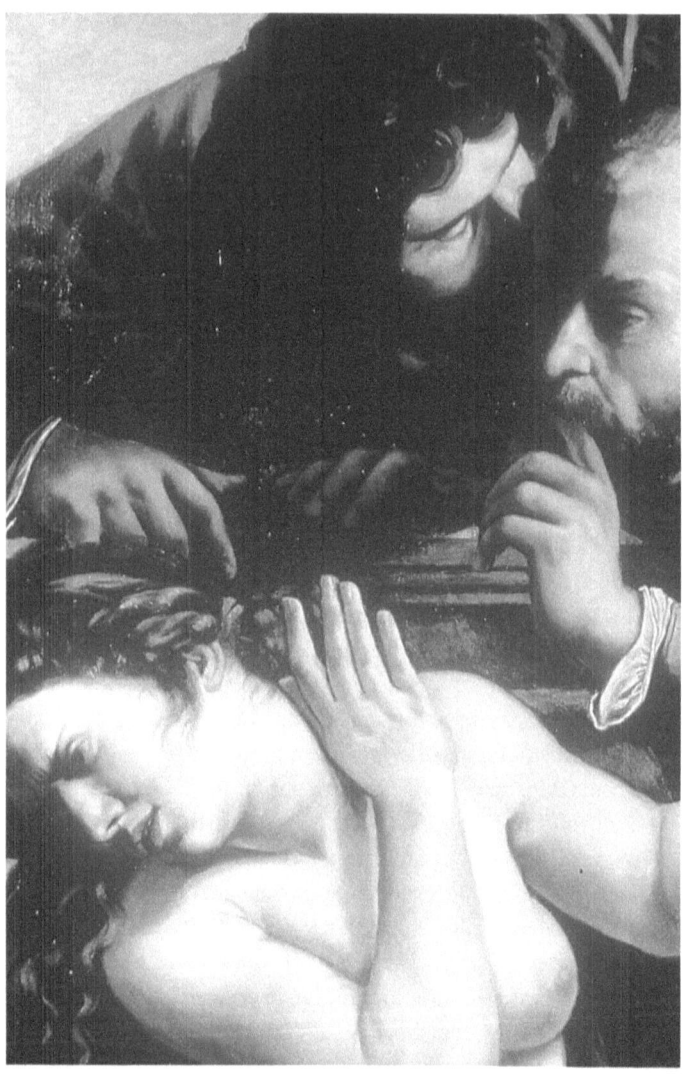

Figure 41. Kathleen Gilje, *Susanna and the Elders, Restored,* 1998. Oil on linen, 78 × 58 in. (framed). Detail of pentimento. New York, Gorney Bravin + Lee. (Courtesy of Kathleen Gilje.)

lomon calls a move toward abstraction, Artemisia narrows narrative time. Narrowing time, just as she narrows the band of private space, she presses the threat toward the rape, so that we as viewers experience the inevitable next step, soon to come, and share Susanna's moment of the instant dilemma: rape or death. But today, *after* public exposure to catastrophe in abundance, Gilje seems to have been aware that simply repeating history risks being both ineffective and dangerous.

She thus invokes a second comparison that works to protect the first comparison from misunderstanding. Using the tools of art history's scientific tradition but turning these upside down, Gilje gave her "restoration" of Artemisia's *Susanna* the by-now conventional treatment of X-ray examination, revealing the so-called *pentimenti*, corrections made by the artist (fig. 42). In the privacy of the indecent, unexposable underpainting, she "discovered" that underneath the contained scene, the moment of catastrophe itself appears. The two men actually physically attack the woman, the one pulling her head back by the hair, the other pressing her down so that she cries out in pain. The fictional painter's hesitation multiplies the number of hands, suggestive both of filmic movement (so utterly suppressed in Merlet's film) and, simultaneously, of the inescapable violence. The woman's arms almost stretch out in reminiscence of crucifixion, the classic emblem of martyrdom in Western culture.

Gilje refrains from recasting rape as sexual fulfillment and liberation, as happens in the disturbing conflation of pre- and postfeminist romanticizing—which throws the aesthetic baby out with the catastrophic bath water. Instead, this work—the underpainting and the overpainting together with the *pentimenti* shimmering through—*represents* the violence in its actuality, proposes its revenge by putting a dagger in this woman's hand, and *raises* the dilemma of repetition versus actualization, instead of resolving it in one direction or the other.

In the finished, "restored" painting, beautifully framed and ready to be objectified in a museum space, traces of what happened inside the allegedly private space remain visible. Viewers who are willing to

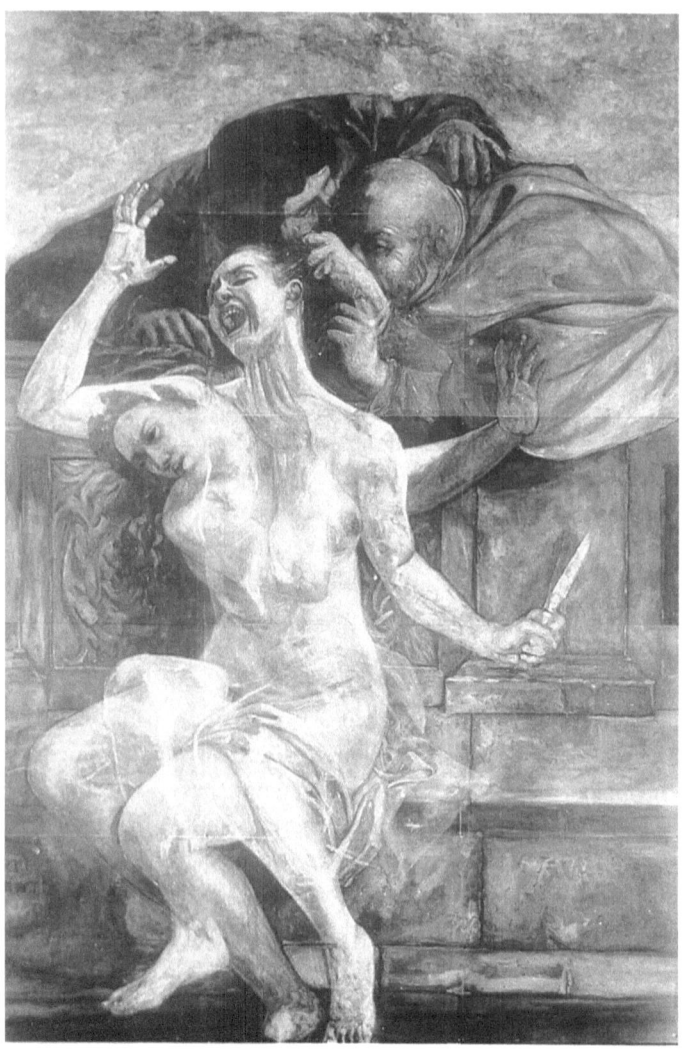

Figure 42. Kathleen Gilje, *Susanna and the Elders, Restored*, X-ray, 1998. 67 × 47 in. New York, Gorney Bravin + Lee. (Courtesy of Kathleen Gilje.)

engage the past within the present can detect, between the hands of the younger elder (Tassi?), the face of the African-American model, which comes through screaming in the underpainting, as if to compel us to realize that violence happening elsewhere, outside our own purview, still concerns us (fig. 42). That this mouth with its teeth recalls Caravaggio's *Medusa* seems to me a felicitous reminder that around 1600 gender trouble was already brewing on the horizon. Depicting his own face in the universal femme fatale/victim of violence, thus disturbing the categories we tend to rely on, this colleague of Artemisia's was, preposterously speaking, ahead of today's "postfeminist" culture. Putting his own subjectivity on the block— beheaded as a woman by a man in *Medusa,* as a man by a woman in *Judith,* and as an older man by a younger man in *David*—he no more refrained from aestheticizing catastrophe than Artemisia did. Both of these baroque artists played out their own subjectivity in their aesthetic works, so that the personal and the political had to merge, the private could no longer be ostensibly severed from the public, and catastrophe could neither be suppressed nor voyeuristically exploited. Here, comparison, across time, unexpectedly yields insight into a similarity otherwise unnoticeable.

Inspired by Gilje's work, I would like to end my essay with one last comparison. By making such aesthetic works, and despite all their historical and aesthetic differences, Gilje and Gentileschi share a common commitment. The thrust of their work is to bring aesthetics and catastrophe to bear on one another, so that each can enforce public participation in the other, and so that every attempt to recast aesthetics from the collective affective into the lightheaded domain of "taste" is stopped in its tracks. Our culture is not ready to forget catastrophe or to reduce aesthetics or political movements such as feminism to the flimsy alibi of "fun."

Exorcism

Like a homeopathic cure, then, comparison of one kind must be mobilized against comparison of another. One way to do this is to inquire about the structure of the comparison: What are its grounds, its standards, its directions? This is what I attempted in the first case, the comparison between Caravaggio and Artemisia. But chronology is an accident of history. The idea of a common ground—the emergent baroque in Rome—between the two artists does not automatically yield a standard, established so that the streamlining chronology becomes a question of influence. Although Caravaggio was "present" in Rome when Artemisia made her *Judith,* the almost systematic opposition between the two compositions suggests a relationship that the word "influence" can only obscure. Instead, comparison can also be performed in the opposite direction. Reversing the chronology "pre-posterously," we can use Artemisia's radically baroque composition and its viewer-oriented three-dimensionality to notice, as we might not have been able to before seeing her picture, how the blood spurts, and how the face of the victim in the Caravaggio also hails the viewer physically.

This last result of the reversed comparison guides us toward a second way of mobilizing comparison against itself. Taking the clue from Artemisia's viewer-oriented composition and generalizing its point, the second case, comparing Artemisia with her father, was premised on the affective relationship between viewer and painting. Putting that relationship first, and using the affect most frequently associated with visual imagery—namely, identification—to get a handle on that relationship, the dynamic of art itself, not the historical biographies of the artists, becomes the grounds for comparison. Its standard, then, is neither predetermined nor predicated on the banality of realism.

In Artemisia's *Madonna and Child,* realism is the tool for soliciting identification. And if in Orazio's painting the baby is the focus—hence, if the adult viewer becomes, for a short while, a feeding child—this is a more exciting experience than seeing naturalism yet again. For, in this painting, it is not such a deployment of realism that orients identification. In Artemisia's painting the emphasis is shifted from the baby to the mother's face, and the face as a site of identity is thus mobilized in ways it wasn't in

Orazio's painting. It is the scenography of the tactile and the mother's response to it. The issue is so different that only the ground of comparison, the relationship between painting and viewer, remains. Standards can be bracketed; judgment can be redundant. Art is what matters.

If the third case—Gilje's "restoration" of Artemisia's *Susanna*— holds the cure, it is because comparison is here both pushed to the extreme of simulacrum and made redundant by a turning within. The painting is compared to its fictional self, the *pentimenti* that Artemisia did not make. These imaginary changes seem to mock art-historical method. They also assert that each work of art is unique—not because of romantic exultation but because each moment in history creates its own interaction with the canonical works of art we cherish but from which comparison distracts us. Artemisia, more than any other artist, has been obscured by comparison. This volume offers an attempt to counter that effect of this primary tool of art history. This countering is not meant to eliminate comparison but to reorient it. Instead of an instrument of judgment, it becomes a source of differentiation.

FEMINIST DILEMMAS WITH
THE ART/LIFE PROBLEM

Griselda Pollock

"None of it's true, of course. But it's still an interesting film," I said.

"Does that matter?" she replied. "Do you really believe in historical truth?"

"Well, there has to be some accountability to the historical record, doesn't there?" I asked, "Even if I know that archives themselves are selective and, dare I say it, already historically overdetermined?"

"History doesn't exist," she retorted. "We just tell ourselves stories. They must meet some criteria of plausibility. But the real question is How is this or that story valuable, and for whom?"

This brief exchange is typical of the conversations I found myself having with other feminist art historians about Agnès Merlet's dramatic biopic based on the "case" of Artemisia Gentileschi (1593–1652/3) titled simply, typically, and yet, with some historical justification, *Artemisia* (France, 1997). Taking Merlet's biopic as a starting point for several interrelated arguments about the troubled relations between an artist's life and work, between biography and

art, fact and fiction, history and truth, document and text, I want
to revisit both the fictions of the artist, Artemisia Gentileschi, created in and by art history, literature, and film on the one hand and,
on the other, the recent legal-historical studies of the infamous rape
trial. I do this in order to stress what I propose as an ethics of reading rather than a politics of truth.

The article, therefore, argues with, and at times against, feminist
critiques of Merlet's film for its radical "distortion" of the "truth" of
the key event, the rape of the painter by her teacher, an "event" that
has figured in the literature on the Artemisia Gentileschi as the
defining "fact" from which interpretation of her work has stemmed
in diverse directions since the middle of the nineteenth century.
But I also want to challenge the new historicist readings of the legal
evidence in this case, which entirely dismiss from the study of
Artemisia Gentileschi the concept of rape in our modern understanding of a sexual violation of the body that has traumatic psychological effects on the subject. Reading for the historically and
culturally specific social conventions and value systems in which
premarital sexual assault was framed and its selves discursively
fashioned through testimony in the seventeenth century, new historicists practice a mode of reading [the trial transcripts as] texts
rather than using [the trial documents as unmediated] evidence.
Yet new historicist writers still claim a *truth* status for their *readings*
of the historical-legal texts.

These new historicists, with all their unresolved questions about
the historically accessible register of subjectivity and embodiment,
are then mobilized by revisionist art historians studying the Gentileschis, Orazio and Artemisia, to discount as completely anachronistic feminist interpretations of Artemisia Gentileschi's life and
work as a site of a feminine subjectivity subjected to patriarchal violence. I consider *feminist desire* for ethical narratives that function
in our present moment of encounter with paintings and their inherited framings, and seek also to maintain a theoretical self-
awareness of the ethics of my situated reading.[1]

Thus, I shall play back across the new historicist debate an analysis of the first fictional response to the Italian painter in the novel, *Artemisia*, published in 1947 by the art historian Anna Banti. Following other scholars, I argue that this complex piece of fictional memory work is an exemplary text in its self-critical engagement with its own desires, projections, and identifications, as well as in its acceptance, by means of its own fictional strategies, of the resistance and otherness of history, and the "absence" or recalcitrance of the historical "Artemisia Gentileschi." Yet the novel makes the case that thinking about the historically lived lives of women artists such as Artemisia Gentileschi does matter for women now. It is a necessary if challenging part of a contemporary, critical self-fashioning of feminine subjectivity and creativity.

Returning from this dual investigation into the problematic status of the historical "truth" and the strategic modes of dealing with the complexity of its absence, I ask of Agnès Merlet's film, the first full-length, fictional film about this archive: What is the discourse of this film? Merlet's film either radically distorts a historically verifiable fact, that is, the rape of Artemisia Gentileschi—such has been the feminist critique of the movie—or it offers a particular, interested and even possible "reading" of a series of equivocal texts, namely, paintings, legal documents, and existing art histories, in order to acknowledge female sexuality and desire as the defining feature of this corpus figured through its author. Thus we need to consider if Merlet's cinematic reading can be defended as a film for addressing the scandal of a woman's desire, starting from the alleged evidence of seventeenth-century paintings saturated with an intense corporeality and sense of the ambiguities of sexuality, desire, and violence. The key question to be posed to this much-contested representation of an artist and her work is this: Does the film text merely rehearse an inherited *mythos* about gender and creativity, or does it transform and displace it? I conclude that, in the end, this brave but conventional piece of cinema, unlike Banti's radically self-critical work of fiction, fails to find a semiotically critical means of evading the collapse of femininity, sexuality, and cre-

ativity into the mythic norm of feminine submission to masculinity, the woman artist to the phallus.

The Film and Its Critics

What place does Agnès Merlet's film have in our present speculations about art history, cultural analysis, and "Artemisia Gentileschi" as the site name of images, histories, texts, debates, readings, cases, arguments, fantasies? The film *Artemisia* was first
released in France in 1997 and elsewhere in 1998 (fig. 43). It starred
Valentina Cervi as Artemisia Gentileschi, Michel Serrault as the
artist's father, Orazio Gentileschi, and Miki Manojlovic as Agostino
Tassi, her father's collaborator, the artist's perspective tutor, and her
convicted rapist. The film was the French director's third feature
film, and its making was inspired by Merlet's own discovery of the
work of Artemisia Gentileschi in art history classes at the university
she attended during the 1980s. The film influenced what was at the
time the very recent feminist reclamation of Artemisia Gentileschi
from relative obscurity in the canonical story of art. Nominated for
the Golden Globe Award for Best Foreign Language Film in 1998,
Merlet's *Artemisia* received mixed critical acclaim. It was praised for
its vivid evocation of the seventeenth-century Roman art world.
Such endorsement was tempered by others who found the film flat,
unintelligent, and predictable as a historical romance despite its
breathtakingly gorgeous colors and compelling acting. In feminist
art historical circles, however, Agnès Merlet's treatment of the Italian painter generated considerable controversy, if not outright condemnation.

At the U.S. premiere of *Artemisia* on April 28, 1998, in New York,
Gloria Steinem and other women in the audience circulated a fact
sheet prepared by Steinem and the art historian Mary Garrard, the
leading expert on this artist and author of the major feminist analysis of Artemisia Gentileschi (see Garrard 2003). They challenged
the film's representation of the artist's life. This led Miramax to
withdraw the claim that the film was a "true story": a claim that ap-

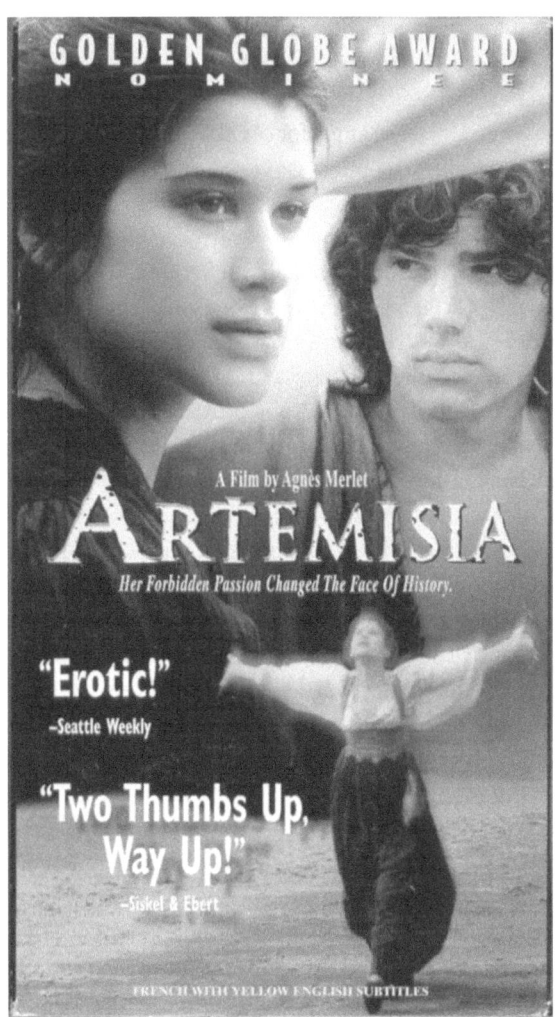

Figure 43. Poster for Agnès Merlet's film *Artemisia*, 1997.

peared on a poster that still blazons these epithets for its epony-
mous heroine: "sexy, provocative, defiant." On one feminist art history Internet discussion list, contributors encouraged women all
over the United States to apply for copies of this leaflet and to picket
the film's screenings. Its title was "Now You've Seen the Film, Meet
the Real Artemisia Gentileschi."

There was a symposium on the controversy held in New York,
addressed by Mary Garrard and Simon Schama, and an exhibition
at the Richard Feigen Gallery where one could, postcinematically,
view a dozen or so paintings by its major characters: Artemisia
Gentileschi; her father, Orazio; and Agostino Tassi. In July 1998,
Sotheby's New York auctioned one of Artemisia's presumed self-
portraits. All this contributed to an unusual and heated interaction
between cinema and the art world.

The key reason that Agnès Merlet's film has fallen foul of its potential feminist audience is her representation of the relationship
between the young painter and her older perspective-in-painting
tutor, Agostino Tassi. What has been largely viewed and argued
over as a rape that took place in May 1611 and was brought to trial
in March 1612, and for which Tassi was sentenced, is presented in
the film as an understandably distressing but desired defloration
within the context of a powerful sexual and intellectual attraction
between the young woman and the older man.

This "event"—the rape and the subsequent trial of Tassi—has
become central to the literature on Artemisia Gentileschi, either
trailing after her as salacious notoriety or rendering her a heroic
survivor of a traumatic violation. The whole axis of interpretation
of the painter's work has rested upon this violent and traumatic life
event, apparently leaving its indelible trace in choice of subject
matter and energetic engagement with images of sex, violence, and
female vulnerability that characterize her painted oeuvre (Cohen
2000, 47). To change the script, however, as radically as Merlet
seems to do by imagining the artist as a desiring sexual partner un-
willingly torn from her lover by her father's intervention and the

trial potentially changes the image of the artist whose personality and experience are typically taken to be the source of the meanings of her work in the typically limited expressive or reflective readings of the oeuvre.

Merlet's film is a costume drama that claims to be a filmic biography. Naming its subject by a known historical figure, carefully representing costume, sites, and the making of dated paintings, it presents its cinematically visualized narrative "picture" to the viewer as a window onto a historical moment, bringing to life the paper characters of art history's chronologies and documents. But perhaps we would be better off to read this film instead as a secondary reflection by one creative woman about another. It must be read intertextually at that level, bringing into view contemporary pressures and interests staged through its making in the 1990s, in which "Artemisia Gentileschi" becomes a contested site for definitions of gender and creativity. It is also intertextual in relation to a series of cinematic investigations into artistic biography and creativity that have given us biopics about Van Gogh, Gauguin, Michelangelo, Caravaggio, and Picasso, to name a few.

But what makes it important to consider the film's place in relation to the art histories of Artemisia Gentileschi that are contemporaneous with its making—that is, of the later twentieth and early twenty-first century—is precisely what Merlet's reading offers as such a radical dissent. Is it merely "wrong" on the basis of "evidence" to change a rape into a love affair? Or is it an act of daring to address the body of work from another angle that, given the rhetorical and political structure of sexuality, and the legal management of marriage and rape in seventeenth-century Rome, may be just as possible a reading of the still undecidable "evidence"? A lot is at stake for both feminist studies, art history, and perhaps what "Artemisia Gentileschi" as fiction of the artist and as author-name of a series of paintings might mean for us. In this article, therefore, I address both fictions of the artist and the legal histories of her case to stress an ethics of reading rather than a politics of truth.

Myth, Fiction, Gossip, and Sex(ism)

The reason for Artemisia Gentileschi's persistent bad press in art history was sex, and the sexism of its later interpretations (Wittkower and Wittkower 1963). Artemisia Gentileschi alleged that she was raped in her own room in May 1611 by a colleague of her father's, Agostino Tassi, an innovative, outdoor sea-painter and collaborator with Orazio on a major fresco series in Rome. Tassi was hired to teach Artemisia the complex rules of perspective: a new way of organizing a seen world on the canvas. In March 1612, significantly ten months later, the artist's father, Orazio, brought a suit against Tassi for raping his daughter, procuring, and the theft of a painting. The latter two charges were ignored.

There was a lengthy legal proceeding in which, as an expected part of the process, Artemisia was tortured by the *sibille*—fine cords wound around the fingers and progressively tightened, causing potentially permanent damage to the fingers. According to one historian, this "ritualised pain" served to strengthen her evidence, which was otherwise devalued as that of a dishonored woman (Cohen 2000, 59). In the no-holds-barred cut and thrust of accusation and counter-accusation typical of Roman lawsuits in this period, each witness made further accusations and self-justifications. Tassi was also accused of the murder of his wife and incest with his young sister-in-law.

He was, we now know because of novelist Alexandra Lapierre's extensive research, convicted of the rape of Artemisia Gentileschi, but because of his wife's existence, he could not make amends by offering marriage and a dowry, and he was sentenced to five years' banishment (Lapierre 2000, 411). He seems merely to have moved a few kilometers out of Rome for a while. Within a year, his sentence was annulled through his powerful patrons. We have the transcript of the trial depositions and investigations, a sordid record in which the married Tassi alleged that Artemisia was sexually active before and after his contact with her and that he never had sex with her. Her defense was that he had promised marriage after the rape, during which she had wounded him and thrown a dagger at his chest, drawing blood. So how can we reconcile what appears to be a form of legal evidence concluding that there was a rape with the narrative exploration of the event offered in this film? What are its ethics as well as its politics?

Perhaps history should be understood as a domain of transference, projection, and fantasy that tells us more about ourselves, the dreamers, than about those about whom we do this projective and often identificatory dreaming. There is a growing industry in fictions about artists—novels and films about paintings and their painters. In the last few years, I have read novels about Vermeer's *Girl with the Pearl Earring,* by Tracy Chevalier (2000); about his painting *The Allegory of Painting,* by Susan Vreeland, *The Girl in Hyacinth Blue* (1999); one about Mary Cassatt's paintings of her dying sister Lydia, and at least two about Artemisia Gentileschi: *The Passion of Artemisia* (2002) by Susan Vreeland, and the major research work *Artemisia: The Story of a Battle for Greatness* (2000) by Alexandra Lapierre. These works use the recent documentary research by scholars, or in Lapierre's case, the author herself, to provide a framework around which to weave the substance of the novelistic construction of personalities for otherwise shadowy historical personae: the feelings, words, and daily experience of characters in paintings, or of artists for whom we have none of the modernist tools of access such as diaries, personal letters, memoirs, photo-albums, or anecdotes in contemporary accounts.

Furthermore, in recent historical scholarship we find a new kind of microhistory being practiced that reads documents as texts to learn about the everyday experience of ordinary people that is not usually recorded in the official archives used in traditional historical research. So are these novelists and filmmakers merely the grosser symptoms of a relentless contemporary hunger for gossip and the everyday, or are they creating images of the artist that are as much part of the archive of "art" as the official evidences and the works themselves? Is the myth of the artist mythic in the sense of being untrue or in the sense of be-ing exemplary of cultural narrative and desire?

The *Kunstlerroman* and a Feminist Intervention, 1947

This spate of novels about art and artists joins a long-established tradition of the *Kunstlerroman* (the artist novel) that dates back to the Romantic period in Europe or even to the foundations of art history in Giorgio Vasari's *The Lives of the Most Eminent Painters, Sculptors, and Architects,* his multivolume history of the art of his time that elaborated biographies of his famous contemporaries as the means to understand art (Vasari 1912–15).[2]

The novelistic refashioning or fictionalization of the life of Artemisia Gentileschi began in 1947 with a structurally innovative novel by Anna Banti (fig. 44), the writing pseudonym of Lucia Lo-presti (see Banti 1995; see also Cannon 1994, 233–41). It was written by an art historian turned writer, who was married to the Italian art historian Roberto Longhi, writer of the first published scholarly ar-ticle on Artemisia Gentileschi (Longhi 1916). Banti's novel *Artemisia* attains both a literary and historiographical interest by a profound self-reflexivity that marks it off from the recent attempts fictively to recreate an accessible historical past and show us Artemisia Gen-tileschi in flesh and blood.

Anna Banti's novel opens in the summer of 1944 as the author-narrator sits sobbing in her nightdress amidst the ruins of Florence, partially destroyed by the retreating Nazis. Along with the bridges and other parts of the old city, Lopresti's home was blown up, and with it her hundred-page manuscript on the life of the then little-known Italian painter Artemisia Gentileschi. The novel is written in its narrator's present tense, and her writing becomes the site of a transaction between the lost manuscript, the lost "artist" created in that manuscript, the author's mourning for both, and her reflec-tions through her own "research" on the perennial question for the "modern" woman writer/thinker/artist about how to reconcile so-cial models of femininity regarding love, marriage, and the domes-

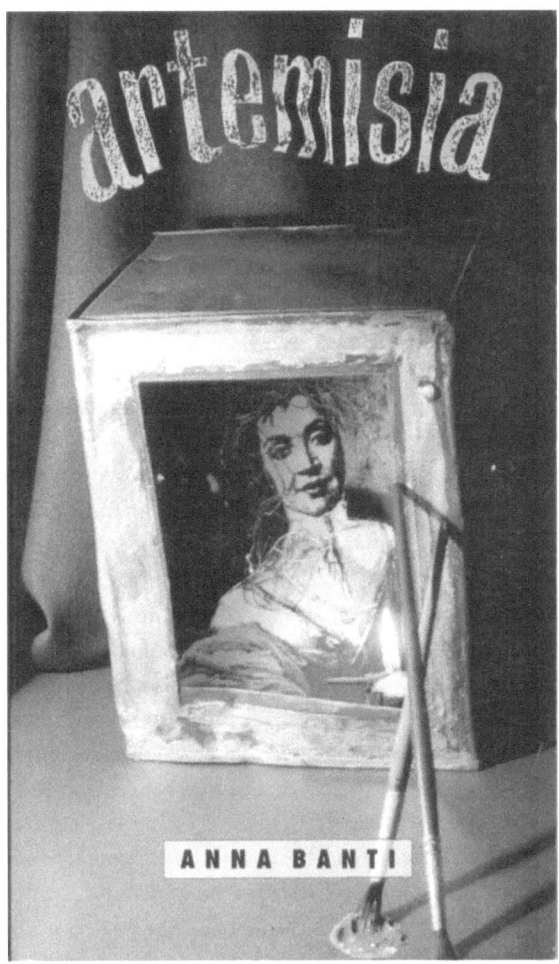

Figure 44. Cover illustration for Anna Banti's 1947 novel, *Artemisia*.

tic persona with the drives of creative intellectuality. As JoAnn
Cannon writes in her subtle analysis of this text,

> Banti here acknowledges that her text does not represent the dis-
> covery of a lost, authoritative, true account of Artemisia's life.

> Rather it is a revision of patriarchy's "reading" of the life of an ex-
> ceptional woman. The author's nostalgia for the lost manuscript
> allegorizes the notion of a story to be found in history. By relin-
> quishing that nostalgia, the author narrator recognizes the illusory
> nature of such a notion of history. (1994, 332)

Cannon further explains, "Banti's novel sets forth both the dilemma of the woman artist and of the writer of a woman's life" (332). She thus introduces a specifically gendered dimension to the act of a woman writing about a woman's life, which must deal both with transforming an inherited genre of artistic biography and also with the specific weight that the meaning any life of another woman might have for the writer in her own predicament under "patriarchy." The complex relations between writer and subject, present and history, might be called, in LaCapra's use of the Freudian term, transference (LaCapra 1996). But that would be an unconscious identification. Or we might think of it with Hayden White, as Cannon does, as something akin to what I name through the theoretically incorrect neologism, *feminist desire* (Pollock 1999). Cannon cites White: "A specifically historical enquiry is born less of necessity to establish that certain events occurred than of the *desire* to determine what certain events might mean for a given group, society or culture's conception of its present tasks and future prospects" (1994, 333). In these comments, I note two different elements. One concerns the general problem of historical study that is launched from the present for the present's purposes. The other concerns the fact that the project is different for feminism.

The scattered and fragmented past of women, irregularly recorded in, or frankly erased from, the archives and largely ignored in each culture's desire to build its present and future upon a selectively created, male-biased history, is reinvented precisely because of the pain of its *absenting*. This missing support for contemporary feminine subjectivities and identities becomes politicized in the struggle to understand current structures of gender and sexual difference that are shaped by culture's active erasure of women from what it uses as its self-defining histories.

Thus, not only the archive of paintings and documents, but also the "story" of Artemisia Gentileschi spoke to Lucia Lopresti, a young, twentieth-century art historian discovering this hitherto unknown woman artist of the seventeenth century through the scholarly researches of her older husband as she struggled with her own sense, as a writer, of the compromises of Italian women's lives in the mid-twentieth century. In saying this, I am not placing Lopresti's life transparently before her own writing, making her novel semi-autobiographical. My interpretation is a reading of her novel's knowing structure of dialogic voices, which formally establishes the desiring first-person narrator, who is interrupted from time to time by another interrogative voice, a spectral "Artemisia" of the writer's own creating in the lost biographical study. Most significantly, the novel is structured by an invented relation between these two fictive feminine subjects that, while it tells the story of the historical events between Artemisia, her father, Tassi and others, refocuses the novel's discourse on the writer's desire for self-knowledge through imaginary exchanges with this feminine alter ego—the Other as Woman (Artist).

By self-reflexively creating a novel form for the invention of feminine subjectivities in play across the gaps of time, Banti, the novelist, further poses what she sensed as pressing questions that she could not otherwise articulate or negotiate. The novel dramatized and rendered speakable through its apparent structure of quest and loss questions about being a woman and being an artist that seemed at odds in the culture of the writer's present and which were mirrored, if differently, by another moment of encounter between femininity and creativity signified by the site "Artemisia Gentileschi." Thus "Artemisia" emerges from the text as also embroiled in this conflict; the ideological bent of the novel is created by the persona of "Artemisia," the allegorical personification of a split femininity. Such conflicted identity, however, recurring across centuries, then appears to become endemic for women, installing the tragedy of a divided femininity at the heart of both the archive and the modern feminine subject.

In her reading of the novel, JoAnn Cannon sees in the allegorization of the woman artist in Banti's work a "rhetoric of uncertainty" that makes her novel very different from the trope of the classic masculine life: a story of progressive achievement, triumph, and recognition of genius.[3] Banti manages to hold open the space between the created figure of "Artemisia," who articulates, through a scripted inner monologue, constant inner doubts and is hurt by the continuing slights she receives from patrons and other artists, and the paintings that, in contrast, are read as the signs of a determined and assertive creative agency. Using the device of imagining women viewers for the paintings as they are being made in Gentileschi's studio, Banti installs yet another feminine subject position: the readers, diversified, shifting over time, receivers of what has been deposited in the paintings in ways that they will in turn into something for themselves. "By focussing on the public perception of the painting, Banti invites each member of the artist's public, including the reader, to attend to the significance of Artemisia's work" (Cannon 1994, 337).

Cannon makes a further point. Banti understands "that the life story of the female artist matters." It is this simple: of the painting *La Pittura,* painted in England (dated now to 1638–39), which is a formal allegory of Painting thought to bear a resemblance to the features of its painter, Banti writes, "Whether it is a self-portrait or not, a woman who paints in sixteen hundred and forty is very courageous, and this counts for Annella, and for at least a hundred others, right up to the present. 'It counts for you too,' she concludes, by the light of a candle, in this room rendered gloomy by war, a short, sharp sound. A book has been closed, suddenly" (1995, 199).

Laura Benedetti reads Banti's novel as the site of its author's anguished and unresolved struggle as a writer: Artemisia is "an ideal precursor, torn apart by the same contradictions and struggles." But she also notes that the author "did not lose sight of the risks implicit in collapsing past into present." Thus the novel textually produces an Artemisia resisting the narrator's desire, "jealous of her individuality and sceptical of the narrator's chances of success" (1999, 59). It is this internalization within its own textual procedure of a monitory "voice" impersonated by the other woman—the histories of women—that the text desires to explore. It then radically marks the gap between Banti's modernist engagement with the archive and the postmodernist collapse into uncritical fictional reconstructionism that presents itself transparently, unmarked as a text, through the lure of cinematic or novelistic realism.

The Ethical and the Historical:
Feminist Time and the Question of Rape

Given the centrality of the rape to the negotiation of the complex meanings that "Artemisia" as a historic and a fictional image of woman as creative artist proffers, we need to be warned indeed against what Foucault might define as the "monumentalization" of rape; that is, against the attempt to render it ahistorically invariable, whereas it is a historically variable, even possibly nonpertinent, category for the past. Recent feminist research into the history of sex and the law in seventeenth-century Rome opens onto a complex field of patriarchal management of sexual transgression. This management operates within the maintenance of family honor and property that barely concerns the individualistic or psychological issues that characterize twentieth century discourses. Some feminist microhistorians of the seventeenth century challenge the clear–cut notion of the 1611–12 rape and trial on the grounds that early modern society's concepts of sexuality, the body, identity, and the family were very different from modern psychological definitions of the same array. The key word *rape* may not work here. They warn us of anachronistic transference. Yet it is an easy step from their caution to recent art historians' wholesale dismissal of any feminist concern with the issue of rape and this archive.

None of the argument about the social organization of sexuality is new to feminists primed by Gayle Rubin's founding text of femi-

nist anthropology, "The Traffic in Women" (1975). Rubin identified
what she calls the sex-gender system. Society is defined by the system of exchange within which women are trafficked between men
as a foundational mode of social-cultural organization: woman as
objects of exchange establish the networks of sociality between the
male exchangers. Knowing that sex-gender is a structure of social
management does not diminish its subjective effects or its cost,
however, and Rubin significantly elaborated her Lévi-Straussian
analysis of woman as object of exchange with a psychoanalytical
reading of how these social rules are installed in subjects, who are
subjectivized as the bearers and sufferers of these hierarchies. Thus
feminist research in this area, using structuralism or Foucault's
more recent studies of the history of sexuality, has always sought to
balance the structural and its subjectivities in order to hold in view
the pathos of patriarchy for women whose subjectivities are precisely sacrificed to their role as the bodily currency of exchange between men.

    Rape was, in seventeenth-century Italy as now, classified as
forcible, nonconsensual sexual assault. Historians have argued that
it was also used as a technical crime to force a marriage or to claim
damages when a higher-class man abused a socially vulnerable
woman. Clearly there are different ways to argue the case based on
different kinds of evidence. Taking the transcript of the Agostino
Tassi trial in conjunction with other rape-trial transcripts of the period researched by Elizabeth Cohen and other feminist scholars
produces an "event" whose surface—accusations, proof of defloration through blood, assertions of resistance through crying out or
attempting to wound the assailant—reveals a pattern, or a recurrent legal formalization of the crime and the evidence expected by
the courts. Reading these texts in their historical specificity as le-
galizing discourse shaping in its own terms the forever unknowable
experience of the witness and plaintiffs, it would be possible to de-
dramatize the "rape" of Artemisia Gentileschi.

    As the event comes before the Papal court, its discursive presen-
tation apparently conforms to social patterns that all attest to the

priority given to the *status* of the woman's virginity in the social exchanges that defined relations of family honor, property, and social
identity through the preservation of the intactness of the "house."
Here "house" means both the actual domestic space and the family's name. The body of the virgin daughter kept safe indoors before
being legally trafficked in marriage is both a literal entity and a socially communicable signifier of that honor.

Elizabeth Cohen argues that the spaces of "respectable" femininity were the convent or the home, interiors within which
women's sexuality and socially productive labor were regulated by
heads of families or the church (Cohen 2000). Yet I would argue
that the law courts, which deal with crimes and complaints, are precisely the site and sign of the irregular that is judged against an ide-
alized regularity, which is itself revealed by the judicial process as always vulnerable to pressures for change or resistances inherent in
any exercise of authority.

Writing of a specific nineteenth-century familial social system,
Michel Foucault defined what he named "sexuality" as an especially
dense transfer point for relations of power between men and
women, young and old people, parents and offspring, teachers and
students, priests and laity, an administration and a population. By
this Foucault means that because the body can be subjected to social usage and management, we, whose bodies constitute this in-
strumentalized socio-sexual space, can become susceptible to social and political authorities who determine the proper uses, places,
pleasures, and abuses of the body. In so far as we are in our bodies,
and our bodies are considered socially significant as laborers, pro-
ducers of children, and sites of property exchange, we are subjected,
subjectified, through these transactions and the languages in which
they are couched (Foucault 1976).

But these formal inscriptions and practices do not exhaust either subjectivity or its embodied processes. Neither is the statement
of authoritative regulation proof that power was exercised over
them. Rather, as Foucault argues, power is a contingent effect of
what it then re-presents as resistance or recalcitrance. It is the play,

the pressures, and the irregularities that call forth the attempted regulation, exposing the body and person to power effects. The trial is one such site of the workings of power in all its messiness and resistances.

The new historians, who wish to argue against feminists for introducing "sexuality" and subjectivity into the rape and trial of Artemisia Gentileschi, want to insist on the legal process at face value. They want to deny that patriarchal regulation of women regarded merely as sites of men's negotiations of their honor and property is always an act of epistemic violence as well as, often, an act of actual physical or sexual violation. Elizabeth S. Cohen reads the trial documents as cultural texts across which a "self" was fashioned in relation to systems of words and social conventions and values. She argues against personal traumatization of the rape victim, suggesting that a general cultural acceptance of masculine authority in the seventeenth century made this violence "normal": the "crime of rape had less resonance. What the modern world calls rape was for early modern Italy a number of legal and social offences" (Cohen 2000, 67). Why is it necessary, however, while activating the power of social definition, to diminish all possibility of trauma associated with its defamation and to disavow all subjective dimensions of sexual embodiment? That we, in the early twenty-first century, have politicized the issues of rape, marital rape, and domestic violence is not to say it did not exist as a brutal and violating experience before we raised it to the level of actual politics. But before the late twentieth century there was no political pressure from a women's movement to turn women's resistance to this perpetual violence into cultural acknowledgement sufficient to create new legal regulation.

In her book *Images of Rape,* covering the medieval and early modern period, Diane Wolfthal carefully sifts through a range of textual and visual evidence and concludes that we can rediscover the voices of historical victims of rape and of women who attest to a subjective experience: fear of male assault and trauma at its occurrence. Contesting Roy Porter's famous dismissal that rape was not on the minds of preindustrial women, Wolfthal quotes Margery Kempe's account of her almost nightly fears of being violated, which caused her to feel safe only when she had several other women in her bed with her as protection. Wolfthal quotes Christine de Pizan, who describes rape as "the greatest possible suffering." Wolfthal notes that women are regularly represented in medieval images as struggling to get free, trying to get away, pulling their assailant's hair. She asks why women feared rape. She concludes that not only were they afraid of the act itself, but they dreaded the repercussions, which included injury, death, unwanted pregnancy and the risks associated with it, emotional scarring, and, of course, loss of reputation (Wolfthal 1999, 127).

Following Mieke Bal's model of "hysterics," reading for the victim, even at the risk of what Bal names an ethical anachronism (Bal 1991, esp. 60–93), Wolfthal refuses the binary opposition of modernist psychological trauma versus a historical sense of purely social damage claimed by historians such as Elizabeth Cohen, who opposes the concepts of the psychologically interiorized self allegorized by the vulnerable body and the socially constructed persona with a weaker bond to her own body (Cohen 2000, 65). Why would the loss of *social being* be any less traumatizing than the loss of personal integrity if the terms offered by a culture for one's identity bind modes of subjectivity to social sanction, often with real economic effects? Women have killed themselves over the violation of their social honor just as they have done so because of feelings of sexual contamination. If subjectivity is always intricately constructed in culturally available imaging and discourse, the transactions between the subject and the culture are always open to traumatic effects, which are not the specialty of the modern bourgeois subject alone. The figure of *Lucretia*, also painted by Artemisia Gentileschi and her contemporaries, remains the representational site of this cultural conviction (Bal 1991).

In this debate, seventeenth-century painting itself repeatedly places the stories of sex and violence before our eyes, our psyches, and bodies through vividly embodied forms where we have to read bodily posture and facial gesture in the lurid realism of Caravaggistic painting from a living model, posed theatrically before the painter in embodied translation of a literary, theological, or philosophical text. The Susannas who anxiously clutch inadequate coverings around their vulnerable nakedness as elderly men ogle with intent, the Lucretias who leap naked from the rapist's couch to plunge daggers in their bared breasts figure the culture's texts on sexual violation of women by men in terms of extremely vivid artistic conjuring of the body, physical violence, and emotional anguish.

Artemisia Gentileschi was one of the major Caravaggisti, an artist who looked closely at bodies, posed them to convey intensity of fraught emotion, pathos, determination, and suffering as well as the capacity to inflict a visibly carnal violence. Indeed, if we start with the paintings, rather than arguing about their author's imagined state of mind via the highly contentious legal documents, we might have to ask ourselves why these paintings so heighten the stakes of subjectivized and incorporated drama through every Caravaggist technique: lighting, realism, blood, pressed flesh, furrowed brow, deathly pallor. What else is the baroque but an intensified artistic technology of embodiment and subjectivity?

The Scandal of Woman's Desire

The radical moment in our recent history of "sexuality," or the sex-gender system, could be, as Jane Flax (2001) has argued, in the posing of the question that is never contemplated in this structure: What does a woman want? In Freud's notorious question, often used to berate the old man for not knowing the answer, we must hear, Jane Flax argues, the truly scandalous, the unheard of: the acknowledgment of women's desire, of a feminine subjectivity that had, we might say, never counted for anything with regard to matters of family, honor, property, and social exchange that constitute a patriarchal, phallocentric society.

The question of a subjectivity for a feminine subject bearing the name "Artemisia Gentileschi" across the archive that records the rhetoric of a Roman papal court hearing a case brought by a father is not to be dismissed by arguing that the "evidence" relieves us of the need to imagine the events—the sexual assault and its public examination in a trial—as subjectively traumatic. How traumatic they were or were not for Artemisia Gentileschi is irrecoverable. We must not posit our novelistic projections as the cause of her paintings or our readings of them: that would be biographical reductionism again.

What does matter is the temporality of the trauma of sexuality and its public determination. Without denying the possibility, indeed the probability of trauma in the historical event, effectively the trauma can only be ours, that is, those of us who, reading this material, animate its textuality with subjectivities that may be differently historically formed and experienced, but which bring another kind of evidence, feminism, to the work of thinking with and about historical materials. If we allow "gender-based readings" to be sidelined as anachronistic, overidentified, ahistorical impositions of "attitudes characteristic of feminists of the late twentieth century," we fail our own moment. We acquiesce in another, but contemporary, shuffling off stage of the violation that is rape.

I prefer not to use the claim for conventionality and standardization in the depositions at trials for rape in seventeenth-century legal archives to suggest that Artemisia Gentileschi was not "raped" but participated in a discourse in which her father had of necessity to claim "damages" against his property in his daughter's marriageability and future social status. Instead we might pose the unanswerable but still important question: What did she want? Is there any way that the messiness and rhetorical theatricality of the trial reveals more than the conventions of the time as given frames of self-understanding? To this reader, they reveal the tensions pressing upon a system buckling under the difficulties of perpetuating a particular sex-gender order in certain urban settings where the relations between the artisan-artist-producers and their patrons required some negotiations between potential social mores and practices. These negotiations only became vivid, however, in the exceptional situation created precisely by the professional talent and evidently saleable artistic ability of the daughter, Artemisia.

At this level, the relations between social context and artistic practice cease to be mediated by the individual author; they become complexly structural. Artistic representation becomes one of the many practices within the social complex that is negotiating similar pressures and limits through its own, significantly semiotic and phantasmatic resources of figurative, narrative, and, after Caravaggio, dramatically corporeal theatricality. Hence the effects of paintings will be different, not reducible to the social or legal, but not unrelated in asymptotic ways with their own, unpredictable effects on viewers led to other ways of experiencing their embodied social subjectivities through encountering these paintings in their specific spaces.

Artemisia according to Merlet: Rape or Love Affair?

In my book *Differencing the Canon* I drew upon Sartre's analysis of the coming to class consciousness in Flaubert's biography to read the public ordeal of the Gentileschi-Tassi trial of 1612 as a moment crystallizing the relations between sexuality and gender power in seventeenth-century Rome across the field of artistic practice and its patronage (Pollock 1999, chaps. 6–7). The process of the public re-presentation of her sexual and social trauma might have revealed, or articulated, to Artemisia Gentileschi how her sex placed her as an object of exchange between men, so that her sexual violation signified not her personal suffering but the legal rights of men over women's bodies and the society's use of the state of those bodies to decide women's social status in this sex-gender economy. Nanette Salomon has analyzed the structure of meaning that the trial enacts in order to place the "experience" within a historical representation of gender relations:

> While the proceedings of the trial may or may not add anything to
> our understanding of Gentileschi's art, they can do so only when

seen as part of the highly coded discourse on sexuality and the politics of rape in the seventeenth century. Perhaps more than anything, they emphasize the fact that Artemisia, body and soul, was
treated as the site of exchange between men, primarily her
father/mentor and her lover/rapist/mentor. . . . This process of exchange began when she was "given" to Tassi as a pupil, and it continued when he violently "took" her, when her honor was "re-
deemed," and when she was given and taken again. The homo-
social bonding ritual enacted and re-enacted among these men
make "Artemisia" an historically elusive construct. If the testimony
of the trial reveals anything, it is a person with an obstinate sense
of her own social and sexual needs. Her paintings look less like
"heroic women" than like the nexus of a series of complicated
negotiations between convention and disruption, between
"Artemisia" and Artemisia. (Salomon 1998, 351–52).

There is as yet no scholarly consensus on what happened between Artemisia Gentileschi and Agostino Tassi in 1611. But however we may contest the evidence, it is certainly not possible to derive from the records a simple love story in the terms offered by
Agnès Merlet. Artemisia Gentileschi's distressing testimony at the
trial describes a violent rape, and her account exhibits not unexpectedly an obsessive recall of every detail including the excessive
pain and her violent struggle, when she scratched both his face and
his penis in her attempts to fight him off. Banti, writing without the
more recent research to guide her, thought that a fourteen-year-old
(for that was the age of the artist according to Longhi's research,
which had not found her birth certificate confirming that she was
born in 1593) would only have known of words like *penis* and *vagina*
as a result of her examination by court midwives.

Merlet's film does not follow the trial transcript in this respect.
But she is not alone in suggesting that its surface conceals as much
as it confusingly reveals. Thus others too have speculated about
Tassi's genuine attraction to and interest in Artemisia Gentileschi,
and they have argued that the delay of ten months reflects Orazio's

impatience at Tassi's recalcitrance over a marriage that would otherwise have been acceptable to him (Cohen 2000). Merlet's film imagines a blossoming relationship between a handsome but dissolute tutor and a willful and eager pupil in which the artistic frankness of the young woman leads a personable and fascinating Tassi to think she is already sexually active.

She shows him some Michelangelesque drawings of a young man's body, and he asks her, "How do you capture such physicality without knowing what the body is capable of?" She replies, "I never said I did not know." "Who modelled for these?" No answer. Pause. "Will you model for me?" He begins to pose, lying on the bed in the posture of the dying Holofernes. She watches him, and then, in her repositioning of his passive body, there is an awkward moment of sexual tension that is rapidly cut off by Tassi. In the next scene, they are on the beach but jointly turn to go indoors. In a moment of admittedly sudden and forceful sexual desire that she reciprocates with growing anxiety about such unimagined forcefulness, he penetrates her (on the same bed)—an act that is interrupted immediately by her cry at the violent pain she experiences from a defloration that draws blood. Confused, distressed, and bleeding ("I am hurt"), Artemisia begins to beat Tassi and then hurries away. After an anguished night, she is shown in subsequent shots actively soliciting his sexual touch in scenes of continuing intimacy at his studio, whereas all the trial documents stress that Tassi invaded her domestic and artistic space with the collusion of the woman Orazio had hired as his housekeeper, Donna Tuzia, in the absence of his wife, who had died when his daughter was twelve.

This sequence moves beyond anything that Anna Banti speculatively drew from the narratives in trial depositions. It defies precisely the sense of historically specific social frames and regulations in which a young artisan woman would have been kept. Moreover, it presents Artemisia Gentileschi as a draughtswoman of the male body when she never painted a male nude, as far as we know, but was remarkable for her paintings of the dramatic female nude body. This misrepresentation significantly affects the meanings produced by the film for the audience to which it is introducing the idea of a woman painter.

Typically, the film locates itself around the rape by interweaving into the sexual relationship the making of the painting of *Judith Beheading Holofernes,* dated 1612–13 (Naples, Museo di Capodimonte; see fig. 22). The sexual scandal has always clung to Artemisia's posthumous reputation, fixing, in both seventeenth-century Italy and modern art history, the image of a *femme fatale* bent on sexual revenge an imputed motivation that is then read into her dramatic representations of Judith killing Holofernes so that Artemisia herself becomes identified with the murderously sexy Judith. Merlet undoes this by redefining her Artemisia/Judith as a seduced and desiring woman, without any thought of revenge. The painting's theatrical prop, the bed, and the role play between the two figures located there become the sites of a significant shift under Merlet's staging. Thus the identification of painting and painter moves in another direction, making not the rape but the sex the foundation for Gentileschi's art. My point is that this still produces the woman artist as a creature revealed to herself by a man's desire.

The Gendered Politics of the Biopic

Clearly, the conflation of an artist's biography and the works of art by that artist functions very differently if the artist is a woman or a man. In the latter case, his art appears to give us access to the generic mystery of (masculine) genius; in the former case, blurring life and art merely confirms the pathology of the feminine, saturated by her sex, of which she becomes emblem and symptom. Her biography, therefore, is always made to hinge around a powerfully sexual, male figure. Think back to Bruno Nuytten's film *Camille Claudel* (1988), where the unspeakable tragedy of a major sculptor secluded and imprisoned in a mental asylum in her forties by her family and violently denied access to her artmaking for the remaining thirty years of her life was reduced to the story of a young and beautiful woman driven mad by her passion for and rejection by

the robust genius Rodin (Gerard Depardieu) for whom she modeled in the nude. Sexual desire in the creative female body leads to
tragedy, and these films then punish the woman for both her transgressive desires: ambition and love. Merlet's film is here both typical and exceptional.

Since 1970, feminists have reclaimed Artemisia Gentileschi as a
heroic figure, reinterpreting the creative dialectic between her sexuality, her gender, and her works within the historical context of
seventeenth-century aesthetics, patronage, and early feminism.
Merlet has creatively used the materials of this historical story to
imagine a passionate professional and sexual relationship between
the young artist and her teacher that is blocked by her father's and
her society's condemnation. Out of the pain of enforced separation,
Artemisia leaves Rome and her father, and matures into the creative
artist she became—after the film has ended. The film's key premise
is that the young woman's sexuality was part of her artistic creativity—a confluence that founders, however, on the inequities of gender embodied in official institutions of her historical moment: the
convent, the Papacy, the academy, and the law.

In her present-day encounter with the work of this seventeenth-
century artist, the filmmaker and art-history student Merlet "sees"
in the paintings by Artemisia Gentileschi traces and forms that
attest to a powerful sensuality and a profound embodiedness, a
richness of color, a density of forms, a fleshiness that cries out for
serious feminist analysis. In a sense her film is trying to answer
the question How did Artemisia Gentileschi learn to paint the
body when she was forbidden by Catholic convention to see her
own body let alone to study the male or female nude from the
model? In an intriguing supposition, Merlet shows Artemisia
Gentileschi first stealing a candle from the convent's chapel to use
in her convent bedroom to study and draw her own body. Later,
she is shown using the promise of sexual favors to persuade a
working-class male friend to strip for her to study his musculature
and to draw his naked torso and genitals. The problem is that, in
fact, Artemisia Gentileschi devoted most of her attention to paint-

ings of *women*, single women whose sexuality, and even lives, were
threatened by men: Lucretia, the suicidal victim of rape; Susanna,
the victim of sexual harassment even to the point of a death sentence; Cleopatra, a great queen dying to save herself the humiliation of being led in captive triumph to Rome. Undraped men are
not part of the oeuvre.

Despite these troubling alterations of rapist to lover and
women's bodies to men's, Agnès Merlet's film is interesting at a
mythic level, even if her reading of Gentileschi is, as Anna Jameson
once declared of Artemisia Gentileschi's genius, "atrociously mis-
directed" (Jameson 1834). This may sound heretical. But there is a
case to be heard for something more than the attempt to match biography to art in a reflexive circle.

The stories we tell do matter. Agnès Merlet's film is clearly not
true at any level that accords with the historical records that sustain
some notion of a legal sense of truth. But if we start from the paintings that present themselves for our encounter, irrespective of their
seventeenth-century Roman, Florentine, Neapolitan provenance,
rather than from the trial records and the plethora of fiction to
which they have given rise, must we not confront this question of
sexuality, but differently? The paintings keep happening in the
present of the viewing.

The film irritates me with other nontrivial inaccuracies.
Artemisia Gentileschi is shown painting an allegorical self-portrait
in 1610 that was produced in 1638–39 when she was a mature
woman visiting her father to work at the English court of Charles I.
She is shown, as I have already said, painting one of her most famous compositions of Judith and Holofernes using Agostino Tassi
as the model for Holofernes when the painting (fig. 22; 1612–13,
Naples, Museo di Capodimonte) postdates the trial for rape. These
are significant misrepresentations not because "truth" lies in
chronology but because whatever we can know about an artist as
the author produced by the practice must honor the relations between artistic productions and the "project" we can only know
through tracking the body of art works that collectively constitute,

post facto, the corpus we name the author "Artemisia Gentileschi." The sequencing of their production may not follow a simple line of development, but much that is important lies in respect for this unconscious structure of appearance, repetition, and divergence, as Nanette Salomon shows in her contribution to this volume.

Feature films about artists fall into the bog where bourgeois ideologies of biography and the creative individual—highly gendered constructs—and fictional narrative cinema collide in that impossible neologism: the biopic. The biopic about the artist tries to show the causes of artistic greatness and often-tragic failure in a hybrid space between the antique tradition of heroic biography and the equally antique concept of the pathological otherness of the artist. The trajectory of the artist's biopic is not simply the biographical line from birth, to childhood, maturity, and decline. Such a simple linearity makes for little drama and no real narrative. The biopic usually builds toward and around a single major event or series of events that appear to offer the key to the characterization of the artist that is being invented for an author name. Thus Minelli's *Lust for Life* (1956) focuses its dramatic structure on the episode of Van Gogh's encounter with Gauguin and his self-mutilation, which in other narratives represents a digression from his art interrupted by the episodic affliction of epilepsy (Pollock 1993, 217–39). Even if Merlet's film is a product of European art cinema rather than Hollywood commercialism, it exhibits its affinity with the latter's popular imaginary.

Within the Hollywood system, films about artists—mostly men to date—signal a curious encounter between popular culture and *its* image of High Art, symbolized by the personification of the artist. These films negotiate a historical contradiction between avant-garde culture and kitsch but from the hybrid point of view of intellectually sophisticated directors working in popular cultural forms. This can produce ultimately very significant reflections on the relations between mass culture and the symbolic figure of individualist ambition, the artist. A series of films by one-time painter turned Hollywood director, Vincente Minnelli, made in the 1950s, repeatedly thematized this contradiction in terms that demand serious consideration: *An American in Paris* (1952), *The Bandwagon* (1953), *Lust for Life* (1956). The artist, like the writer or the musician, functions for Minelli as the embodiment of an idea of creativity that renders the life of the person who is an artist significant and emblematic. By making a narrative picture of this life—the biopic—the film about an artist promises to reveal to us the magical but also blighted nature of genius. Defiant, unconventional, driven, and willful, the artist is always set against a society that litters his path to self-realization with obstacles and misunderstandings. Tempered in the fire of this conflict, the artist is exceptional in a heroic sense and utterly unbearable. He is doomed to a human failure as the price of his cultural contribution to humanity. Thus the biopic's fidelity to the downs as well as the ups ensures that the ordinary viewer walks away confirmed in his view of art's otherness because of the self-alienation of the artist. The recent film *Pollock* (2001), directed by and starring Ed Harris in the title role, is an exemplary repetition of this structure and, in passing, erases entirely the counterexample of the painter Lee Krasner, whose life and career survived her encounter with Pollock but did not thereby attract biopic celebrity. *Love Is a Devil*, directed by John Maybury (1998), was a film about Francis Bacon that focused on a single, traumatic love affair as the core of his disrupted and extraordinary art and life.

But the visual artist has also acquired in the popular imaginary a mythic function partly because of the increasing remoteness of artistic practice from the public in general. There is a long history of treating the artist or poet as a figure apart, melancholy, suicidal, mad, driven, asocial. In the high modernist moment of the twentieth century, the artist became paradigmatic of the pathology of creativity and was represented as a hysterical figure of difference and marginality that functioned as an ideal, heroic figure of resistance to the bourgeois social order, rather like the unassimilable cowboy or the wild man (see Pollock 1980; 1999). The artist is also a problematic figure falling perilously, but often desirably, into tragic feminization. Mythically, the artist is Western society's sacrificial victim, aligned with a Christ figure, or mad and feminized, and yet embodying the creativity of masculine sexuality unfettered by the familial restraints of bourgeois ideology.

Michelangelo (*The Agony and the Ecstasy*), Rembrandt, Gauguin (*The Moon and Sixpence*), Toulouse-Lautrec (*Moulin Rouge*), Van Gogh (*Lust for Life*), and Picasso (*Surviving Picasso*) have been famously portrayed by Hollywood in biopics that were at once "untrue" in a prosaic factual sense and totally "true" to the mythic or imaginary functions of the artist in twentieth-century popular culture. But there have been moments of difference in this genre. Derek Jarman's *Caravaggio* (1986) stands completely apart as a film made by a painter as a kind of subliminal self-portrait, lending a different value to the meaning of marginality by identifying with the subcultural struggle of the homosexual artist in the seventeenth century. This film's achievement is enhanced by its resisting historical costume drama or the conventions of the biopic through self-conscious fictionalization. These conventions tend to be marked by the use of contemporary dress and mannerisms, mixed with elaborately staged compositions that echo the style of the paintings while yet endowing that aesthetic with the cutting edge of its own confused politics of sexuality, class and difference. Jarman skillfully avoided them all.

The Hungry Eye

Consciously arty but succumbing to the lure of historical reconstruction without that ironic self-consciousness and reflexivity, Merlet's film opens with the extreme close up of an eye, huge and disturbing, as the credits roll. A voice whispers a description of fragments of male nudes from a scene of the *Last Judgment.* Thus are we introduced to the concept of the artist as a hungry eye, desiring to see, to know, to participate in the jumble of expressively naked bodies, in the mysteries of representation. A different kind of struggle—transgression—is about to take place before us that is signified by the relations between this voice, this eye, these images and the scene at which the event takes place. The scene is a chapel in a convent, and the eye belongs to a young girl peering through her hands folded at prayer towards the mannerist assemblage of naked men signifying this violent moment in Christian mythology. In itself, this scene dramatizes the question I was arguing above: What were the effects of the Tintoretto or Michelangelo extravaganzas of embodied passion and ecstasy on the praying congregations who daily confronted these visual invocations of human passion? However the theologians worked to accommodate the incarnation of Christian ideas with Catholic doctrines of meditation, their writ did not exhaust the spectacular presence of these visual machines.

The young girl steals a candle from the chapel, and later that night she uses its light and a mirror to examine and sketch her own naked body. Human anatomy was the grammar of seventeenth-century painting: without a knowledge of its physical articulations and musculature, the rhetoric of gesture and expression by means of which stories were told, ideas conveyed, and dramas evoked was inaccessible. Because of their sex, women were forbidden this knowledge by the Papacy and excluded from academies. But how else would Artemisia Gentileschi have gained the necessary mastery of this fundamental element of her art if not through clandestine examination of her own body? Merlet's supposition of this scene is remarkable because it marks not only the young girl's transgression of contemporary Catholic mores but a reflexive relation to her own female corporeality. She is learning aspects of her own craft in a radically different relation from that in which the female nude emerged in its typical structure of male vs. female and artist vs. model, which we see later in the film in Tassi's brutal assessment of the naked models brought before him in the hurly-burly of the workshop. In the cinema, however, the viewer watches Artemisia undress to learn this, and thus the gendered hierarchy of viewing and viewed is returned to the conventional cinematic order that the actual scene is narratively collapsing and shifting by intimating the

political transgression of this artist-woman's Pandoran (in Laura
Mulvey's feminist sense) curiosity about her own body (see Mulvey
1996, 53–64).

Removed from the convent by her father, who realizes that "she
is the daughter of a painter and has much to learn, but not here,"
Artemisia works in the studio of her successful father, hungry for all
that she needs to know but cannot access because of her sex. The
film shows her going to the sea to meet up with a young fisherman,
Fulvio, and she catches sight of a couple making love in the sand
whom she watches with fascinated attention, even laying her own
body in the imprint of their coupling in the sand, miming its gestures while the camera remains in her former viewing position,
watching her. This repeated dislocation of woman as eye and
woman as seen, fantasizing sexual receptivity, marks the key point
where the filmmaker's lack of familiarity with feminist film theory
and cinematic poetics constantly undoes the potential covenant between Gentileschi's historical negotiation of regimes of representation and contemporary feminist interventions in cultural languages. Merlet's narrative imagination is not matched by a critical
semiotic practice in cinematic terms.[4]

With this scene, the trope of Gentileschi the artist as hungry eye
now begins its sexualization. This becomes the underlying theme of
the film and its narrative logic that will take her into a passionate
love affair with Agostino Tassi, whose arrival in Rome is defined by
two scenes. The first shows Artemisia Gentileschi watching him
paint on the beach in daylight. He was a landscape and marine
painter, and he used a perspective frame to see "the world." Tassi
apparently became her teacher of perspective, a skill that she hardly
ever used in her closed and single-figure compositions. In a second
scene she sneaks up to his house at night and secretly peers in at the
licentious sexual revels for which this dissolute artist was notorious. These two moments of Artemisia Gentileschi as aspiring artist
and sexually curious adolescent converge in the critical scene
where, between lovemaking scenes, she is shown painting Agostino
Tassi as Holofernes from her 1612 painting through his perspective

frame in the very room in which the sexual orgy had earlier taken place. Merlet's reading of Artemisia Gentileschi is entirely based on that painting, and the sensuous and swarthy Miki Manojlovic has been chosen to play the otherwise dissolute and effete Tassi because of his resemblance to the hairy Assyrian general in this painting. This is how the biopic fills in the potential gaps.

Readings of Judith

The story of Judith and Holofernes has long fascinated male writers (and musicians like Vivaldi, in *Juditha Triumphans*).[5] In more modern times, speculation has shifted the hitherto religious and patriotic motives to play with the ambiguities of the woman's sexuality: Was she a virgin momentarily seduced, killing her seducer in the guilty aftermath (Hebbel 1960)? Was she a frigid girl who was so ambitious for glory that out of love for her the general Holofernes offered himself to her attack (Bernstein 1922)? Was she the passionate object of the general to whose compelling ardor she yielded before again recovering her political purpose (Girardoux 1932)? Despite the original story, which charts a very carefully plotted trap for Holofernes, modern writers have always returned to the fatal idea: Did sexual desire undo the woman who killed out of revenge for having been made to feel that desire?

The lengthy biblical narrative of the Book of Judith that appears only in the Catholic Bible and the Apocrypha foregrounds the selectiveness of the later cultural focus on only the moment of Judith's action, on the scene in the tent, which the original story embeds in a larger political narrative that includes a strategic war, an endangered culture, and the fascinating creation of a warrior-virgin heroine whose substitution of violence for sexual submission radically inverts the relations between a subject people and their all-powerful enemy. This trope of the weak undoing the strong, of the adolescent shepherd David killing the giant Goliath, of the stay-at-home wife doing in the enemy general, contains a mythic element and a dream element: a wish that invokes the power

of the mother, the adult sexual woman, to counter and overcome
the violence and hatred of the father.

Judith's status as widow-virgin, as a beauty never again pos-
sessed but used only in the service of freeing the oppressed com-
munity, allows elements counter to patriarchal mythology to peep
through while also suggesting the competing fantasies of the powerful mother figure who can resist, and undo, and, yes, castrate, but
who can also deprive of his leadership, and thus his power, the father's menacing representative. If we take the text of the victory
song of Judith at the end of the biblical book, its framing as a hymn
to a powerful God is progressively undermined by a slippage into
the first person, in which Judith speaks of her own great deed.

By returning to the textual elements of the mythic biblical narrative as a staging of a cosmic as well as psychic competition between paternal and maternal imagoes, we see more clearly the inscription of different kinds of cultural projection typical of the
visual narratives familiar to us through the emergence of this theme
as a popular subject for painting in the sixteenth and seventeenth
centuries. What did Judith signify for early modern European culture in that moment of killing Holofernes? What did paintings visually narrate? Only when we allow this creative gap can we approach Artemisia Gentileschi the painter without placing her life
and her work inside this other narrative of Judith and Holofernes.

Merlet does not manage this. Her film tells a love story of an ambitious and sensual young woman and a dissolute but entranced
older man who sacrifices himself for love of her. Her father Orazio's
rage and jealousy forces the trial for rape when we are shown con-
sensual lovemaking, and Tassi confesses to rape only in order to
save Artemisia's hands—her painting hands—from the permanent mutilation of the thumbscrew torture to which she is subjected. In the historical trial Artemisia Gentileschi, accused by Tassi
of sexual promiscuity, was tortured because she insisted she was
raped; in the film she is tortured because she refutes the charge.

Despite its total fictionalization of the events in the life of
Artemisia Gentileschi that we know from historical evidence, I take

this film seriously because it belongs in a long history of Western mediations on and abuses of the story of Judith and Holofernes. It has an imaginative agenda that explores a relationship between two people in which sexuality and violence have become complexly interwoven under the sign of that story, painted by Gentileschi many times in her career. In his appraisal of Artemisia Gentileschi's 1612–13 painting of *Judith Beheading Holofernes*, Roland Barthes argued that any painting "checkmates" interpretation, suspending its viewers between a range of possible meanings of the event that never quite takes place. Its stillness and monumentalization of bodies captured permanently "in the act" generates its tumult of potential resonances within each viewer and for each period (Barthes 1979). Cinema's relentless narrativity, however, situates the moment of the painting's coming into being within a story that renders it not as such a polysemic text but as a decodable reflection of the life that narrative embeds in a plot, making it both explicable and knowable and the secret key to the whole story that surrounds it.

For my money Artemisia Gentileschi's painting of *Judith Beheading Holofernes* has nothing whatsoever to do with rape or her life experience.[6] It was a popular and much-commissioned subject in baroque Italy. As the major trope of sex and violence for the baroque era, the subject had been painted by both Gentileschi's father and her major artistic reference, Caravaggio. Whomever is being so calculatedly decapitated, the painting may be equally read as the art of these "artistic" fathers in a crucial act of aesthetic space-clearing and self-definition as a painter among painters, but space-clearing "in and for the feminine." It borrows the heroic mold of the political conspirator, Judith, to create, within the world of public and visual representation, a figure of identification for woman as self-creating artist.

In this hypothesis, the relation between Artemisia Gentileschi and Judith is not dissimilar in structure to that between Anna Banti and Artemisia Gentileschi. In each case, the latter term, Judith or Artemisia, is an existing fiction offered by the culture to a creative woman artist or writer as the mythic means by which to explore through an artistic/writing practice possible identities and their socio-psychic complexities in a patriarchal world. The regular collapse of Artemisia into Judith precisely prevents us working with the gap, the creative gap, the gap of signification, and the structuring of inchoate subjectivity by the semes and tropes offered through cultural representation.

The point, however, is that in unconsciously identifying with Judith as a creative agent, it would seem that "Artemisia Gentileschi" the painter did not become a figure of anguished conflict, or even a figure of abundant sexuality. Who knows how she read this figure? Through other paintings? Inevitably. Through some theological discussions and iconographical traditions? Probably. All we can do is keep rereading the painting with as much evidence as we can muster to shatter the mythic collapse of a vengeful and man-hating Judith onto the violated woman painter whom cultural narratives repeatedly invent. If in the end I do not agree with Merlet's reading, I acknowledge her attempt to see something else, to effect what I call a *differencing* of the canon, including the feminist canon. She asks why Gentileschi's paintings have the effects they do. Could it be because of desire rather than hatred?

As I have tried to show, the question of what happened between two people between May 1611 and March 1612 is subject to its own kinds of microhistorical textual analysis and the politics of interpretation of subjectivity, culture, and its representations. It is interesting that the most diligent of archival historians, Alexandra Lapierre, felt able to represent her research only as a novelistic biography. While presenting itself as a biopic that makes the biographical subject the source and explanation of the artwork, Merlet's film, despite itself, has the effect of opening up a space between person and painting. It does this precisely by offering a dissident biographical interpretation.

I have also wanted to stress that the theology of the Judith story itself does not support either the theme of revenge or of desire. Nonetheless, Merlet's "wrongness" on several counts brings the painting into view in this film text as the signifier of a desiring woman-creator-subject, Artemisia—as the scene of her painful initiation into a sexuality that the filmmaker proposes as a vital part of the character she creates for the woman as painter. But if this case is made only through what ultimately becomes a conventional love story that, unlike Banti's novel, never really situates Artemisia in any relation but to father or lover, does this not radically compromise the image of feminine desire as always confined within a phallically defined circuit of exchange?

At What Price?

Mine is just a different story, and it is no more "true" than any of the others, but it is shaped by a feminist ethics that intends to undermine the cultural tropes in the popular imaginary, with which cinema is so often complicit. It has become impossible to figure the terms *woman* and *artist* outside of the tropes of sex and death. Merlet's film is, I would argue, not really a biography, for there is no analysis of the impact of the early death of the artist's mother and her bereavement, no exploration of how she made a massively successful career in Italy and beyond after the horrors of the trial and her torture, how she married and mothered several daughters who also became artists, how she negotiated with some of the major patrons of her time for the commissions on which she lived and through which she, not their father, accumulated dowries for her daughters. No one wants to tell that story.

Jarman's film *Caravaggio* is structured as a flashback in which a whole complex life of sexual, social, and artistic interactions and events are rerun before the eyes of the exiled, dying man—a figure of subcultural identification and political compassion in all his violence. Like most of the art historians before her, Merlet has published—in the sense of exposed—only the sexualized body of the raped or, in her version, deflowered but desiring Artemisia Gentileschi. The film reduces the life and work of the woman artist to one complex and probably deeply formative and traumatizing moment of her otherwise long and productive life. In ignorance of all the histories of women artists so faithfully recovered by feminist scholars since 1970, Merlet's film signs off with the mistaken and misleading phrase that Artemisia is considered the first woman painter in the history of art—again asserting that woman as artist is a rare exception, a belated oddity in the history of art.

Opening this essay, I asked if a myth was being disrupted and transformed or rehearsed and desired. In the end, despite being hopeful about the film's address to "Artemisia's"—that is a feminine—desire as a force in her painting, I think that a myth is being perpetuated in that huge audience of the cinema who will never be exposed to feminist revisionism: the myth that the terms *woman* and *artist* are rarely conjoined and only come together out of heterosexual initiation of the sexually vulnerable but precocious woman who opens herself to the big prick. Whether for love or through violence, it comes to the same thing, and we wait in vain for a film about women, sexuality, intellectuality, and creativity that does not make the woman the sacrificial victim.

NOTES

Artemisia's Hands

1. Bernard Berenson's connoisseurship principles were founded on those of Morelli.

2. The painting, which turned up at auction in 1995, has been connected with a work owned by the eighteenth-century English collector Ignazio Hugford.

3. There is reason to believe that the association of Artemisia with the Allegory of Painting—epitomized in her *Self-Portrait as the Allegory of Painting* of 1630 or later—began during her Florentine period, in the 1610s. See Garrard 2001 and fig. 37.

4. For differing opinions about the attribution of the *Cleopatra,* see Christiansen and Mann (2001, no. 17). Unusually, the painting is included in both the Orazio and Artemisia sections of the exhibition catalogue, where the coauthors present opposing positions.

5. On Artemisia's alleged posing nude for Orazio, see Christiansen, in Christiansen and Mann (2001, 98); and Elizabeth Cropper (2001, 274–75). The rumor that Orazio had improper relations with his daughter, or wished to, can be found in the rape trial testimony; it was suggested by a witness for Tassi's defense and also stated by Tassi himself (Garrard 1989, 481, 453).

6. For the poem, and a different interpretation, see Bissell (1999, 355-56).

7. Baldinucci, writing in the 1680s, as cited in Bissell (1999, no. 15).

Judging Artemisia

1. While the exhibition included the subtitle Father and Daughter Painters in Baroque Italy, the catalogue is simply called *Orazio and Artemisia Gentileschi;* see Christiansen and Mann (2001).

2. For a full discussion of this phenomenon, see Bourdieu and Darbel (1990, especially 108–13).

3. The intricacies of the ideas of this period are insightfully explored in Smyth (1992).

4. On issues of taste, see Summers (1987, 23).

5. See Elizabeth Cropper's introduction to Smyth (1992).

6. This very complex problem of narrative in still images has been addressed in several texts by Mieke Bal. For a recent bibliography of her work, see Bal (2002).

7. The knowledge of good and evil is interpreted here as sexual knowledge, with reference to the "tree of life." The notion is that sexual knowledge is indispensable to overcome death and perpetuate life. For this interpretation, see Bal (1987, chap. 5).

8. The concept of the subaltern was developed by Gayatri Chakravorty Spivak in her article "Can the Subaltern Speak?" (1988).

9. For the relationship between Vasari, Janson, and the Janson-like survey books, see Salomon (1998) and the references there.

"Gran Macchina è Bellezza

1. Although the exhibition began in Rome and ended in St. Louis, I have focused here on its New York venue (February-May, 2002), because of its scale and its convenience for repeated viewings. I will therefore refer to it as the Metropolitan show throughout. I must also acknowledge the opportunities provided subsequently by the St. Louis Art Museum, where two of Artemisia's and two of Orazio's *Judiths* were on display. My visit there was under the academic circumstances of the museum's Gentileschi symposium in September of 2002 and, in any case, occurred after the initial drafting of this article.

2. The fullest expression of this phenomenon is provided by the catalogue by Christiansen and Mann (2001) of the exhibition, with its extensive bibliography. Landmarks in the previous scholarship which inform every aspect of this essay are the foundational monograph by Garrard (1989) and the invaluable catalogue raisonné by Bissell (1999). Unless otherwise indicated, all allusions to Garrard and Bissell refer to these two works. Also important is the Florentine exhibition catalogue by Contini and Papi (1991).

3. Difficulties begin at the most basic level, because the Hebrew original has not survived, and the version in the Latin Vulgate bible is now considered a paraphrase of diverse antique sources. The preferred text is that of the Greek Septuagint. As one of the Hebrew Apocryphal scriptures, the Book of Judith is excluded from the biblical canon by Jews and most Protestants, but included (as Deuterocanonical) by Roman Catholics. For a useful compendium of a variety of versions, see *The Parallel Apocrypha* (Kohlenberger 1997); my verse citations refer to the Douay English translation of the Vulgate there. For samples of modern commentaries by biblical scholars, see the essays in *"No One Spoke Ill of Her"* (VanderKam 1992) and also Craven (1983; 2000). For the afterlife of the story, see the synthetic treatment by Stocker (1998).

4. See the catalogue by Christiansen and Mann (2001, 308–11), with relevant bibliography. In every case, my descriptions of the Gentileschi paintings of Judith have been considered with regard to the catalogue entries and to the discussions of Garrard and Bissell cited there.

5. The first challenge was by Spike, in his review of the exhibition by Contini and Papi at Casa Buonarroti (1991). More recently, Bissell, who in his monograph of 1999 supported the familiar attribution to Artemisia, announced a change of heart and defended an ascription to Orazio at the Gentileschi symposium held in conjunction with the exhibition at the St. Louis Art Museum in September of 2002.

6. My discussion here is indebted to both conversations with and publications by Toni Craven, beginning with her monograph (1983, 67); more recently, see her entries in the encyclopedic *Women in Scripture* (2000).

7. My use of this text here is indebted to Pietropaolo's study (1989), which is full of resonance for the topic of the iconography of Judith in the baroque period.

8. A convenient discussion of major criticisms inspired by her feminist conclusions is provided by Garrard herself (2001, esp. xvii–xxii). See also the survey of the critical literature by Spear (2000b).

9. This topic is necessarily addressed in the discussions of the Gentileschi *Judiths* by Garrard (1989) and Bissell (1999), as well as in the relevant entries in the Metropolitan catalogue of Christiansen and Mann (2001). There is also a growing literature on this topic that is not focused on Artemisia's paintings. See, for example, Ciletti (1991), Stocker (1998), and the Judith entries in the recent exhibition catalogues by Baumgaertel and Neysters (1995), and by Dixon (2002).

10. See Christiansen and Mann (2001, 347–50). Incidentally, the height measurement given (100 centimeters, or 39 3/8 inches) is incorrect; it is about half of the actual vertical dimension, which is 199 centimeters, or almost 78 inches.

11. In order to simplify the citation of the flurry of positions enumerated in the following two sentences, I'd like to point the reader to some recent overviews of Artemisia's interpreters: the entries and essays in the Christiansen and Mann catalogue (2001) by Mann and by Elizabeth Cropper; Bissell's chapter 6 (1999), and the assessment by Spear (2000), which includes a most helpful bibliography. It is telling that more than half of Spear's argument is organized around the literature on the Uffizi *Judith,* with particular attention to psychoanalytic and/or semiotic readings (by Pointon, Slapp, Taylor, Hersey, Pollock, Barthes, and Bal), as well as to the feminism of Garrard. Beyond the authors discussed in these surveys, my list of interpretations comes from such diverse sources as Almansi (1991, 24); Topper and Gillis (1996, 10–13); Rossi (1998, 19–20); Greer (1979, 189); Redig de Campos (1939, 321–22); and Korsmeyer (2002).

12. I am perplexed by the statement in the Metropolitan catalogue entry (Christiansen and Mann 2001, 347), which locates the signature "at bottom right, on the sword blade."

13. On this painter, see the monograph by Monducci, Negro, and Pirondini (2002).

Grounds of Comparison

1. As Ciletti mentions, some of this effect may be due to a cropping of the canvas. Nevertheless, the effect is undeniable.

2. Elsewhere, in relation to another *Judith* painting, I have discussed this inquiry as part of a larger posthumanistic inquiry in what constitutes a human individual. The result of beheading—the isolation of head from body—partakes of the same inquiry (2002, 133–73).

3. For a brief description of baroque thought, see the introduction to this volume. For a more elaborate discussion, see my *Quoting Caravaggio* (1999).

4. On the distinction between commensurable and incommensurable or radical otherness, see Spivak (1984). On different interpretations of allegory, see Fletcher (1964). The interpretation of allegory as a discourse of otherness is developed by Paul de Man (1979).

5. On this painting, see Garrard 1980. The term "allo-portrait" is explained by Marianne Hirsch (1997, 86–94) in a discussion with Philippe Lacoue-Labarthe (1979).

6. For the idea, essential to deconstruction, of "homeopathic" arguments, see Derrida's chapter "Plato's Pharmacy" and Barbara Johnson's explanation of it in her introduction to Derrida's *Dissemination* (1981).

7. On the complexities of the anxiety of influence, see Harold Bloom's pi-

oneering study (1973). Norman Bryson takes up Bloom's idea for an analysis of visual art (1984). In an astute reversal, Catherine Lord argues for an intimacy of influence, which might be relevant for some of the discussions of the relationship between Artemisia and Orazio (1999).

8. For a critique of this traditional concept of portraiture and a discussion of contemporary alternatives, see Van Alphen (1996). Other contributions to that volume develop the humanistic conception of portraiture in Brilliant's sense.

9. Since Leo Steinberg's 1983 eye-opener, the insistence of the reality of the Christ child's sex need no longer surprise.

10. All Adorno's writings about art "after Auschwitz" have recently appeared in English (2003). Perhaps this availability will put an end to the popular practice of indirectly citing without nuancing Adorno's position.

11. On the problem of the public-private distinction, see Rössler (1980). Of course, painting is not always meant for the general public, especially not in the seventeenth century. But even if a painting is made for private patrons, the representation does leave the strictly private domain of the artist.

12. See Pollock (1999). On problems of canon formation, see Salomon (1998).

13. For an extensive discussion, see Bal (2001).

14. On this important meaning of aesthetics, see Schaeffer (1997).

15. On quotation of historical art in contemporary art, see Bal (1999).

16. The allusion, of course, is to the popularized interpretations of Kant's 1790 requirement that aesthetic judgment be grounded in disinterested looking. Whereas this requirement may indeed have been intended to make art the reserve of gentlemen of the leisure class, the meaning cannot be abducted to become indifference.

Feminist Dilemmas with the Art/Life Problem

1. For the concept of "feminist desire," a desire for different knowledges and meanings, see Pollock (1999).

2. Originating in the Romantic period with Goethe's *Werther,* the novel about the artist or writer developed in the nineteenth century, with Balzac and Zola playing leading roles in making the artist the central character of a psychological drama of creativity and its dooms. Vasari's *Vite* [Lives] on the other hand, forms the foundation of a different tradition, the biographically focused study of art history, seeing in the life of the artist the clues and keys to the character of the artist and hence the value and meaning of the work. The romanticization of the artist draws on this biographical bias, but also reworks more classical cultural narratives in which the condition of the artist or poet

was perceived to be singular as a type, with psychological tendencies toward melancholia or mania, suicide, or intensity and obsession. See Wittkower and Wittkower (1963) for this tradition from antiquity to modern times; see also Kris and Kurz (1979) and Pollock (1980).

3. This is a very significant point that Cannon makes in the context of other texts, such as Lapierre's novel, which is subtitled for British publication as a "battle for greatness" implying struggle, and Germaine Greer's perplexing reading of the failure of Artemisia Gentileschi in *The Obstacle Race: The Fortunes of Women Painters and Their Work* (1979).

4. This argument is indebted to Mieke Bal's critical analysis of iconography and semiotics in *Reading Rembrandt* (1991). There she contrasts the critical transformation of a reference text in Alice Walker's novel *The Color Purple* with Spielberg's mistranslation of that novel into cinematic signification. The radical work of Walker's own text is undone by Spielberg's failure to think that "work" through in his own medium, genre, and practice. How could a critical film about race and gender be made without undoing cinematic tropes and traditions that institute racism and sexism?

5. For further information on this, see Garrard (1989) and Pollock (1999).

6. My argument is elaborated in Pollock (1999).

REFERENCES

Adorno, Theodor W. 2003. *Can One Live After Auschwitz? A Philosophical Reader.* Ed. Rolf Tiedemann. Trans. Rodney Livingstone et al. Stanford, CA: Stanford University Press.

Almansi, Guido. 1991. "Artemisia: Una donna in pittura." *FMR* 86:24–25.

Andreini, Isabella. 1995. *La Mirtilla.* Ed. Maria Luisa Doglio. Lucca: Maria Pacini Fazzi Editore. Orig. pub. in Verona, 1588.

Arslan, Edoardo. 1960. *Le Pitture del Duomo di Milano.* Milan: Electa.

Bal, Mieke. 1987. *Lethal Love: Literary Feminist Readings of Biblical Love Stories.* Bloomington: Indiana University Press.

————. 1988a. *Murder and Difference: Gender, Genre and Scholarship on Sisera's Death.* Trans. Matthew Gumpert. Bloomington: Indiana University Press.

————. 1988b. *Death and Dissymmetry: The Politics of Coherence in the Book of Judges.* Chicago: University of Chicago Press.

————. 1991 *Reading Rembrandt: Beyond the Word Image Opposition.* Cambridge: Cambridge University Press.

————. 1996. *Double Exposures: The Subject of Cultural Analysis.* New York: Routledge.

————. 1999. *Quoting Caravaggio: Contemporary Art, Preposterous History.* Chicago: University of Chicago Press.

————. 2001. "Enfolding Feminism." In *Feminist Consequences: Theory for the New Century,* ed. Elisabeth Bronfen and Misha Kavka, 321–52. New York: Columbia University Press.

———. 2002 *Travelling Concepts in the Humanities: A Rough Guide.* Toronto:
University of Toronto Press.

———. Forthcoming. *Political Art Now.*

Banti, Anna. 1995. *Artemisia.* London: Serpent's Tail. Orig. pub. 1947.

Barasch, Moshe. 1985. *Theories of Art: From Plato to Winckelmann.* New York:
New York University Press.

Barthes, Roland. 1979. "Deux Femmes/Two Women." *Mot pour Mot/Word for
Word Artemisia* 2:8–13. Paris: Yvon Lambert.

———. 1991. "The Reality Effect." In *French Literary Theory Today,* ed. Tzvetan
Todorov, trans. R. Carter, 11–17. New York: Cambridge University Press.

Baumgaertel, Bettina, and Silvia Neysters. 1995. *Die Galerie der Starken
Frauen: Regintinnen, Amazonen, Salondamen.* Exhibition catalogue.
Kunstmuseum, Duesseldorf: Klinkhardt & Biermann.

Baxandall, Michael. 1971. *Giotto and the Orators.* Oxford: Clarendon Press.

Benassi, F., Manenti Valli, Z. Davoli, and F. M. Gobbo. 1983. *La Madonna della
Ghiara in Reggio Emilia.* Pordenone, Italy: n.p.

Benedetti, Laura. 1999. "Reconstructing Artemisia: Twentieth-Century
Images of a Woman Artist." *Comparative Literature* 51:43–61.

Berenson, Bernard. 1902. "Rudiments of Connoisseurship (a Fragment)." In
The Study and Criticism of Italian Art, 134–36. London: George Bell & Sons.

Bernstein, Henry. 1922. *Judith: Comédie dramatique en trois actes et cinq
tableaux.* Théâtre Nouvelle, série no. 8. Paris: La Petite Illustration.

Bevilacqua, Mario, and Elisabetta Mori, eds. 1999. *Beatrice Cenci: La storia e il
mito.* Rome: Fondazione Marco Besso.

Bissell, R. Ward. 1999. *Artemisia Gentileschi and the Authority of Art.* University Park: Pennsylvania State University Press.

Bloom, Harold. 1973. *The Anxiety of Influence: A Theory of Poetry.* New York:
Oxford University Press.

Blunt, Anthony. 1940. *Artistic Theory in Italy, 1450–1600.* Oxford: Clarendon
Press.

Bohn, Babette. 2002. "The Antique Heroines of Elisabetta Sirani." *Renaissance
Studies* 16:52–79. Reprinted in Broude and Garrard, forthcoming.

———. 2004. *Ludovico Carracci and the Art of Drawing.* Turnhout, Belgium:
n.p.

Bos, Johanna W. H. 1988. "Out of the Shadow: Genesis 38; Judges 4:17–22;
Ruth 3." *Semeia* 42:37–68.

Bourdieu, Pierre, and Alan Darbel. 1990. *The Love of Art.* Stanford, CA: Stanford University Press.

Brilliant, Richard. 1991. *Portraiture.* Cambridge: Harvard University Press.

Broude, Norma, and Mary D. Garrard. Forthcoming. *Reclaiming Female Agency: Feminist Art History after Postmodernism.* Berkeley and Los Angeles: University of California Press.

Brown, Beverly Louise, ed. 2001. *The Genius of Rome: 1592–1623.* London: Royal Academy of Art.

Bryson, Norman. 1984. *Tradition and Desire: From David to Delacroix.* New York: Cambridge University Press.

Bulwer, John. 1974. *Chirologia; or, The Natural Language of the Hand,* and *Chironomia; or, The Art of Manual Rhetoric,* ed. James W. Cleary. Carbondale: Southern Illinois University Press. Orig. pub. 1644.

Cannon, JoAnn. 1994. "*Artemisia* and the Life Story of an Exceptional Woman." *Forum Italicum* 28:233–41.

Cavazzini, Patrizia. 2001. "Artemisia in Her Father's House." In Christiansen and Mann 2001, 293–95.

Cecchi, Alessandro. 1992. "Cigoli's 'Jael and Sisera' Rediscovered." *Burlington Magazine* 134:82–91.

Chevalier, Tracy. 1999. *The Girl with the Pearl Earring.* London: HarperCollins.

Christiansen, Keith, and Judith Mann, eds. 2001. *Orazio and Artemisia Gentileschi.* Exhibition catalogue. Metropolitan Museum of Art. New Haven, CT, and London: Yale University Press.

Ciletti, Elena. 1988. "Questa e la donna terribile!: Artemisia Gentileschi and Judith." Lecture given at Hobart and William Smith Colleges, Geneva, NY.

———. 1991. "Patriarchal Ideology in the Renaissance Iconography of Judith." In *Refiguring Woman: Perspectives on Gender and the Italian Renaissance,* ed. Marilyn Migiel and Juliana Schiesari, 35–70. Ithaca, NY: Cornell University Press.

Cohen, Elizabeth S. 1991. "No Longer Virgins: Self-Representation by Young Women in Late Renaissance Rome." In *Refiguring Women: Perspectives on Gender and the Italian Renaissance,* ed. Marilyn Migiel and Juliana Schiesari, 169–91. Ithaca, NY: Cornell University Press.

———. 1992. "Court Testimony from the Past: Self and Culture in the Making of Text." In *Essays in Life Writing: From Genre to Critical Practice,* ed. Marlene Kador. Toronto: University of Toronto Press.

———. 2000. "The Trials of Artemisia Gentileschi: A Rape as History." *Sixteenth Century Journal* 30, no. 1:47–75.

Cohn, Samuel K., Jr. 1996. *Women in the Streets: Essays on Sex and Power in Renaissance Italy.* Baltimore, MD: Johns Hopkins University Press.

Contini, Roberto, and Gianni Papi. 1991. *Artemisia.* Exhibition catalogue. Casa Buonarroti, Florence. Rome: Leonardo–De Luca Editori.

Cox, Virginia. 2000. "Fiction, 1560–1650." In *A History of Women's Writing in Italy,* ed. Letizia Panizza and Sharon Wood. Cambridge: Cambridge University Press.

Craven, Toni. 1983. *Artistry and Faith in the Book of Judith.* Chico, CA: Scholar's Press.

———, Carol Meyers, and Ross Kraemer, eds. 2000. *Women in Scripture: A Dictionary of Named and Unnamed Women in the Hebrew Bible, the Apocryphal/Deuterocanonical Books, and the New Testament.* Boston: Houghton Mifflin.

Crespi, Luigi. 1769. *Felsina Pittrice, Vite de'pittori bolognesi.* Bologna: Arnaldo Forni Editore.

Croce, Benedetto. 1929. "Le tragedie di Federico della Valle di Asti." *Critica* 27:377–97.

Cropper, Elizabeth. 2001. "Life on the Edge: Artemisia Gentileschi, Famous Woman Painter." In Christiansen and Mann 2001, 262–81.

———. 1993. "New Documents for Artemisia Gentileschi's Life in Florence." *Burlington Magazine* 134:760–61.

Della Valle, Federico. 1978. *Iudit.* Ed. A. Gareffi. Rome: Bulzoni.

Derrida, Jacques. 1981. *Dissemination.* Trans., with an introduction and notes, Barbara Johnson. Chicago: University of Chicago Press.

Dixon, Annette. 2002. *Women Who Ruled: Queens, Goddesses, Amazons in Renaissance and Baroque Art.* Exhibition catalogue. University of Michigan Museum of Art. London: Merrell.

Fewell, Danna Nolan, and David M. Gunn. 1990. "Controlling Perspectives: Women, Men, and the Authority of Violence in Judges 4 and 5." *Journal of the American Academy of Religion* 58, no. 3:389–411.

Firenzuola, Agnolo. 1992. *On the Beauty of Women.* Trans. and ed. Konrad Eisenbichler and Jacqueline Murray. Philadelphia: University of Pennsylvania Press. Orig. pub. 1541.

Flax, Jane. 2001. "Der Scandal des Begehrens." In *Verhandlungendes Geschlechts,* ed. Ewa Vaniek and Silvia Stoller. Vienna: Verlag Turia &

Kant. Forthcoming as "The Scandal of Desire" in *Contemporary Psychoanalysis.*

Fletcher, Angus. 1964. *Allegory: The Theory of a Symbolic Mode.* Ithaca, NY: Cornell University Press.

Foucault, Michel. 1976. *The History of Sexuality.* Vol. 1. Trans. Robert Hurley. Harmondsworth, UK: Penguin Books.

Friedländer, Max J. 1942. *On Art and Connoisseurship.* Trans. Tancred Borenius. London: B. Cassirer.

Frisoni, Fiorella. 1975. "Lionello Spada." *Paragone* 27, no. 299:53–79.

Garrard, Mary D. 1980. "Artemesia Gentileschi's Self-Portrait as the Allegory of Painting." *Art Bulletin* 62: 97–112.

———. 1989. *Artemisia Gentileschi: The Image of the Female Hero in Italian Baroque Art.* Princeton, NJ: Princeton University Press.

———. 1993. "Artemisia Gentileschi's *Corisca and the Satyr.*" *Burlington Magazine* 135:34–38.

———. 2001. *Artemisia Gentileschi around 1622: The Shaping and Reshaping of an Artistic Identity.* Berkeley and Los Angeles: University of California Press.

———. 2003. "Artemisia's Trial by Cinema." In *Singular Women: Writing the Artist,* ed. Kristen Frederickson and Sarah E. Webb, 21–29. Berkeley and Los Angeles: University of California Press. Orig. pub. 1998.

Girardoux, Jean. 1932. *Judith: Une tragédie en trois actes.* Paris: Emile Paul.

Gombrich, Ernst. 1978. *Meditations on a Hobby Horse, and Other Essays on the Theory of Art.* London: Phaidon.

Good, Edwin M. 1988. "Deception and Women: A Response." *Semeia* 42:117–30.

Grandi, Renzo, Massimo Medica et al. 1987. *Museo Civico d'Arte Industriale e Galleria Davia Bargellini.* Bologna: Industria Grafica.

Greenshields, Malcolm. 1994. *An Economy of Violence in Early Modern France: Crime and Justice in the Haute Auvergne, 1587–1664.* University Park: University of Pennsylvania Press.

Greer, Germaine. 1979. *The Obstacle Race: The Fortunes of Women Painters and Their Work.* New York: Farrar, Straus and Giroux.

Gunn, David M. 2005. *Judges.* Blackwell Bible Commentaries. Oxford, UK: Blackwell.

Hebbel, Friedrich. 1960. *Judith: Eine Tragödie in fünf Akten.* Dizingen: Broschiert. Orig. pub. 1840.

Hirsch, Marianne. 1997. *Family Frames: Photography, Narrative, and Postmem-ory.* Cambridge, MA: Harvard University Press.

Jacobowitz, Ellen S., and Stephanie Loeb Stepanek. 1983. *The Prints of Lucas van Leyden and his Contemporaries.* Washington, DC: National Gallery of Art.

Jameson, Anna Brownell. 1833. *Characteristics of Women, Moral, Practical and Historical,* London: Saunders and Otley.

——. 1834. *Visits and Sketches at Home and Abroad.* 4 vols. London: Saunders and Otley.

Kemp, Martin. 2000. "The Handy Worke of the Incomprehensible Creator." In *Writing on Hands: Memory and Knowledge in Early Modern Europe,* ed. Claire Richter Sherman with Peter M. Lukehart, 22–27. Carlisle, PA: Dickinson College, Trout Gallery; Washington, DC: Folger Shakespeare Library.

Kohlenberger, J., ed. 1997. *The Parallel Apocrypha.* New York and Oxford: Oxford University Press.

Korsmeyer, Carolyn. 2002. "Savoring Disgust." Paper presented at the American Philosophical Association, Central Division, Chicago, April 25.

Kris, Ernst, and Otto Kurz. 1979. *Legend, Myth, and Magic in the Legend of the Artist: A Historical Experiment.* New Haven, CT: Yale University Press, 1979.

LaCapra, Dominick. 1996. *Representing the Holocaust: History, Theory and Trauma.* Ithaca, NY: Cornell University Press.

Lacoue-Labarthe, Philippe. 1979. *Portrait de l'artiste, en général.* Paris: Christian Bourgeois.

Lapierre, Alexandra. 2000. *Artemisia: The Story of a Battle for Greatness.* Trans. Liz Heron. London: Chatto and Windus.

Lavin, Irving. 1995. "Why Baroque?" In *Going for Baroque: Eighteen Contemporary Artists Fascinated with the Baroque and Rococo,* ed. Lisa G. Corrin and Joaneath Spicer, 5–8. Baltimore, MD: The Contemporary and The Walters.

Levine, Amy-Jill. 1992. "Sacrifice and Salvation: Otherness and Domestication in the Book of Judith." In VanderKam 1992, 17–30.

Longhi, Roberto. 1961. "Gentileschi padre e figlia." In *Opere compete di Roberto Longhi.* Vol. 1. *Scritti giovanili, 1912–1922,* 245–314. Florence: Sansoni. Orig. pub. 1916.

Lord, Catherine. 1999. *The Intimacy of Influence: Narrative and Theoretical*

Fictions in the Works of George Eliot, Virginia Woolf, and Jeanette Winterson. Amsterdam: ASCA Press.

Luther, Martin. 1976. *First Lectures on the Psalms.* St. Louis, MO: Concordia.

Mahon, Denis. 1969. *Guercino (Giovanni Francesco Barbieri, 1591–1666): Catalogo critico dei disegni.* Bologna: Edizioni Alfa.

Malvasia, Carlo Cesare. 1841. *Felsina Pittrice, Vite de' pittori bolognesi,* ed. G. P. Zanotti. Bologna: Tipografia Guidi all'Ancora. Orig. pub. 1678.

Man, Paul de. 1979. *Allegories of Reading: Figural Language in Rousseau, Nietzsche, Rilke, and Proust.* New Haven, CT: Yale University Press.

Mann, Coramae Richey. 1996. *When Women Kill.* Albany: State University of New York Press.

Matthews, Victor H. 1991. "Hospitality and Hostility in Judges 4." *Biblical Theology Bulletin* 21:13–21.

Monducci, E., E. Negro, and M. Pirondini. 2002. *Leonello Spada: Bologna 1576–Parma 1622.* Brescia: Merigo Art Books.

Mulvey, Laura. 1996. "Pandora's Box: Topographies of Curiosity." In *Fetishism and Curiosity.* London: BFI; Bloomington: Indiana University Press.

Niditch, Susan. 1989. "Eroticism and Death in the Tale of Jael." In *Gender and Difference in Ancient Israel,* ed. Peggy L. Day, 43–57. Minneapolis, MN: Fortress Press.

Parker, Rozsika, and Griselda Pollock. 1981. *Old Mistresses: Women, Art and Ideology.* London: Rivers Oram.

Pietropaolo, Domenico. 1989. "Iudit, *femme fatale* of the Baroque Stage." In *Donna: Women in Italian Culture,* ed. Ada Testaferri, 273–83. Ottawa: Doverhouse Editions.

Pollock, Griselda. 1980. "Artists, Mythologies, and Media or Madness: Genius and Art History." *Screen* 21, no. 3:57–96.

———. 1988. *Vision and Difference: Femininity, Feminism, and Histories of Art.* London: Routledge.

———. 1993. "Crows, Blossoms and Lust for Death: Cinema and the Myth of Van Gogh the Modern Artist." In *The Mythology of Van Gogh,* ed. Tsukas Kodera, 217–40. Amsterdam: John Benjamins.

———. 1999. *Differencing the Canon: Feminist Desire and the Writing of Art's Histories.* London: Routledge.

Rabb, Theodore K. "Orazio, Artemisia, and Rome Revived." *Times Literary Supplement,* April 5, 2002, p. 16.

Réau, Louis. 1956. *Iconographie de l'Art Chrétien*. Vol. 1. *Ancient Testament*.
    Vol. 2. *Iconographie de la Bible*. Paris: Presses Universitaires de France.

Redig de Campos, Deoclecio. 1939. "Una 'Giuditta' opera sconosciuta del
    Gentileschi nella Pinacoteca Vaticana." *Rivista d'Arte* 21:311–23.

Riviere, Joan. 1986. "Womanliness as a Masquerade." In *Formations of Fantasy*,
    ed. Victor Burgin, James Donald, and Cora Kaplan, 35–44. London:
    Methuen.

Rossi, Sergio . 1998. "Il mistero della luce glauca. Verità dell'immagine e attesa
    del miracolo nella pittura del Seicento." In *Scienza e miracoli nell'arte del
    '600 alle origini della medicina moderna*, 14–21. Exhibition catalogue,
    Palazzo Venezia, Rome. Milano: Electa.

Rössler, Beate, ed. 2004. *Privacies: Philosophical Evaluations*. Stanford, CA:
    Stanford University Press.

Rubin, Gayle. 1975. "The Traffic in Women." In *Towards an Anthropology of
    Women*, ed. Rayna Reiter, 157–210. New York: Monthly Review Press.

Rublack, Ulinka. 1999. *The Crimes of Women in Early Modern Germany*. Ox-
    ford: Clarendon Press.

Russell, H. Diane, and Bernardine Barnes. 1990. *Eva/Ave: Woman in Renais-
    sance and Baroque Prints*. Washington, DC: National Gallery of Art and
    The Feminist Press at the City University of New York.

Salomon, Nanette. 1998. "The Art Historical Canon: Sins of Omission." In
    The Art of Art History: A Critical Anthology, ed. Donald Preziosi, 344–55.
    Oxford: Oxford University Press. Orig. pub. 1992.

Schaeffer, J. M. 1997. *Les célibataires de l'art*. Paris: Editions du Seuil.

Smith, Susan L. 1995. *The Power of Women: A Topos in Medieval Art and Liter-
    ature*. Philadelphia: University of Pennsylvania Press.

Smyth, Craig Hugh. 1992. *Mannerism and Maniera, with an Introduction by
    Elizabeth Cropper*. Vienna: IRSA.

Spear, Richard. 1971. *Caravaggio and His Followers*. Exhibition catalogue.
    Cleveland, OH: Cleveland Museum of Art.

———. 1985. "The Critical Fortunes of a Realist Painter." In *The Age of Car-
    avaggio*. New York: The Metropolitan Museum of Art.

———. 2000a. *The "Divine" Guido: Religion, Sex, Money and Art in the World
    of Guido Reni*. New Haven, CT: Yale University Press.

———. 2000b. "Artemisia Gentileschi: Ten Years of Fact and Fiction." *Art
    Bulletin* 82, no. 3:568–79.

Spicer, Joaneath. 1991. "The Renaissance Elbow." In *A Cultural History of*

Gesture, ed. Jan Bremmer and Herman Roodenburg, 84–128. Ithaca, NY: Cornell University Press

Spike, John. 1991. "Review of Contini and Papi's *Artemisia.*" *Burlington Magazine* 133:732–43.

Spivak, Gayatri Chakravorty. 1984. "Overdeterminations of Imperialism: David Ochterlony and the Ranee of Sirmoor." In *Europe and Its Others,* ed. Francis Barker, 1–21. Proceedings of the Essex Conference on the Sociology of Literature, July 1984. Colchester: University of Essex.

———. 1985. "The Rani of Sirmur: Reading the Archives." *History and Theory* 224, no. 3:247–72.

———. 1988. "Can the Subaltern Speak?" In *Marxism and the Interpretation of Culture,* ed. Cary Nelson and Lawrence Grossberg, 271–313. Urbana: University of Illinois Press.

Steinberg, Leo. 1983. *The Sexuality of Christ in Renaissance Art and Modern Oblivion.* New York: Pantheon Books.

Stocker, Margherita. 1998. *Judith—Sexual Warrior.* New Haven, CT: Yale University Press.

Strinati, Claudio, and Rossella Vodret. 1998. *Caravaggio and His Italian Followers, from the Collections of the Galleria Nazionale d'Arte Antica di Roma.* Venice: Marsilio Editori; see cat. no. 19.

Summers, David. 1987. *The Judgment of Sense: Renaissance Naturalism and the Rise of Aesthetics.* Cambridge: Cambridge University Press.

Topper, David, and Cynthia Gillis. 1996. "Trajectories of Blood: Artemisia Gentileschi and Galileo's Parabolic Path." *Woman's Art Journal* 17 (spring/summer): 10–13.

Turner, Nicholas, and Carol Plazzotta. 1991. *Drawings by Guercino from British Collections.* London: British Museum Press.

Vaccaro, Alessandra M., ed. 1996. *Historical and Philosophical Issues in the Conservation of Cultural Heritage.* Los Angeles: Getty Conservation Institute.

Valdez, Sarah. 2002. "Every Picture Tells a Story." *Time Out New York,* March 7–14, p. 67.

Van Alphen, Ernst. 1996. "The Portrait's Dispersal: Concepts of Representation and Subjectivity in Contemporary Portraiture." In *Portraiture: Facing the Subject,* ed. Joanna Woodall, 239–56. Manchester, UK: Manchester University Press.

VanderKam, James C., ed. 1992. *"No One Spoke Ill of Her"—Essays on Judith.* Atlanta, GA: Scholars Press.

Vasari, Giorgio. 1912–15. *Lives of the Most Eminent Painters, Sculptors, and Architects.* Trans. Gaston du C. de Vere. London: Macmillan. Orig. pub. in Italian in 1550; expanded ed., 1558.

Vreeland, Susan. 1999. *The Girl in Hyacinth Blue.* Denver, CO: MacMurray & Beck.

———. 2002. *The Passion of Artemisia.* London: Headline Books.

Wittkower, Rudolph, and Margaret Wittkower. 1963. *Born under Saturn.* New York and London: W. W. Norton.

Wolfthal, Diane. 1999. *Images of Rape.* Cambridge: Cambridge University Press.

CONTRIBUTORS

Mieke Bal, a well-known cultural critic and theorist, is professor of the theory of literature at the University of Amsterdam and the A. D. White Professor-at-Large at Cornell University. Her most recent publications are *Travelling Concepts in the Humanities: A Rough Guide* (University of Toronto Press, 2002) and *Mieke Bal Kulturanalyse* (Suhrkamp, 2002). Among her many other books are *Louise Bourgeois' Spider: The Architecture of Art-Writing* (University of Chicago Press, 2001) and *Quoting Caravaggio: Contemporary Art, Preposterous History* (University of Chicago Press, 1999). She has recently taken up filmmaking and video installation.

Babette Bohn is professor of art history at Texas Christian University in Fort Worth, Texas. Her recent publications include "Female Self-Portraiture in Early Modern Bologna" (Renaissance Studies, 2004), "Elisabetta Sirani and Drawing Practices in Early Modern Bologna" (Master Drawings, 2004), and *Ludovico Carracci and the Art of Drawing* (Harvey Miller, 2004).

Elena Ciletti teaches art history and women's studies at Hobart and William Smith Colleges in Geneva, NY. Her articles, reviews and presentations have addressed topics including the iconography of Judith in the Renaissance, art patronage in late Medici Florence, opera, and African American art. She is currently working on a book-length study of Artemisia Gentileschi and the iconology of Judith in the Counter-Reformation.

Mary D. Garrard is professor emerita of art history at American University, Washington, DC. She is the author of *Artemisia Gentileschi: The Image of the Female Hero in Italian Baroque Art* (Princeton University Press, 1989).

Her recent publications include *Artemisia Gentileschi around 1622: The Shaping and Reshaping of an Artistic Identity* (University of California Press, 2001) and (coeditor, with Norma Broude) *Reclaiming Female Agency: Feminist Art History after Postmodernism* (University of California Press, February 2005).

Griselda Pollock is professor of social and critical histories of art and director of AHRB Centre for Cultural Analysis, Theory, and History at the University of Leeds. She writes extensively on feminist cultural theory and cultural analysis and is currently completing a book on Charlotte Salomon. Recent publications include *Differencing the Canon: Feminist Desire and the Writing of Art's Histories,* "Cockfights and Other Parades," *Oxford Art Journal* 26, no. 2 (2003): 141–59, and "The Grace of Time: Narrativity, Sexuality and a Visual Encounter in the Virtual Feminist Museum," *Art History* 26, no. 2 (2003): 174–213.

Nanette Salomon is professor of art history in the Performing and Creative Arts Department of the College of Staten Island of the City University of New York. She also curates the college's art gallery. Her most recent book is *Shifting Priorities: Gender and Genre in Seventeenth-Century Dutch Painting,* Stanford University Press, 2004.

INDEX OF NAMES AND TITLES

Boldface page numbers indicate illustrations.

INDEX OF TERMS AND CONCEPTS